Fear in Bongoland

STUDIES IN FORCED MIGRATION
General Editors: Dawn Chatty and Chaloka Beyani

FEAR IN BONGOLAND

Burundi Refugees in Urban Tanzania

Marc Sommers

Berghahn Books
NEW YORK • OXFORD

Published in 2001 by

Berghahn Books

www.berghahnbooks.com

Library of Congress Cataloging-in-Publication Data

Sommers, Marc.
  Fear in Bongoland : Burundi refugees in urban Tanzania / by
  Marc Sommers.
      p. cm.
  Includes index.
  ISBN 1-57181-263-6
  1. Refugees, Hutu–Tanzania–Dar es Salaam–Social conditions.
2. Hutu (African people)–Relocation–Tanzania–Dar es Salaam.
3. Hutu (African people)–Urban residence–Tanzania–Dar es Salaam.
4. Dar es Salaam (Tanzania)–Ethnic relations. 5. Dar es Salaam
(Tanzania)–Economic conditions. 6. Dar es Salaam (Tanzania)–
Social conditions. I. Title

DT443.3.H88 S66 2001
306'.09678'232–dc21   00-051891

British Library Cataloguing in Publication Data

A catalogue record for this book is available from
the British Library.

Printed in the United States on acid-free paper

Cover photo: "Mimi ni Jobless, Dar es Salaam" © Marc Sommers

To Christine

and

to the Burundian people,
who so richly deserve lasting peace

Contents

List of Illustrations

Foreword

The author of this book stimulates the reader with insights on a variety of interrelated subjects. Dar es Salaam as "Bongoland" and the commentary on urban youth culture and language enrich the discourse on urbanization in Africa. Those interested in social networks will be intrigued by the importance of Pentecostal patronage and the distorting impact of fear and suspicion on rural-urban (chain migration) and intra-urban (social support) social networks.

Our understanding of a particular refugee population, Burundians in Tanzania, is enhanced through the author's revelations concerning internal schisms (by class, region, and generation) and contradictions in what had been projected to be a homogeneous (empirically and as imagined) Burundian Hutu national consciousness in exile. The volume's approach in addressing emotion and ethos, and analyzing the importance of the transgenerational institutionalization, or crystallization, of an emotion such as dread, is a welcome antidote to the usual materialistic analysis of refugees ("All they need are food, shelter, and medical care"). In addition, of relevance to the more general field of forced migration and displacement studies, this conceptualization of cultural fear and its influence on the behavior of subsequent generations could be utilized as a linkage to post-Holocaust studies.

However, the primary focus of this book is on self-settled urban refugees, and the information and insights that the author provides about these Burundian refugees in Dar es Salaam are, in my mind, the primary contributions of this pioneering work. Conducting this research was not easy. Classes in research design will benefit from this cautionary tale of the difficulties of conducting research on sensitive populations and the all too frequent necessity of transforming one's research design in the field (the "making lemonade from lemons" analogy). In this case, the author's preparedness, creativity, tenacity, ability to establish trust with informants who were living clandestine existences, and use of snowball sampling allowed him to successfully conduct innovative research on representatives of an important and seriously understudied population.

Each reader may be stimulated by and respond to a different subject in this book. Instead of trying to summarize the author's findings, I wish to concentrate on how this innovative and pioneering research contributes to our knowledge about African refugees and, in particular, to our knowledge about self-settled urban African refugees.

There is much that we do not know about the millions of African refugees coming from and currently living in scores of countries across the continent. Most of what we think we know has been gleaned from official statistics and reports or, in terms of field research, has been learned from studying people living in official camps and agricultural settlement projects in rural areas. Most African governments require, as a matter of law or policy, that almost all refugees live in these officially demarcated and supervised rural areas. The exceptions to these laws and policies are small numbers of officially recognized refugees living in urban areas.

International attention focuses on, or is exclusively dedicated to, protecting and caring for refugees in transit or living in these camps and settlements. Official reports are based on official statistics and on the movements, activities, care and feeding, and supervision of the refugees living in these camps and projects.

All of us who study African refugees recognize that the official statistics of refugee populations and flows should be considered to be, at best, rough approximations of reality and, at worse, seriously misleading. Similarly, we recognize that many—perhaps as many as half—of Africa's refugees live off the official map. They have chosen to settle themselves unofficially (in what is referred to as "self-directed" or "spontaneous" settlement) in villages, towns, and cities instead of living in the official settlements. These self-settled refugees live and work interspersed among the local residents and deliberately do not call attention to their refugee origins and (usually illegal) presence because they do not wish to be confined to official settlements or to have their movements and socioeconomic activities limited.

Governments and researchers know almost nothing about these self-settled refugees. The clandestine nature of self-directed settlement means that these refugees do not want to be identified. This makes it extremely difficult for researchers. The little that we know about the (presumably) millions of self-settled refugees and their activities comes from a few rare and scattered research projects that, by intent or fortuitous accident, managed to penetrate the secrecy and enlist the cooperation of refugee informants. What we do know from this research is that the conditions of life and processes of settlement of self-settled refugees vary significantly from what is typical of officially settled refugees, who have been the subjects and informants for almost all research about African refugees.

Officially settled refugees are relatively easy to study. Their identity and location are known. They live in locations that are supervised and managed by the national government or by international organizations (the United Nations or nongovernmental organizations) and are already in contact with international organizations that are providing assistance (food, medical care, shelter, clothing, etc.). Thus, there already exists a link between these refugees and international staff members of humanitarian assistance organizations. In migration terminology, this existing link facilitates the chain migration of local and expatriate researchers to these refugee locations and populations.

Saying that research on officially settled refugees is relatively easy does not imply that it is easy. No field research on refugees is easy. The author originally intended to study refugees living in an official rural settlement, but permission to conduct this research was not granted by the Tanzanian government. Governments are suspicious about refugees themselves (foreigners associated with, and perhaps inciting, cross-border conflict) and about activities in refugee-affected (unsettled) areas. The mantle (or mantra) of national security makes it easy for governments, which are generally distrustful of research anyway, to refuse researchers permission to study refugees or even to enter refugee-affected areas.

The author persisted in trying to study refugees in Tanzania and, finally, was given permission to study the few officially recognized refugees residing in Dar es Salaam. This was undoubtedly seen by the government as a relatively contained and secure activity. Fortunately, the researcher is an anthropologist and managed to turn this unpromising permission into an opportunity to learn about an important and unrecognized clandestine population of self-settled and urbanized Burundian refugees.

The author's academic orientation facilitated his being able to recognize and establish contact with these wary informants. Most academic disciplines emphasize accessing and analyzing existing documents and statistics. Thus, what is most important is a control of the administrative and archival language. Researchers are not required or expected to speak local languages or dialects, or to understand local cultures. On the other hand, all anthropologists, and some individuals from the cognate social sciences (social geography and sociology), are expected to learn much more about the language and ways of life of common people. The author speaks Swahili, the local language, but the real opening to young urban refugees was the author's exploration of the dialect, or jargon, of urban youth (*Lugha ya Wahuni*).

This research also demonstrates the complementarity of formal and informal, and quantitative and qualitative, research methods. Formal research methods, such as surveys, are designed to efficiently collect representative information about the society. These methods rely upon people's willingness to answer questions honestly. Unfortunately, these methods do not work well in an atmosphere of mistrust and suspicion and will not stimulate clandestine peoples to identify and reveal themselves. Identifying and studying these elusive and fearful persons requires a combination of informal methods (usually participant observation and unstructured interviews) and the expenditure of time (months or years) to build relationships that are the foundation for allaying mistrust.

The informal research reported in this book identifies and opens up a new world to us. We learn about the networks and processes that enable these young men to leave their rural settlements and establish themselves in Dar es Salaam, and we learn about their traumatized culture and society. Much remains to be learned. How many self-settled refugees from different refugee populations are living in this city? How representative are the lives of the young men to whom we are introduced in this volume? Hopefully, the author's research will stimulate others to expand upon this opening, this portal to Bongoland.

Art Hansen

Preface

Perhaps no other country in the world is as enmeshed in fear as is Burundi. The torment and latent terror in Burundian psychologies are the wellsprings of ethnic violence in that country. Eminent scholars of the region have pointed out how the genocide of 1972 has become the touchstone for all politically-inspired violence since that time. Burundi's ethnic majority, the Hutu, are constantly afraid that the ethnic Tutsi-dominated army will descend upon them as they did in 1972. The country's ruling Tutsi minority is equally fearful of Hutu revenge.

This book is about that fear, particularly its imprint on the lives of second generation Burundi refugees whose experience of genocide has been indirect: they were either infants when their parents fled the country, and do not recall the details of the tragedy, or they were born in refugee settlements in Tanzania. Either way, these youths have heard about the 1972 tragedy from their elders, over and again and in scorching detail.

This book is also about a particular subset of the second refugee generation: young men who are urban refugees living clandestinely in Dar es Salaam, the capital of their country of exile, Tanzania. In addition to examining the impact of fear in their lives, the following story details how they constructed city lives in accordance to a coping strategy they called *kujificha*, the Swahili verb for "to hide oneself."

The tension between the practicalities of *kujificha* and the subtle penetration of *kuogopa* (Swahili for "to fear") played out differently in the earlier rendition of this book, my dissertation. The first dissertation draft, which I shared with my wife, and my primary dissertation advisor, Professor Allan Hoben of Boston University, was entitled "Fear in Bongoland." Both my wife and my advisor noticed a similar orientation: I was ascribing fear to lives that did not seem to be in particular or acute jeopardy. On the surface, this was true: though the refugees talked incessantly about fear in private, they were never harassed, threatened, beaten, or arrested. Indeed, the refugees lived and worked in tailoring shops in a way that seemed fairly straightforward, nondescript, and safe. What, then, had led me to highlight fear in the telling of their stories?

My arguments in response to this question proved a hard sell, and I ultimately decided to abandon an in-depth exploration of *kuogopa* and shift my focus to the mechanics of *kujificha*. The dissertation became "Hiding in Bongoland" (1994). I got my degree and moved along. Two years later, with the encouragement of Professor Thomas Barfield (also of Boston University), I decided to revisit my dissertation and see if it would turn into a book. I immediately realized that task would lead to a thorough revision of the manuscript. So I returned to my data. With a fresh eye on my fieldwork experience, I considered the issue of fear.

For the final months of field research in Dar es Salaam, I lived with my wife and son in a house on a spit of Dar es Salaam shoreline between the houses of Jane Goodall and Julius Nyerere. The President of the country at the time, Ali Hassan Mwinyi, was building a new house across our road. A small neighborhood of family houses lived between our two more substantial ones.

Even though Dr. Goodall and the *Mwalimu* (Teacher), ex-President Nyerere, were scarcely ever present in their particular houses (Dr. Goodall traveled constantly and Mr. Nyerere resided in his primary residence upcountry), and President Mwinyi only occasionally visited to inspect the progress on his new house, the tangle of Tanzanian officialdom in which we lived was strange—especially for me, a researcher working with refugees in hiding. But as I was a graduate student with a family on limited funds, facing a housing market for expatriates that typically required two thousand U.S. dollars a month to rent a house or apartment, paid for in advance as a two-year lump sum, we had been relying on house sitting arrangements. When I was hit with a bad case of hepatitis while facing the end of our last viable house sit, my wife looked for a feasible living arrangement for our family. She was eventually hired by Jane Goodall. It was a straightforward *quid pro quo*: in exchange for running the Jane Goodall Institute in Tanzania, my wife received a house for our family to live in.

Though the arrangement worked out for all involved, the circumstances of my own research made the situation particularly challenging. As I proceeded in my field research, I was repeatedly told that surveillance on me was continuing. The information, I was told by people in and out of the government, was pretty innocuous—getting paid for reporting information about any number of expatriate activities to state or party bureaucrats is one of a multitude of ways that Tanzanians made ends meet—but my file was growing. Just before I left the country, in fact, one man told me he'd seen my file and it had gotten so large that it no longer fit in the filing cabinet where it once resided but now lay atop it. Knowing that I was being watched in town, I had created, and repeatedly revised, an array of diversions to deflect attention from my work. And though my efforts ultimately succeeded—my relations with government officials were always friendly (if distant) and no harm ever came to the refugees I was involved with—the work itself was exceedingly tense. The tension was also exacerbated by the nature of the data I was receiving about genocidal horrors, ever present fears, and elemental distrust between refugees.

In the time that has passed between completing my dissertation and finishing this book, I conducted field research with Rwandans and Burundians in Central Africa several times. I also took time to reexamine the field data for this book and reflect on the context of my fieldwork in Dar es Salaam. At home on the beach, I had lived in a Bermuda Triangle of officialdom, while in the field I had worked in another universe, marginal and tenuous. The dissonance was intense. I came to realize how the refugees' fear had, for a time, made an imprint on my perceptions as well. I was experiencing what a psychologist friend told me is known as vicarious traumatization.

Be that as it may, my time away from the field research, while keeping involved with Central Africans and their concerns, allowed me to analyze the field data with more precision. It has enabled me to develop the concept of cultural fear, which will be considered in detail in this book, and see the refugees' fears, and the context of those fears, more clearly.

It is in this way that this book has returned to its original title, *Fear in Bongoland.*

Acknowledgments

I am grateful to a wonderful array of people for their contributions and support over the course of the researching and writing of this book. First and foremost, I want to thank the refugees who are featured in this study and are the most remarkable group of young men that I have ever met. A large number of other refugees also provided me with essential information and endless hospitality. I wish I could name them all, but will continue to respect their wishes for anonymity. My deepest gratitude goes to the pastor, referred to in this book as Albert, who helped me enter the clandestine Burundi refugee world in Dar es Salaam. Though my presence in the refugees' lives undoubtedly complicated their lives, I was nonetheless consistently received with kindness and patience, even when the reasons for some of my fieldwork activities seemed unusual or tiresome, or both. They did not have to allow me into their lives. I am truly grateful that they did.

I am indebted to many others as well. Early in the fieldwork period, Allan Hoben, my primary dissertation advisor, visited me and my family in Dar es Salaam. He urged me to follow my intuition and feature the lives of the young Burundi refugee men. His support, guidance, and friendship proved instrumental in the development of this book. Special thanks are also due to my other dissertation advisor, Jane Guyer, for her creative intellect, inspiring insights, and kindness. Among those at Boston University whose assistance remains deeply appreciated are: Eduard Bustin, Maddie Goodwin, Robert Hefner, Joanne Hart, Meredith Kirkpatrick, Sutti Ortiz, James Pritchett, and Gretchen Walsh and all of her helpful and friendly colleagues in Boston University's African Studies Library (David Westley, Loumona Petroff, Richard Alessio, and Augustus Kwaa). Special thanks are reserved for James McCann, the Director of the African Studies Center and Thomas Barfield, Chair of the Anthropology Department, who urged me to re-visit my data and write this book.

A number of people in Dar es Salaam were instrumental in helping me carry out my research. Sincere thanks are offered to a number of people at the University of Dar es Salaam, especially Abel Ishumi, Dr. Kaijage, Prof. Mkude, P. Mlama, and C.K. Omari. Most especially, thanks to Maurice Mbago, my local contact and friend, and Francis Sichona, without whose insistent support I may have never received permission to research refugee lives in Dar es Salaam. Thanks also to Dr. Sichona's wife, Kisa, officials at the Tanzania Commission for Science and Technology, H.N. Nguli in particular, the Refugee Section of the Ministry of Home Affairs, especially Caroline Mutahanamilwa, the late Daniel Mwaisela and Mr. Songoro, officials at the United Nations High Commissioner for Refugees in Dar es Salaam, including Bruno Geddo, Brian Treacy, Ms. Warioba, William Young, Mr. Rugero of the Christian Council of Tanzania (CCT), and Sister Jean Pruitt of the Tanzania-Mozambique Friendship Association (TAMOFA).

Thanks to Patricia Daley and Liisa Malkki for their pre-fieldwork advice and for steering me to the Tanganyika Christian Refugee Service (TCRS), whose assistance and support in Dar es Salaam was both steady and remarkable, most especially Allan Armstrong and his wife, Marian, the late Jan Bayer and his wife, Pernilla, Jim Hart and his wife, Eila, the late *Mzee* Mwakambodya, and Edwin Ramathal and his wife, Dorothy. My deepest appreciation is reserved, however, for Bernhard Staub and his wife, Christa, whose support was unstinting and whose friendship is treasured. I am also grateful for the friendship of others in Dar es Salaam, especially Ahmed Bille, Jerry Brennig of USIS, Bo and Britt Bürstrom, Maria Finnegan, Nick Howard, Greg MacIsaac, Frank Mbago, Tessa Willy, and the Tetlows (Anna, Bevis, Chloe, Julian, and Sue). I owe very special thanks to Christine Heller, my family's contact in the United States, for her unfailing support, reliability, and friendship during our stay in Tanzania's capital.

Grateful acknowledgment is due to the foundations who have supported various phases of this work. The Rotary Foundation was the chief supporter of my fieldwork. Special thanks to members of the Rotary Club of Dar es Salaam North, particularly Shyam Jadeja, Santosh Masson, Evarist Mbuya, and especially Dhiru Pabari and Kaleem Shabbir, and to Daniel India for introducing me to the Rotary Foundation. Thanks also to the Harry Frank

Guggenheim Foundation, particularly Karen Colvard, and to Sigma Xi and the Ford Foundation's Research Enhancement Grant (administered by Boston University's African Studies Center) for their generous support.

During the final stages of write-up, I am grateful for the insights, advice, and input of many friends and colleagues, including Judy Benjamin, Art Hansen, Jim Igoe, Ogbu Kalu, Hugo Kamya, Carolyn Makinson, Susan Pollak, Joost van Puijenbroek, Neal Rantoul, Peter Rosenblum, Ranga Settlur, Simon Turner, Tony Waters, and, most especially, Warren Weinstein, whose wisdom about Central Africa and gentle support of my work are both deeply appreciated.

Final thanks are reserved for Christine, my wife, stalwart partner, and tender friend, and my son, Isaiah.

1

Introduction

Through an Urban Borehole

<hr>

Soon after arriving in Dar es Salaam, just before Christmas in 1990, I discovered that asking young people in Dar es Salaam about their notorious *Lugha ya Wahuni* (Language of the Ignorant) was a useful way to start learning about their world. The outcast language, which was actually a rapidly changing vocabulary that youths invented and continuously revise, has helped establish their identity as a separate yet demographically dominant sector of Dar es Salaam society.

In the *Lugha*, simple responses can be dense with meanings. A young man might respond to a typical greeting, such as *Habari ya mihangaiko?* (How are your anxieties?), with the thumb's up sign. He may accompany this with words such as *kwa soks* (with socks, or condoms), meaning the young man practices safe sex and has not been infected by AIDS. He may also select one of the multitude of borrowed English phrases such as *no sweti* (no sweat) to suggest that he's doing well. A third kind of response might be to say nothing, a signal that his ethnic group practices circumcision and that he views himself as one of the "civilized" youth in town.

Though most adults in Dar es Salaam seem to despise the *Lugha ya Wahuni*, it is spoken so widely that everyone in Dar es Salaam knows at least some of the words, including the Burundi refugees who are the subject of this book. One day, returning to my rented home after a day of interviews and errands, withered by Dar es

Salaam's combination of equatorial heat, city dust, and coastal humidity, I stopped to rest under a tree in one of the city's sprawling informal markets. One young man, a *Rasta*, had claimed the precious shade for his shoeshine and repair operation. He was wearing a knitted cap bearing colors announcing his solidarity with South Africa's anti-Apartheid African National Congress and large enough to contain his lengthy dreadlocks. The *Rasta* was not alone–perhaps fifteen other young men shared the shade with him, some of them sitting on the bench he provided for customers. After not succeeding very well with a number of opening conversational gambits, I began to practice the few *Lugha ya Wahuni* words that I'd already learned.

The other youths in the shade, surprised by the sudden presence of a white foreigner inquiring about their *Lugha*, gathered round, preparing to teach. During the course of my ensuing lesson, I asked my teachers why young people so often asked each other about their anxieties. The self-appointed leader of the group, a young man in a pressed shirt and slacks whom I would later learn was a secondary school graduate spending his days downtown looking for work, responded with a chuckle. "*Taabu za Bongo*" (The troubles of *Bongo*), he explained. When I asked what he meant by *Bongo*, all the youths laughed. "It's where you're living," the *Rasta* entrepreneur joined in. Then, holding his arms outward, toward the market din surrounding us, his palms facing the tree branches just above, he continued in Swahili with a knowing grin. "This is not Dar es Salaam, *Bwana*," he told me. "This is *Bongoland*."

Bongoland is a worthy nickname for one of Africa's fastest-growing cities. The city's real name, Dar es Salaam, means "Haven of Peace" in Arabic, a remnant of the city's beginning as a royal getaway for Zanzibar's Swahili Sultans. The new nickname is drawn from Tanzania's two national languages (Swahili and English) to create "Brainland," the place where those with *bongo* or "brains"– the cunning and the shrewd–thrive. Selling coffee in the streets or working as a day laborer for pennies a day may seem insignificant to outsiders, but for many urban newcomers to the cities of Africa it represents a foothold gained, a minor yet significant success. For these young men and women, calling their new home "Bongoland" signifies that they have the smarts it takes to make it. You may be on your way, and dreams of opening your own market stall or working in an office suddenly seem within reach.

At the end of 1990, I began twenty months of field research with Burundi refugees in the Tanzanian capital because I was denied permission to work in Katumba, a remote settlement for refugees

PHOTOGRAPH 1.1 Downtown

In Dar es Salaam, young hustlers constantly search for opportunities to make some money or find something interesting to do. Here, as a crowd draws around a street magician, young men find a perch to view the scene or sell something, in this case an umbrella and a backpack. Photograph: Marc Sommers.

from Burundi. Unlike most of Dar es Salaam's residents, I was try-ing to work in the countryside, not the city. It was there, I thought, that I could find a large cohort of Burundi refugees, a population whose survival strategies and experience I found compelling.

Visiting Katumba had become politically sensitive, so the Tan-zanian government insisted I remain in the capital instead. But conducting research on Burundi refugees in Dar es Salaam seemed particularly problematic because government and United Nations officials reported that only a small number lived there. My first months seeking out this handful of Burundi refugees, however, revealed that many thousands more actually lived in Dar es Salaam than officials knew. Following leads that refugees supplied, I began to make inroads with this hidden population. Eventually, I received permission to regularly visit two tailoring shops con-taining Burundi refugee tailors who presented themselves to cus-tomers as fellow Tanzanians.

I thought that I had finally gained my own foothold in Bon-goland after several difficult months of field research. Then, on a Sunday in my seventh month of fieldwork, after finally seeming to have gained the trust of several refugee tailors from the Burundi refugee settlements, I made a slip that underscored how much I still did not understand about their clandestine lives. It was a slip that could have ended my research; instead it ended up deepening it.

For months, I had been carefully probing the lives of these clan-destine residents while not betraying their efforts to conceal their refugee identity. I had avoided mentioning issues relating to their refugee status during business hours because my weekday visits occurred when Tanzanians were around. The tailors had forbidden speaking about refugee issues at those times. As the weeks passed, I started joining them at their Pentecostal church services on Sun-days. Attending church with the refugee tailors was a moment of passage and acceptance into their world, and I was anxious to respond to their growing trust in me.

One Sunday afternoon after church, while relaxing back at the shop behind closed doors, I decided that the opportune moment had arrived for beginning to inquire about their refugee, ethnic, and national identities. In response to my initial questions, some of the younger tailors immediately related the outlines of their stories and the quandaries attached to them. They explained that they strug-gled to define their identity while living outside their refugee settle-ment homes. As one tailor put it, "I came from Burundi, and I'm a Burundian. But I don't understand Burundi. I came as a baby [in

1972]. I've never returned. I'm not a Tanzanian, but I only know Tanzania." The refugees knew they could not belong to Tanzania, and the Burundi they knew existed only in the refugee settlement they had left behind.

By the time this breakthrough interview occurred in mid-1991, nineteen years had passed since 150,000 ethnic Hutus had fled genocidal violence in Burundi to seek asylum as refugees in Tanzania. Many of the young men who spoke to me inside the dark, steamy shop that Sunday were born in refugee settlements. I had been waiting months for the right opportunity to ask them about how they saw themselves. But now that I had entered the refugees' secret world, I had to learn how to traverse its complexities.

Excited by this first Sunday conversation on Burundi refugee issues, I eagerly awaited an opportunity for a second interview with refugee tailors. The opportunity arose after Albert, the Pentecostal pastor from Burundi who had first invited me to carry out research in his church-based tailoring shop, introduced me to his Assistant Pastor. This portly, handsome man with a flashing smile and seductive charm offered to arrange a second Sunday meeting with the tailors that he and Albert would supervise. During this meeting, I was careful not to mention my interest either in Burundi or refugees, but the Assistant Pastor eventually turned to the subject of where people had migrated from, and some of the tailors made reference to their Burundian roots.

After the Assistant Pastor had left, two of the older tailors asked to speak with me. It was night, and because Dar es Salaam had virtually no streetlights, the dense darkness provided sanctuary for those with secrets. The two tailors joined me in my car and asked that I drive for a while. They were tense, preferring silence to the usual pleasantries that filled our everyday conversations. Eventually, at the tailors' request, we parked alongside a main road. Immediately one of the refugees warned that I should be careful about what I said with "that pastor"—meaning the Assistant Pastor—around. He was not a refugee, and he seemed too curious, one of the tailors explained. The Assistant Pastor was asking too many questions to discover who was a refugee. "We fear that pastor," he told me, "and do not trust him." When I countered that some of the tailors had readily volunteered information, the two responded that some of the refugee tailors were not "our friends."

Their warning stunned me. Had I been warned about conventional authority figures, like Tanzanian policemen and government officials, I would not have been surprised. Given a chance, they might have seized and returned the refugees to the settlements they had secretly left. But even the youngest refugee tailors had already learned how to interact with Tanzanian authorities. The refugee settlements had taught them that most Tanzanian officials received salaries so low that a small fee might persuade the officials to leave them alone.

Instead, as my nighttime lecture continued, I learned how the refugees' urban fears rested on a double-edged blade: they feared other refugees as well as ordinary Tanzanian citizens. As one of the tailors sitting in my car explained, if their Tanzanian neighbors, customers, or members of their congregation discovered their hidden refugee identity, "they will chase us and destroy our property." Accordingly, Burundi refugees residing illegally in Dar es Salaam had to rely on other refugees to maintain their shared secret. Yet I also learned the ethnic genocide that the refugees had fled, when ethnic Tutsi slaughtered tens of thousands of ethnic Hutu in Burundi in 1972, had created shock waves that the descendants of genocide survivors continued to feel. All the refugees shared a penetrating fear of their Tutsi adversaries. This fear had also inspired refugees to perceive their exiled society as divided between "pure" Hutu survivors and less pure Hutu who colluded with Tutsi killers. The tailors were thus forced to trust "enemy" refugees, whom they feared and distrusted, to help shield their identities from Tanzanians.

Like a paratrooper off course, my conversation in the dark landed me in uncharted territory. After seven months of work on what I had initially planned as a thirteen-month fieldwork foray, I now saw that my most difficult challenge still lay ahead of me. Having learned that refugees who lived and worked together may privately consider each other enemies, I had to develop separate relationships with each and every Burundi refugee from whom I sought information. I had gained entrance into a hidden refugee society. Now I had to navigate through the nervous associations and private apprehensions and resentments that circumscribed these secret lives. In short, to embark upon this deeper voyage into the Burundi refugees' urban world, I had to leave Dar es Salaam behind and enter Bongoland with them.

A New Burundi

This book is about the clandestine lives of a group of Burundi refugee tailors who live and work in Dar es Salaam.[1] The young men in this story are Burundian nationals who have little or no memory of Burundi, and ethnic Hutu who may have never seen their ethnic nemesis, the Tutsi. They reside in Tanzania without the rights of citizenship, sequestered in refugee settlements before voyaging into urban anonymity. In terms of their experience, these young men are, at their core, neither Burundian, nor Tanzanian, nor Hutu: they are refugees, and this status, the uncertain future it implies, and the reason their families originally sought refuge in Tanzania, informs the other aspects and identities of their lives.

As the young men headed out of the familiar "Burundi" of their settlement homes toward Bongoland, the aftershocks of genocide that the second Burundi refugee generation received were felt more keenly. In the Burundi refugee settlements of Katumba, Mishamo, and Ulyankulu, memories of an ethnic holocaust had been shaped into a history that could be used both to strengthen group solidarity and connect the children of genocide survivors to their parents' traumatizing experiences. This mythologized, collective past, described by Malkki about Mishamo settlement refugees (1989, 1990, 1995) and used to help inspire genocidal violence by Rwandan Hutu extremists in 1994, not only laid the foundation for young Burundi refugees' identification as Burundian national, ethnic Hutu and refugee. It also infused their lives with culturally transmitted terror, which will here be called *cultural fear*. The Hutu, they had been told, had been victimized for generations by menacing Tutsi adversaries who sought to destroy them.

Douglas and Wildavsky present a conception of culture as the intermediary level between individual subjectivity and "public, physical science" (1982:194) which functions as a lens through which the world is interpreted and understood. Their conception sheds light on why the refugee tailors took precautions and expressed fears that did not, at first, seem particularly threatening. But through the cultural lens they had carried with them from their settlement homes, city life offered no respite from the genocidal killers of their past. For them, the Tutsi were not phantoms but definite threats to their carefully constructed urban hideaways. Cultural fear, a product of surviving and remembering extreme ethnic violence, magnified the tensions and threat of violence they weathered in Dar es Salaam because it inserted the hidden presence of predatory Tutsi enemies into their urban lives. Tanzanians might drive them back to their settlements, and might even employ violent means to do so. But the Tutsi, the refugee tailors all believed, wanted to wipe them out.

Refugee Realities

Refugee identity is as complex as definitions of home. Staking their claim to new, previously uncharted territory, the second Burundi refugee generation reversed the words which referred to their country of origin and settlement homes. For them, *Kwetu* (Our Home or Homeland in Swahili) referred to Burundi, while *Burundi* referred to the refugee settlements, where the older generation had tried to connect the younger refugee generation to Burundian culture and the ethnic genocide they had survived.

Complexity characterized the Burundi refugees' struggle to balance the tensions that pulled on their lives. On the one hand, refugees outwardly formed a unity, simultaneously sharing the identities of ethnic Hutu, Burundi national, and refugee. On the other hand, Burundi refugee society divided along a cleft that separated refugees who fled from lakeland Burundi (called the Imbo) from the Banyaruguru, who originally hailed from Burundi's highland areas. Each group claimed that they were the "true" ethnic Hutu and castigated the opposing group as distant Hutu relations who served as Tutsi intimates. Ironically, many of the young men in this story told me that they could discuss the Imbo-Banyaruguru rivalry only while hiding in Dar es Salaam because refugee leaders forbade such discussions in the settlements. This form of ethnic censorship enabled refugee politicians to declare that they represented all "Hutu"–not Burundi–refugees.

In Dar es Salaam, Imbo and Banyaruguru refugees often had to live and work together. All refugees may carry mail for each other between the settlements and the city and exchange information that mutually affected them. Yet refugees also maintained a very short list of truly trustworthy urban associates. Each refugee's network was minute, centering on a single patron upon whom they relied heavily to maintain their security and safety in Dar es Salaam. The patron was usually an established urban refugee man who received hardworking, dependable young workers from the settlements in return for his efforts to secure a job and a place for them to stay. The patrons' power over young refugees was plain: if they failed to work hard enough, or behaved in ways that could expose their Burundi refugee identity to Tanzanians, they would be shipped back to the settlements. The patrons knew that thousands of other young refugees were waiting for a chance to work in Bongoland.

The main source of refugee labor for Dar es Salaam was Katumba, the largest of the three settlements for Burundi refugees who had survived the 1972 genocide. Katumba is a sprawl of rich farm-land cut from remote woodland containing twenty-nine villages and nearly one hundred thousand refugees. The settlement's location provided two advantages over the other two settlements for refugees who sought opportunities in the Tanzanian capital. Katumba refugees had access to regular transport to the capital, as long as they utilized caution and an actor's skills to deflect Tanzanian suspicions, because the settlement had a train station in it. Katumba was also surrounded by villages of ethnic Ha, Tanzanians with a language and culture similar to Burundi refugees. Migrating refugees from Katumba were more familiar with Ha tendencies than those from Ulyankulu, the second source of Burundi refugee out-migration to Dar es Salaam (few refugees reached Dar es Salaam from the distant Mishamo settlement), and could present themselves as Ha Tanzanians with relative ease. Since every refugee sought to become invisible in public by assuming the role of model Tanzanian citizen in the capital, the Katumba refugees owned a comparative advantage over their Ulyankulu counterparts.

Migrant Refugees

> There is life in town, and by life I mean pleasures.
>
> –South African schoolgirl (Mayer 1957; 241)

Long considered the most rural of continents, Africa has had the world's highest urban population growth rate for decades, and today is the only world region whose urban growth rate is increasing. In 1965–70, the populations of Africa's urban areas were rising by an average of 4.4 percent a year. The rate increased to 4.9 percent annually by 1975–80 and held at that rate in 1985–90 (World Resources Institute and Institute for International Development 1988: 266–267). In contrast, South America, which had the second-highest average annual urban growth rate in 1965–70 (4.1 percent), saw its annual average decline to 3.6 percent in 1975–80 and then to 3.1 percent in 1985–90. With the rate of population growth in some African cities unprecedented in recorded world history (Linden 1993), Africa's urban population was expected to quadruple between the late 1970s and the year 2000 (Ogbu and Ikiara 1995: 53). By 2020, more than half of Africa's population will reside in urban areas (UN Department of Economic and Social Information and Policy Analysis 1993).[2]

Migration to Dar es Salaam illuminates Africa's demographic transformation. Tanzania's capital is the fastest growing city in East Africa, the region with the fastest growing urban growth rate in the world (Torrey 1998: B6). Ankerl (1986) has noted that Dar es Salaam's population will increase by 1,239 percent over the final three decades of the twentieth century. Since 1965, 69 percent of this growth has been due to migration from rural Tanzania (Harris 1990). The East African nation, which currently has a total population of more than thirty million (UNDP 1998: 177), will likely contain an *urban* population of 47 million by the year 2020 (Harris 1992: 1). With a population of at least 1,747,000 (ibid.: 175)–the actual figure may be much larger–Dar es Salaam is perhaps eight times greater than Tanzania's second-largest city, Mwanza, and will receive the lion's share of this urban explosion. Dar es Salaam, in short, is on the verge of becoming one of the world's mega-cities,[3] and migrating Burundi refugees are contributing to that growth.

Considering the magnitude of Africa's demographic transformation into a continent whose inhabitants live not in rural areas but in cities, the fact that much remains unknown about this phenomenon is discouraging. "One of the most significant problems in addressing urbanization issues … in Africa," wrote Carole Rakodi, "is the dearth of information" (1997: 10). Stresses on urban infrastructure, management capacity, environment, and land use are common topics of concern among those who study African cities.[4] But social scientists often rely on African government statistics, which are notoriously unreliable. African cities are also largely depicted as "essentially locations for economic activity" (ibid.: 4); places where Africans congregate out of economic necessity and endure considerable hardships to do so. The literature's strong emphasis on crisis and impending disaster has, in fact, left the migrants' experience of the social or cultural attractions of cities largely overlooked.[5]

The lack of information on urban refugee lives is even more striking. This is not because a limited number of refugees are thought to be migrating to cities–a growing number of scholars, in fact, are finding the opposite result. Quite simply, Africa's urban refugee population remains largely unknown because their presence is both illegal and clandestine. Host governments and humanitarian agencies such as the United Nations High Commissioner for Refugees (UNHCR) generally prefer that refugees remain in camps, or settlements, designated for them. Refugees not living in camps are thus difficult either to assist or count. As a result, although Bascom has noted that "many cities in Africa have sizable

FIGURE 1.1 Aims for 1992

The cover of a popular magazine depicts one view of what migrant youth seek in Dar es Salaam (in this case, marriage for young women, a car for young men). Note the couple's stylish hairstyles and clothes.

Source: Cover of *Mcheshi: Gazeti la Riwaya za KiTanzania* (1992, Vol. 1).

refugee populations" (1995: 207), it is not at all clear just how many urban refugees there are, in Africa or elsewhere. UNHCR estimates that there are more than thirteen million refugees in the world (UNHCR 1998), and nearly a million more seeking refugee asylum. The U.S. Committee for Refugees (USCR) speculates that there are more than seventeen million more people considered Internally Displaced Persons (IDPs); civilians who have been forcibly displaced but have not sought asylum in another country, as refugees have. USCR has a third category of "people in refugee-like situations ... [who] for various reasons do not meet the narrow refugee definition" (USCR 1997: 11), which totaled, by the end of 1998, about 3.5 million more people. In all of these statistics, however, the proportion of those living in cities, particularly when the majority do so illegally, is not recorded.

Bascom has argued that "the integration of urban refugees" remains "one of two main refugee issues that remain relatively unresearched and poorly understood" (repatriation problems being the other) (1995: 207). He has further observed that refugees "go to great lengths to avoid camps and get into urban centres" (Bascom 1995: 205), moving into cities after first becoming refugees. This correlates with Rogge's finding that "an increasing proportion of [African] refugees of rural origin, in becoming displaced, simultaneously become urbanized" (1985: 128).

In many ways, the refugee tailors' tale dramatizes Africa's headlong rush to urbanize. Like the "young men [who] predominate among [rural-urban] migrants in Africa" (Hope 1998: 352), the refugee tailors were young men of rural origin. They thirsted for the economic opportunities and cultural excitements that cities promise as much as any migrant. Even so, they lacked the rights of citizens and lived illegally in town, personifying the price that must be paid to make it in an African city. They instituted a coping strategy which they called *kujificha* (hiding oneself). But through their success in hiding, they helped create a new category of urban migrant: the sort of refugee that Rogge considered "voluntary migrants to the cities" (1986: 8), or what might be considered *migrant refugees*.

John, William, and James

This book is a gender study. In this case, however, "gender," unlike the increasingly common use of the word, refers to a focus not on women but on men. Two methodological constraints accounted for this. The first was that relatively few Burundi refugee women resided in Dar es Salaam. Most of the migration had been carried out by refugee men, while most refugee women remained at home. The second reason was due to cultural restrictions. Unlike my experience carrying out research with Rwandan Hutu refugees in Tanzania, Burundi refugee women, young women in particular, were difficult to interview. Two other anthropologists, Liisa Malkki and Simon Turner, faced similar frustrations while researching Burundi refugees. Malkki commented that "Efforts to work with women were frustrated" (1995: 50), while Turner noted that "non-elite refugees–especially women–were not very comfortable with expressing their opinions to me in public" (Turner 1998: 24). In Dar es Salaam, one woman warned that she could talk with me only once and only until her husband came home, at which time she would have to return to the back of the house. She explained that Burundi refugee men did not allow "their women" to speak with foreigners, particularly those interested in their lives as refugees. Several other Burundi refugee women, together with numerous Burundi refugee men, confirmed that this was the case.

If many Burundi refugee men wondered why I wanted to talk to Burundi refugee women in the first place, they were equally confused by my particular interest in the experience of those who grew up as refugees and bolted to the cities. Just why would an American venture all the way to Tanzania just to talk to some teenagers? Didn't I realize that the older refugee generation had survived the genocide and could tell the true story of Burundi and its refugees? After talking to a sequence of these men, usually while sipping sodas together in their living rooms, the fundamental difference that lay between members of these two refugee generations became clear. The senior refugee men, whose roles as refugee historians will be detailed in the next chapter, were not simply older than the youths. They were also from a different social and economic class than the younger men in town. They were elites, while the youths came from families with humble backgrounds. This made it hardly unusual that most elite men knew so little about the lives of the younger refugee men who constituted the overwhelming majority of Burundi refugees in Dar es Salaam. The older men considered themselves *Watu wa Juu* (The High People), while young men like John, William, and James were called *Watu wa Chinichini* (The Very Low People) or *Watu Wadogo* (The Little People). The paths of these two groups rarely crossed.

The three central figures in this book will be called John, William, and James. Like every refugee depicted here, their real names are not used in order to preserve the refugees' efforts at *kujificha*. I chose to highlight their stories here for four reasons. First, while some refugee tailors would return to their settlements for prolonged periods, these three were committed to urban life. Their settlement visits were brief and infrequent. This allowed me the opportunity to record a series of private interviews with them, and observe their activities for an extended, near-continuous time period. Second, their patrons granted me regular access to their work sites and private lives. Third, their joint attendance in the same Pentecostal church and neighborhood afforded insight into different perspectives on a community endeavor they all shared. Fourth, they had each developed strikingly different strategies and attitudes toward coping in Dar es Salaam and confronting the problems of living as a refugee in hiding.

My daily visits to the refugee tailors' shops provided me with a borehole into urban African life, as well as the particular perspective and concerns that preoccupied the refugees I sat among. Working in a dark tailoring shop all day long afforded refugee tailors a safe perch for observing the activities of the street while avoiding possible interrogations from policemen and threatening confrontations with Tanzanians. They could also receive neighborhood gossip or commentaries on larger issues from visitors to the shop. Practically every tailor was passionately involved in one of two national soccer clubs based in Dar es Salaam, just as Tanzanians were. Indeed, the current of urban social life split along the *Simba-Yanga* divide during radio broadcasts. Refugees entered this friendly rivalry even when there was no radio in the shop, for groups of men gathered in front of blaring radios along every street during games. News of a goal scored traveled across the neighborhood with the roar from their fans. In these and many other ways, refugees could partake in urban life by letting *Bongo* come to them.

John and William worked together at a Pentecostal church tailoring shop (*kiwanda cha kanisa*) that adjoined the house of Pastor Albert, their patron. James worked as the sole refugee in the nearby shop that was owned by his Tanzanian cousin, Amosi. They all lived in the same neighborhood and attended Pastor Albert's church. None had attended secondary school. Four other refugee tailors figure prominently in the lives of John, William and James. They will be called Luka, Marko, Mathayo and Yona.

John arrived in Dar es Salaam early in 1991 as an apprentice in Pastor Albert's tailoring shop. A seventeen-year-old who had grown up in Katumba settlement, he was quiet at the time. Introduced to him by his boss, Pastor Albert, during my first visit to his shop, I immediately noted his evident caution, shy smile and large, bright eyes. He seemed to be a naive, innocent teen, and despite his tall, wiry frame, he looked young for his age. John spoke only when spoken to in those early days, and when someone asked him something he raised his eyebrows and asked, *Ndio?* (Yes?). His role as a shop apprentice meant that he performed the grunt work: ironing clothes, fetching supplies, cutting cloth. Excepting a one month return to his family in the refugee settlement, John remained in Dar es Salaam.

Over time, I came to realize that even as John steadily assumed increased confidence and authority in his city life, he maintained the innocent demeanor I'd originally noted whenever strangers were present. These performances greatly aided my understanding of how refugees developed Tanzanian personas to shield their refugee identities in public, for as soon as someone new entered the shop, John's behavior changed dramatically. Our private talks, meanwhile, told a different story: John was exceedingly perceptive and shrewd. He also demonstrated his considerable independence by withstanding intense pressure from Pastor Albert and other refugee tailors after deciding to cease his church attendance almost completely. This decision came after completing his first year in the shop, when he shed his apprentice title and received a substantial raise.

John eventually grew sensitive to suggestions that he had left the church entirely and was now living a sinful life. Periodically he would defend himself, proclaiming that he simply disliked going to church and insisting that he was not sinning. He just wanted to be left alone on Sundays.

John's decision not to attend church services unsettled those around him. They had not seen it coming. Some of the refugee tailors began to worry that his decision to act differently would attract unwanted attention from Tanzanians, which might endanger all of them. John's behavior particularly perplexed the pastor and his wife, for it did not look right that one of the pastor's tailors was not attending Sunday services.

John seemed to enjoy the consternation he caused because it signaled that he could no longer be taken for granted. Over the time I knew him, his suspicion of others—Tanzanians and refugees alike—increased. Yet during my final months, John grew eager to have me understand the hidden realities of urban refugee life. He aspired to get a driver's license and hopefully work as a driver for an organization, just as his father had in Burundi before the genocide. Typical of the entrepreneurial spirit that the refugee tailors jointly shared, he proposed a deal to me: that I teach him to drive in my car on Sundays in return for granting me long, private interviews afterwards. As a result, I compiled more information about John than any of the other tailors I interviewed.

William was a proud, secretive, sometimes severe and always intense man. He assumed charge of the day-to-day operations of the pastor's tailoring shop in early 1992. The former shop manager,

Yona, was found to be taking some of the profits, and was slowly eased out of the shop. Once in charge, William exercised his authority over other shop members with cool orders and an aloof manner. A small, wiry man with dark skin and fierce eyes he could contract into an intimidating glower, he also sat in the seat furthest from the front door, shying away from interactions with strangers. William rarely seemed at ease with me, except when discussing some aspect of Christian theology. These conversations usually led him to moral conclusions, which as often as not placed him as a righteous Christian while suggesting that I was not. These methods of gaining the upper hand with me were the only times I saw him laugh. William had a wife and children in Ulyankulu–a fact I dis-covered only at the end of my study period–and was twenty-four years old at the end of the fieldwork period.

Active in the church's choir as guitarist, singer and co-director, William took John's absence from Sunday church as a personal affront. It caused the tension between William and John, who already lived, shared meals, and worked together, to increase dra-matically. William began to regularly express his disapproval of John's absence from church. According to William, a man of rigid morals and uncompromising Pentecostal fervor, John's actions were plainly sinful, and he was not about to let John fall into the hands of Satan. After dinner, William often insisted on reading selections from the Bible to John, who rolled his eyes but received William's evangelizing compliantly.

James was an easy-going, jovial, and popular nineteen-year-old. A stylish dresser with a broad smile, compact build and handsome features, he was far more popular in the neighborhood than John, his cousin. Although the two grew up in the same village in Katumba settlement and attended primary school together, they were never close. James worked as the sole refugee in a Dar es Salaam shop owned by Amosi, his Tanzanian cousin, a product of his uncle's marriage to a local woman in Kigoma, a town located near the Tanzania-Burundi border. Like William, James was active in the *Kwaya* (Choir), but his participation seemed more motivated by the joy of music and social activity than spiritual expression. Many of the congregation's members lived near his shop, and it was the favorite neighborhood hangout for young Pentecostals in the neighborhood. James loved the hum of social activity that sur-rounded him during work hours, and since one of the two Tanza-nians he worked with was his relative, his life was comparatively relaxed. Unlike the refugee tailors who worked in Pastor Albert's shop, James did not have to work with refugees whom he ultimately came to distrust. In contrast, James's living and working situation was significantly more relaxed, which facilitated his aim to steer clear of refugee politics and social conflicts.

Luka, aged twenty-two, was the most economically enterprising refugee tailor I knew. Tall and muscular, with broad features and a large, almost ever-present grin, Luka was confidant and remarkably outspoken. Luka had lost out to William for the head post in the pastor's tailoring shop, no doubt because the pastor considered him too free-spirited and independent. Coupled with two strong but distrustful personalities in John and William, he distanced himself from both, and teased them by engaging Tanzanians in prolonged conversations–something William recoiled from and John avoided. Although all of the tailors displayed high levels of stamina and concentration while working long hours, Luka's vigor and speed at work was extraordinary. Even during the midday heat, Luka would pause only to turn his head and quickly run his index finger across heavy beads of sweat on his forehead like a wiper shoving rain off a windshield.

Like all the refugees described here, Luka was raised as a Pentecostal. He sold maize as a sideline, working for a Tanzanian member of his congregation. Never particularly religious, Luka dared to work on Sundays, something Pastor Albert frowned upon. He briefly sold maize during work hours, but that ended because other tailors feared it would attract the sort of public attention they sought to avoid. Luka returned to assist his widowed mother and seven younger siblings in Katumba in mid-1992. Although he promised to return, he never did.

Marko and John were an inseparable tandem when I first visited the pastor's shop in 1991. Marko was clearly the dominant of the two, in large part because he had already worked as a tailor in Katumba settlement prior to migrating to Dar es Salaam. A quiet, shy man, his face usually wore a worn, tired expression that rarely betrayed his inner emotions. Although only a year older than John, Marko looked thirty.

Marko and John returned to Katumba near the end of 1991, but John came back to Dar es Salaam alone. He carried with him a letter from Marko, in which he asked me for funding to become a mechanic's apprentice in Mpanda, the district capital located near the settlement. I sent him some money and assumed that I would not see him again in Dar es Salaam, yet Marko returned to the capital a few months later. He told me that the mechanic whom he had intended to work for, a Tanzanian, swindled him out of the money I had sent him. Finding his job in the pastor's tailoring shop now filled, Marko stayed at his sister's house in a nearby neighborhood and looked for work.

When I left Tanzania Marko was still unemployed. He talked of his future in vague terms. It was during this time that John and Marko drifted apart. John had a steady job in Pastor Albert's shop and had become a veteran urbanite. By contrast, Marko was now an edgy, contained man who increasingly visited the shop looking worn and worried, his clothes soaked with sweat and dust. Marko was clearly struggling now, but could not depend on John any longer. Where once John would call Marko the best friend he ever had, he now told me that he no longer trusted Marko to keep his intimate secrets. John expected that Marko would not last much longer in Dar es Salaam, and would eventually return to his Katumba settlement home.

Mathayo secretly left Dar es Salaam to return to Burundi in late 1991. He had a slight figure with a broad smile and quiet voice. Mathayo had been a calming presence in the shop, nearly a father figure to John and Marko, who were then working as apprentices. Mathayo patiently taught them various tailoring skills with an air of quiet reassurance. Because Mathayo was an Imbo, neither John nor Marko, who, together with James and Luka, were Banyaruguru, would admit to revering Mathayo. But they did.

Mathayo was the head tailor at James's shop until he was found to be stealing some of the profits. Pastor Albert had then accepted him into his tailoring shop, but not as a head tailor. An active and devoted member of the congregation, Mathayo lived with his wife and two children in Dar es Salaam. Mathayo was about thirty-three years of age, and spoke Kiswahili with a distinct Imbo accent.

Yona was the most secretive refugee I dealt with. Thin and nervous, with large, watery eyes, he could be hostile or aloof with me and abusive to the other refugees. Yona was known to be "doing business"—meeting refugee traders at the train or bus stations and helping them sell their crops for a fee. Because of this, he was well-known among refugee entrepreneurs and their associates in the settlements. Refugee visitors to the shop frequently asked for him. I received most of this information secondhand, since Yona rarely related his activities directly to me.

Yona was a veteran of Dar es Salaam, aged thirty-four, with a family in Dar es Salaam. He did not like me, but the Banyaruguru refugees in Pastor Albert's shop (John, Marko and Luka) told me not to take it personally: Yona seemed only to like William and Mathayo, the other two Imbo in the shop. Yona often delivered sharp lectures to his Banyaruguru colleagues, demanding that they complete their jobs on time.

Yona's tenure in the shop expired during my fieldwork period. Even after he was found to be pocketing some of the profits, he remained as head tailor because his skills as a manager were highly respected. After finally being replaced by William in early 1992, however, I rarely saw him.

Pastor Albert served as the Pastor for all of the refugee tailors in this study, as they all lived in the same neighborhood and attended his Pentecostal services every Sunday. A middle-aged man, he had dark skin, darting eyes, an enveloping smile and a gentle demeanor. After he introduced me to the tailors in his shop, I saw him only occasionally. He was very involved in church business and worked very long days. Albert's unusual legal status–a Burundi refugee who became a naturalized Tanzanian citizen (although he explained that Tanzanian law kept his wife and children as refugees until they applied for citizenship themselves)–briefly made him a controversial figure with Burundi refugee elites in town. His switch threatened and outraged some of them, who spoke of Albert, privately, with contempt. They considered him a traitor and probably a spy. When I asked Albert about his mixed reputation in the city's underground society of Burundi refugees, the bright and upbeat expression he usually wore way gave way to gray fatigue. His decision had attracted attention he had never sought, and it left him exasperated.

As the overseer of the tailoring shop connected to his house (the profits from which went to the church), he bore additional influence over those refugee tailors who worked there. His moral presence in the shop was constant, even when he was not there: refugees were not supposed to listen to the radio because it contained sinful, pagan music, use the slang-filled *Lugha ya Wahuni*, or venture across the street to the shop managed by a refugee official from the rival Pentecostal church. The relationship the refugee tailors had with him as their patron was by far their most important outside the refugee settlements. Without the pastor's help, the refugee tailors in his shop could not hope to retain their situation in Dar es Salaam.

Pastor Albert was the tailors' protector as well as patron. Luka did not get along well with John or William, for example, but he could always rely on the Pastor's assistance in case emergencies arose. As a pastor, Albert commanded sufficient authority to vouch for a tailor's character or claim that the tailor was actually a Tanzanian.

Pastor Albert was an especially able patron because of his close connection to the Swedish Pentecostal mission. He could arrange for refugees to get a church identity card which, while not the official *kitambulisho* that they were required by law to carry, was usually enough: most of Dar es Salaam's huge migrant youth population also lacked government identity cards, and most inquiring policemen considered any sort of identity card proof of urban residence.

Pastor Albert's house betrayed the wear and tear of housing seven children and hosting a near-continuous stream of visitors. The dusty, rectangular courtyard contained broken furniture, sacks of maize, laundry lines and a large chicken coop. His children often did their homework on a table pushed against a shady wall. At night, cooking and study took place beneath the lone light bulb in the courtyard. Visitors frequently waited for Pastor Albert to return from church or business duties on the living room sofa, which was adorned with embroidered covers and matching throw pillows.

Mama was Pastor Albert's wife. Though tall and stocky, Pastor Albert seemed frail when seated next to her. A middle-aged woman of enormous girth, she had small brown eyes and short hair, and was very powerful. She was a commanding presence, and the tailors generally kept their distance from her. Mama was a disciplinarian who tightly controlled the activities of her children. She could be harsh if she found any of her children misbehaving or failing to attend to their house or homework duties. Often her look of distant irritation hid her shyness with visitors. Mama only allowed gospel music to be played in her house. Despite her evident devotion to her husband's church, I never saw her there. She always remained at home with her infant daughter. What I remember most about Mama was her near-constant look of fatigue.

Gathering Information on "The People of '72"

When I arrived in Tanzania at the end of 1990 as a doctoral student from Boston University, I intended to study refugees who lived in a refugee camp, not an underground community of urban refugees. But the Ministry of Home Affairs informed me that conducting research in the settlements would not be possible. My application for research clearance was summarily denied. With the support from officials from a variety of local institutions and government departments, I re-applied, and was again denied clearance. Conducting extended research among refugees was not going to be possible, I was told. Could I not study migrants instead? one government official inquired. I was reluctant to do this, I explained, because I had spent two years preparing myself to research refugee society. Migrants are very different from refugees, I said. "Yes," he replied, "but they are not problematic like refugees."

One University of Dar es Salaam faculty member took up my case with unusual resolve and was eventually rewarded with a meeting in the office of a key Home Affairs official. The meeting itself had come about suddenly. Sitting in the University professor's office one afternoon just before Christmas, we were hoping that our entreaties to Ministry of Home Affairs and University officials would result in a telephone call from the Ministry. A call that day did not seem likely because it had rained that morning, and rain normally cut telephone lines all over town for days. But somehow a call came through: we were to present ourselves at the Ministry's office within the hour. Driving as fast as we could, enduring repeated delays due to roadwork on Bagamoyo Road, we reached the downtown office in just under sixty minutes. I was then told to wait outside while my University supporter met with a Ministry official alone. As I paced and fretted near the office gates, my fate was settled: the Tanzanian Ministry of Home Affairs would allow me to carry out research on refugees living in the capital city. The Ministry official then told my University champion: "He can get his degree, but he's not going to learn anything we don't already know." Thus did research for this book, the first devoted exclusively to clandestine urban refugees in Africa, commence.

It was never clear to me how much government officials actually knew about the hidden refugee community in their midst. I never got the impression that urban refugees were a major concern to the government. The government was preoccupied with far more pressing concerns in the settlements and along their borders. After receiving my research clearance, Ministry officials then awarded me with a list of Burundi refugees that had received permission to reside in Dar es Salaam. I then supplemented this list with others provided by refugee agencies in town. Most of these refugees had not entered Tanzania overland from Burundi, as those living in the refugee settlements had. They had instead found their way into Dar es Salaam from other countries–Rwanda, Uganda, Kenya, Zaire– and had managed to present their refugee asylum cases to United Nations High Commissioner for Refugees (UNHCR) offices in the Tanzanian capital. Some of these Burundians had already received permission to reside in Dar es Salaam; others were awaiting the outcome of asylum negotiations between UNHCR and the Tanzanian government. UNHCR officials explained that Ministry of Home Affairs officials wanted to keep those asylum-seeking Burundians whom they considered politically involved out of the refugee settlements altogether. These Burundians thus had the best chance of being allowed to live in Dar es Salaam. Together, the total number of Burundi refugees listed as living in town included no more than thirty men and their families. I assumed that this more or less constituted the extent of the Burundi refugee community in Dar es Salaam.

The members of this community did not live together, but resided instead in a number of different urban neighborhoods, surrounded by Tanzanians. Tanzanian government and UNHCR officials considered them members of Burundi's exiled elite. Following leads from refugee agency officials and refugees themselves, I eventually managed to meet nearly every member of this group. I found that they had all received at least some secondary school education. Some had university degrees, and had managed to obtain employment in the formal sector in town. Most seemed to participate, in some way, in the city's huge informal market.

The Burundi refugees who legally resided in the capital lived scattered in different neighborhoods, surrounded by Tanzanians, and were considered members of Burundi's exiled elite. Yet despite their apparent advantages, they evinced many of the characteristics I would find later among the refugee youth living in town illegally. Although politically involved and sharing the same social class, these men rarely saw each other and distrusted the intentions of their exiled peers. Still, their residence permits allowed them to speak more freely than any refugee tailor would dare.

Snowball sampling techniques were required to gain access to the hidden Burundi refugee majority. Just as refugees need a patron—a link to a job and residence in Dar es Salaam—so I needed a trustworthy refugee of stature with a residence permit for Dar es Salaam to introduce me to the illegal refugee residents. By initially asking the known refugees where others lived in Dar es Salaam, I began to realize that the Burundi refugee community in Dar es Salaam was large. Eventually, one educated refugee recommended that I meet Pastor Albert. Sitting in his living room, I explained to the pastor that I was looking for prospective research sites. He was among the first Burundi refugees to tell me that considerable numbers of young refugees from the settlements were secretly living in Dar es Salaam: more than one hundred, he said, on his street alone.

All of them were Pentecostals, too. To illustrate his next point, Pastor Albert made a fist with his right hand and hid it underneath a corner of the coffee table between us. Glancing at his hidden fist, Pastor Albert explained that the history of the ethnic Hutu of Burundi had only been written by Catholic priests "who always hide the truth." Hutu and Tutsi authors, he added, had never written a good history of their relationship, either. There thus was a need to tell the true Hutu story, and for this reason Pastor Albert agreed to help me. He then gave me permission to visit the tailors in the shop adjoining his house, provided they agreed to cooperate. But he said he could at least explain to them that I was not a spy. Without his stamp of approval, Pastor Albert explained, "The refugees would all lie to you. They are afraid of outsiders and they hide themselves." In this second sentence, the pastor used two verbs, *kuogopa* (to be afraid) and *kujificha* (to hide oneself), that refugee tailors would repeatedly use to describe their situation to me over the coming months. Following my round of introductions to the refugee tailors working in the tailoring shop adjoining his house, and a series of subsequent visits there, it became my primary research site.

Pastor Albert's assistance eventually led me to a second tailoring shop in his neighborhood where I conducted research. This shop was run by Amosi, a member of Albert's Pentecostal congregation, and it contained one refugee, James, working alongside Tanzanians. His family had come from a village in Burundi located near the Tanzanian border. One of his aunts had married a Tanzanian, and her son, Amosi, employed James in Dar es Salaam. Amosi was the only person in the shop who knew the refugee's true identity.

After I had arranged to carry out research at these two primary research sites, I started to visit the two tailoring shops on a regular basis. Subsequent field research employed many standard participant observation techniques, which included becoming an accepted regular visitor to the shops, observing and recording ordinary and extraordinary social interactions, and, when possible, asking the tailors questions, followed by nightly write-ups of all relevant observations.[6] The pre-arranged Sunday afternoon individual interviews with one refugee at a time allowed me to explore a wide range of issues that I was not able to ask about during shop hours.

Another important research site was the Pentecostal churches that the refugee tailors attended. Regularly attending church services became an unspoken research requirement for three reasons. First, it lent credibility to the integrity of the research endeavor, as it both increased my standing with Burundi refugees in the congregation and incorporated a vital aspect of their urban lives into the research. Equally important, however, it provided the refugee tailors with cover in case any inquiries were ever made about the presence of a foreigner in their tailoring shops. It did not take long for the issue of my identity to arouse curiosity from the refugees' Tanzanian neighbors—not only because I was a white man visiting specific communities regularly, but because of my car. Each car has a license plate whose letters indicate an identity for the owner of the car. There were coded vehicle plates for United Nations vehicles, for military personnel, for diplomats, for CCM officials,[7] and for many other types of car owners. My car had a "TX" plate, signifying that the owner was a "Tanzanian expatriate." Thus, the mere presence of my car in a neighborhood indicated that a foreigner was nearby. And since white-skinned foreigners were rarely seen in the communities I visited, my presence had to be explained.[8] Refugees asked that I tell inquirers either that I was a missionary or a visiting lecturer at the University of Dar es Salaam. The ruse seemed to work well.

Like most Tanzanian youth in town, John, James, and most of the refugee tailors were drawn to the urban youth culture of Bongoland. It seemed to captivate their private thoughts. Literacy in the culture was important to their urban identities, and dissecting different aspects of the culture were popular topics of shop discussions, particularly the intricacies of the *Lugha ya Wahuni*. Involvement in the culture enabled them to connect to Tanzanian youth as fellow urbanites by sharing information about the latest words, hairstyles or clothing. These urban enjoyments also served a very useful purpose. Mixing in with their Tanzanian peers in public helped reduce the chances that their undercover identities would become known. For Pentecostal refugees like William, however, urban youth culture compromised their moral positions and created another fissure that divided Burundi refugees into opposing groups.

To improve my proficiency in the culture, I also interviewed Tanzanian youths who were tailors, day laborers, market hawkers, or unemployed hustlers who congregated in groups. Entering discussions with young men in Dar es Salaam was easy. They were found in large numbers in every community and downtown street. Their culture and language were readily accessible as well, as it was a popular topic of conversation.

I conducted all interviews with refugees firsthand and in fluent Swahili, and translated interview tapes, field notes, and written materials from Swahili to English. A Tanzanian research assistant, recommended by a Tanzanian scholar on refugee issues, helped me translate and transcribe interview tapes and compile information on contextual issues, such as migration, urbanization, and government security. I personally conducted all interviews with relevant government, United Nations, and non-governmental organizations. I also conducted all of the private interviews with the refugee tailors and with nearly thirty of the Burundi refugee men on the original lists I had received just after New Year's Day, 1991, from the Ministry of Home Affairs and refugee agencies in Dar es Salaam, including UNHCR. Similar to interviews carried out with refugee entrepreneurs who ventured into Dar es Salaam from the refugee settlements, these discussions usually centered on Burundian history and the 1972 genocide.

Researching urban refugees in hiding is akin to researching a moving target. It was never clear how large the Burundi refugee population was in Dar es Salaam. The total probably amounted to several thousand refugees. It may have been considerably larger. But such estimates are necessarily sketchy, as it was not a population that could be accurately counted. The research also uncovered very few Burundian Catholic refugees living in Dar es Salaam, though their numbers in the refugee settlements were quite considerable, and this was also a challenge to account for. It might be concluded that I simply did not receive leads into the Catholic refugee network, but there were reasons to doubt this. First, the few Catholic, or even Anglican, refugees present in Dar es Salaam all told me that the number of respective cohorts was tiny. They also were at a loss to explain in any detail why Pentecostal refugees from Burundi dominated the urban refugee population. Catholic church officials interviewed in the capital were also not aware of Burundi refugees in their urban congregations. Though firsthand data on Catholic refugees proved to be exceedingly thin, the issue itself—the overwhelming presence of Pentecostal refugees in the Tanzanian capital—is considered in Chapter 6.

Both in the field and since returning from Tanzania, I have taken precautions to protect the identities and locations of my informants. My writings about refugees in Dar es Salaam do not identify specific locations or people, although one must suppose that their location could conceivably be discovered. After interviewing officials and scholars about this subject, however, I am confident that their situations will remain safe. Officials in the Ministry of Home Affairs in Dar es Salaam are already aware of the presence of illegal Burundi refugees in their midst, and know that the population is not a troublesome one. They don't need to read here that refugees can buy a train ticket directly from the settlements to Dar es Salaam. Though the Tanzanian government has conducted a series of sweeps of Burundian nationals over the years, attempting to collect and deposit those living outside of refugee settlements into refugee settlements, the focus has always been on areas along the Burundi-Tanzania border or towns located near refugee settlement areas (such as Kigoma, Mpanda and Tabora). The presence of Burundi refugees in Dar es Salaam has never been considered a significant problem by government officials, and it shouldn't be. City officials are overwhelmed with far more pressing concerns (garbage disposal problems, for instance, reached crisis proportions during my stay in Dar es Salaam), and most refugees in the capital, after all, try to keep a low profile by quietly following the rules and norms of urban life.[9] Because of the precautions I continue to maintain regarding this study's informants, and since the urban presence of Burundi refugees has largely been recognized by the government, I do not believe that my research will endanger either the refugees described in this study or the urban refugee population in general. Hopefully the opposite will occur–that learning about the contours of the Burundi refugees' clandestine strategies will encourage recognition and acceptance of their quiet urban lives.

Presenting portraits of the urban lives of John, William, James, and the other Burundi refugees in this story required that I try to comprehend city life as they did. After almost two years of following their rules for self-censorship and deception, hanging out with them in their shops, attending their church on Sundays and talking to them privately, I began to understand why fear dominated their lives and became the central theme of the story I sought to tell. I found that, in a strange way, the genocide their parents had fled lived on within them.

As boys growing up in refugee settlements, the tailors had been told that they were "the people of '72," the year the genocide took place. Hearing stories of extravagant evil and massive violence left them feeling vulnerable and afraid. They had come to believe that there would always be some people in their midst who hid dark secrets and were out to get them. Yet they could never be sure who those people were. From those uncertainties and worries arose a kind of culturally received fear that circumscribed an urban lifestyle centered on hiding oneself: *kujificha.*

Surveillance, I also learned, was an accepted part of life in Dar es Salaam. Given their refugee status and illegal urban residence, the young refugees in this story recognized that they had to be careful to remain in the city. Yet the array of fears that John, William, James and the others expressed, and the extensive precautions they took, could only be understood by considering their connection to "the people of '72." For although their families had been forced to leave Burundi, Burundi had never left them.

Notes

1. For matters of clarity, I have chosen to use terminology commonly found in English literature on refugees from Burundi. I have not used the Kirundi language prefix "Ba," which means "people," when mentioning a Burundian's nationality or ethnic affiliation. Thus, refugees from Burundi are called Burundi refugees instead of Barundi refugees, and Burundi's main ethnicities are simply called Hutu and Tutsi instead of Bahutu and Batutsi.

2. Cited in Rakodi 1997: 1.

3. The term "mega-city" is used to describe cities with populations of over eight million (Harris 1992; Watts 1992).

4. See, for example, significant edited volumes such as Richard E. Stren and Rodney R. White's *African Cities in Crisis: Managing Rapid Urban Growth* (1989); Carol Rakodi's *The Urban Challenge in Africa: Growth and Management of Its Large Cities* (1997); and Jonathan Baker and Tade Akin Aina's *The Migration Experience in Africa* (1995).

5. See, for example, the author's 1997 review of "The Migration Experience in Africa" in the *International Journal of African Historical Studies*, 30, no. 3: 636–638, which argues that the book is actually "less about the *experience* of African migration than the study of African migration as a phenomenon."

6. Bernhard observes that participant observation "involves establishing rapport in a new community; learning to act so that people go about their business as usual when you show up; and removing yourself every day from cultural immersion so that you can intellectualize what you've learned, put it into perspective, and write about it convincingly" (1988: 148). The research in Dar es Salaam expanded on this foundation.

7. *Chama Cha Mapinduzi*, or the Revolutionary Party, was Tanzania's only political party until 1992, although it continues to reign as the party of government.

8. It was not at all unusual for young children to shriek in terror in my presence, as often I was the first white man they had ever seen.

9. Whether refugees should be allowed to openly migrate from the settlements is a separate issue.

2

Empowered Victims

Growing up in Burundi refugee society taught the young men in this story about victimization, fear, secrecy—and how to work the system. While growing up in refugee camps, their elders had never allowed them to forget how their Hutu identity forced their families to flee Burundi in order to survive. At the same time, their refugee identity reminded them that they were foreigners in Tanzania, the only country they had ever known. In both cases, the young refugees learned that they were outsiders—exiled from the old country and less than citizens in their country of residence. Growing up unsettled by stories of their violent, distant homeland and frustrated by living inside a remote refugee settlement, it is hardly surprising that thousands of young Burundi refugees wanted nothing more than a chance to escape to Bongoland, an adventure that might distance them from their bloody past as well as their difficult, but more frequently boring, present.

This chapter will explore the effect of two kinds of movements on Burundi refugee lives and ideas: the flight from genocide in Burundi to refugee asylum in Tanzania, and out migration from their new refugee settlement homes. Like so many other features of Burundi refugee perceptions, these two categories stood in opposition to each other. Cultural fear, created in the aftermath of flight from genocide, made refugees feel vulnerable. The stories that young refugees had heard in the refugee camps about their ethnic adversaries, Burundi's Tutsi population, created a fearful picture of powerful predators bent on exterminating all Hutu. But while cultural fear arose from a struggle to survive, the act of migration was done by choice. Dating back at least to the colonial era, Burundian men have migrated from their homes to make money. The young refugee men in this story have thus had to balance a sense of empowerment that migration had instilled in them with the lasting sense of terror and vulnerability that the stories of violence had created.

Fear and Violence

Cultural Fear in Central Africa

While Tanzanian migrant youth often spoke of their *mihangaiko* (anxieties), which were part of living in Dar es Salaam, John, William, and James spoke of *kuogopa* (being afraid). This difference illuminated the emotional gap that separated migrants from refugees. The fears that refugees described went far beyond their awareness of living in the Tanzanian capital illegally. Their deepest fears were generated by the experience of the refugees' survival of an extensive genocide in Burundi in 1972, and it is this source that constitutes the central contributing element to what will here be called cultural fear.

The concept of cultural fear arose during my search to determine exactly what John, William, and James were so afraid of in Dar es Salaam. For while their lives were circumscribed in large part by the fears they consistently described, they did not seem debilitated by them. In fact, in many respects their lives did not seem scary or fearsome at all. The tailoring shops could be fairly pleasant work places, and church was, especially for James and William, mostly enjoyable.

The core of the refugee tailors' fears was shaped by the unknown. Neither John, William nor James could recall much of what took place in Burundi that caused the flight of ethnic Hutu from Burundi. John and James had left Burundi as infants, and William, five or six when the genocide took place, remembered little. Though they would not admit it, it is probable that John and James had never seen a Burundian Tutsi, much less any Tutsi. They had grown up in refugee camps where no Tutsi lived and migrated to a city populated by Tanzanians. But as second generation refugees, and among the survivors of a horrifying and brutal "selective genocide" (Lemarchand and Martin 1974) of Burundian Hutu in 1972, fear was cultivated in the refugee culture they grew up in. As will soon be described, elite Burundi refugee men, who will here be called refugee historians, assumed the role of relaying the story of traumatizing ethnic violence, devastation, flight, and survival.

The historians depicted the Tutsi as fundamentally evil. This characterization was embodied not only in their tales of ferocious Hutu-Tutsi animosities but also in the everyday Imbo-Banyaruguru rivalry that divided Burundi refugees into two mutually suspicious groups. John, William, and James fervently believed that Burundian Tutsi wanted to kill them. Perceived as unusually cunning and clever, seeking collaborators from every possible source, the refugee camps' climate of fear conjured up evil specters that moved secretly in the shadows of refugee lives. The cultural fear emerging from this environment proved portable: detached from their refugee communities in the settlements, John, William, and James still felt surrounded in Dar es Salaam. They believed that the Tutsi or their accomplices could be anywhere, observing them and plotting their destruction. No matter where they went, the Tutsi seemed to hold the upper hand.

The well of cultural fear that nourished the tailors' fear of the unseen appears to have had much deeper sources; an underground river of collective terror that has fueled Burundian and Rwandan societies for generations. Of course, in two countries overwhelmed by waves of violence and controlled for decades by repressive, controlling governments, it has often been difficult for researchers to tap into this river directly. But its existence has been repeatedly suggested in the form of strange, and strangely similar, explosions of violence that have repeatedly overwhelmed Rwandans and Burundians since at least 1959.

Violence in Central Africa has generated significant analysis not only because the slaughters have repeatedly been so extensive but because of the macabre nature of the killings themselves. In Burundi and Rwanda alike, not only have people been killed in extraordinary numbers, the victims are mutilated as well. This type of killing has astounded outside observers, both in Africa and elsewhere. Tanzanians living along the Kagera River marking the Rwanda-Tanzania border in late 1994–after the genocide had ended but while Rwandan corpses were still being fished out of the river–made it clear during interviews that they thought Rwandans were "crazy." They described how waterlogged corpses floating down the Kagera were disfigured not only from their time in the river but also from the gruesome slashes from *pangas*, or machetes, made by their Rwandan killers. To these Tanzanians, and to so many other observers, such actions seemed incomprehensible.

A sequence of Central Africa experts have argued that the desperate and seemingly depraved actions of Rwandans and Burundians are indeed understandable. Most–from Reyntjens to Lemarchand to Prunier–have centered on the political manipulations of ethnic elites. Reyntjens, for example, has argued that "the violence [in Burundi and Rwanda] has been political rather than ethnic in nature" (Reyntjens 1995: 6). Lemarchand's arguments (1996) envision political elites as mythmakers whose manipulations inspire their followers to carry out "ethnocide" (the author's term for ethnic genocide). This approach, in general, has led to a greater understanding of the elite manipulators than the non-elite citizens, and their fears, that are being manipulated. And it is these fears that have driven ordinary Rwandans and Burundians to repeatedly display desperate violence on a massive scale.

Methodological constraints on research have much to do with this gap in our understanding of Central African violence. Lemarchand, for example, details how his "'guardian angel' assigned to [him] by the Ministry of Foreign Affairs"(Lemarchand 1996b: xxx), limited his ability to dig beneath the level of ethnic politicians to "the clandestine discourse of the powerless" (ibid.). As will be discussed shortly, Burundi refugee elites also sought to constrain the ability of researchers to learn about non-elite refugee concerns. Yet evidence nonetheless exists in the historical record to suggest that intensely emotional connections between ordinary Rwandans and Burundians have promoted the growth of extreme fear in the region. A similar kind of culturally inspired fear, vulnerable to political manipulation, appears to afflict Burundians and Rwandans in very similar ways. Uvin indicates that Rwandans and Burundians alike are afflicted by "the vicious dynamic between the two neighboring countries, with [violent] events in each country presenting to the other, in a kind of distorted mirror, the proof of its worst fears, its worst nightmare" (Uvin 1998: 34). The fear that Uvin refers to is mentioned by other scholars of Central Africa as well. Lemarchand describes Burundi during the killings in 1972 as having "an atmosphere saturated with fear" (Lemarchand 1996b: 98). Prunier considered the relationship that had arisen between Rwandans and Burundians beset with a "constant and almost obsessive mutual scrutiny" (Prunier 1995: 198).

As a result, extreme violence arising in one country has repeatedly sent shock waves through the other. Fear–of ethnic violence in one country being duplicated in the other–has become the catalyst for still more repression and violence. Prunier cites a sequence of examples of this phenomenon: "the fear aroused in the Tutsi community of Burundi by the Rwanda massacres of 1959–63" leading to "the construction of a Tutsi dominated political system in Bujumbura [Burundi]"; "fear caused by Rwanda-inspired Hutu restlessness in the late 1960s which drove Tutsi extremists to start the 1972 mass killings of Hutu intellectuals in order to deprive any future Hutu movement of its potential elite"; fear arising from "the 1972 Burundi horror which led [Rwandan] President Gregoire Kayibanda to think in 1973 that a demagogic persecution of the Tutsi community in Rwanda would help him prop up his faltering dictatorship." (ibid.: 198) And so on, until late in 1993, when Burundi's first democratically elected president, a Hutu engineer named Melchior Ndadaye, was assassinated by extremist Tutsi military officers, leading to ethnic slaughter that has continued to the present. This, in turn, spurred Hutu extremists in Rwanda to "rally many simple or hesitant [Hutu]" by playing to Rwandan Hutu fears at many levels: (1) "fear of losing one's privileges (rational level)"; (2) "fear of losing one's life (visceral level)"; and (3) "fear of losing control of one's world (mythical level)" (Prunier 1995: 200). As Weinstein noted in 1972 but is equally true today, "Burundi politics has never been able to escape the possibility that what happened in Rwanda was fated to happen in Burundi" (Weinstein 1972: 28). The reverse could be said for politics in Rwanda, and it is this creeping, shadowy fear that scholars refer to and local ethnic politicians manipulate that also permeates the Imbo-Banyaruguru rivalry within Burundi refugee society.

Noses

To discern whether an apprehended person was Hutu or Tutsi, a survivor of the 1994 genocide in Rwanda reported how *Interahamwe* militiamen sometimes stuck a thumb into a person's nose. If their thumb could enter a nostril, the militiamen would release the prisoner, concluding that he or she was a Hutu. But if their thumb could not fit, the prisoner's life was over. Small nostrils meant the person was a Tutsi, and all Tutsi had to be killed.

In 1996, while carrying out field research among Rwandan Hutu refugees, I hired a translator who resembled a Tutsi. He was tall and thin, he had very dark skin, a thin nose and almond-shaped eyes. Given his presence among a huge Rwandan Hutu population containing many who had carried out mass murder during Rwanda's 1994 genocide, I asked him, in private, about his identity. "I am a

Hutu," he said. Then he described his escape from Rwanda. One day, in the Rwandan capital of Kigali just after the genocide erupted in April, 1994, he was surrounded by hooded young men who knocked him down and threatened to kill him on the spot. As they raised their machetes, he called out that he was a Hutu. The drunken *Interahamwe* militiamen didn't believe him. He pulled his identity card from his pocket, and begged them to read it. Finally, he recognized one of the men and asked him by name to do so. The man relented, confirming that the identity card identified my translator as a "Hutu." The killers left.

In Burundi, Colonel Michel Micombero, the Tutsi dictator who assumed power in his mid-twenties and then supervised the 1972 genocide, actually looked like a Hutu. Short, stocky and brown-skinned, with a broad, flat nose, Micombero had physical features that were much closer to the Hutu stereotype that German and, especially, Belgian colonial rulers had institutionalized. "Some thought I was a Hutu because of my physique," Micombero once explained, but then "someone went to have a look at my father and say that he had a Tutsi nose. From then on no one asked me any question" (Livre Blanc 1972: 59; in Lemarchand 1996b: 7).

"You know," a Rwandan Muslim leader explained to me in a refugee camp, the 1994 Rwandan genocide "was an affair of the nose." As the stories described above relate, when ethnic violence erupts in Central Africa, the shape of one's nose, among other characteristics, can determine whether one lives or dies. To understand how such racial stereotypes can play a peculiarly destructive role in history, a brief examination of ethnic ambiguity in Central Africa is helpful.

Rwanda and Burundi have long been thought to contain similar proportions of Hutu (85 percent), Tutsi (14 percent) and Twa (1 percent). A fourth group, the Ganwa, or "Princes of the Blood," constituted the royalty of pre-colonial Burundian society and had no corollary in Rwanda. Against their will, the Ganwa eventually became identified as Tutsi, a group they considered well beneath their own. The two central groups, Hutu and Tutsi, have been described as ethnic identities, but also as caste designations (Kesby 1977), racial distinctions (Greenland 1973), and sometimes as tribal groupings by the Western media. Field investigation of this problem has been difficult because Burundi's government continues to outlaw the mere mention of "Tutsi" and "Hutu," and the Rwandan government has also assumed this policy. The tendency to define the two groups as "ethnic" is clouded by the fact that they share a common language, culture, history, geographic space,[1] and some-times even the same clan affiliation (D. Newbury 1980).

In both Rwanda and Burundi, Tutsi and Hutu can be deadly adversaries yet united in their disdain for the Twa. Greenland notes that "It would be defilement for [Burundian Hutu and Tutsi] to eat, drink or sit under the same roof as a Twa," and that the story of the Twa of Burundi and Rwanda "is one of continuous exploitation by the rest of Burundi and Rwanda society" (Greenland 1976: 129). Illustrative of this, many Burundi refugees casually refer to the Twa as monkeys.

Unlike the lowest-status Twa, Hutu and Tutsi have inter-married since the arrival of Tutsi migrants to Central Africa centuries ago from, some argue, the Oromo area of modern-day Ethiopia.[2] This inter-marriage helps explain why ethnic stereotypes describe the Hutu-Tutsi differences more accurately than does reality: a Hutu may resemble a Tutsi, and vice versa, even while stereotyped stan-dards of ethnic difference have not changed. Thus, while Central Africans such as the scholar Alexandre Kimenyi insist that "In real-ity there is no way a Mututsi [Tutsi person] can be distinguished physically from a Muhutu [Hutu person]" (Kimenyi 1989: 12), the power of stereotypes to influence reality has proven lasting.

It is striking to reflect on the remarkable power of Hutu and Tutsi stereotypes. The conception of Tutsi arising from a superior race of people (the Abyssinians, or Ethiopians) emanates directly from the speculations of the first European explorer to the area, John Han-ning Speke. In what now is Uganda, while meeting with a king of one of a sequence of Central African peoples thought to contain Tutsi-like immigrants, Speke declared that he "admired [the king's] race," adding that he "believed them to have sprung from our old friends the Abyssinians" who "were Christians like ourselves" (Speke 1922: 171). As a young boy, more than a century after Speke's 1863 visit to Central Africa, I recall reading in a record book that the Tutsi were the world's tallest people. There was also a dance popular in the United States called "the Watusi," which had apparently arisen from the European fascination with Central African court culture. In his book, *In the Heart of Africa,* the German traveler Duke Adolphus Frederick of Mecklenberg vividly described the sort of wonder that overtook so many European vis-itors to Central Africa regarding "the high degree of civilisation existing among the Watussi" (Frederick 1910: 50). To the Duke and most other Europeans entering "Ruanda-Urundi," Tutsi culture constituted an island of refinement surrounded by uncouth Bantu tribes. The Tutsi's apparent superiority could be seen in a host of ways, including their war dances, which Duke Mecklenberg said were "measured and dignified" and "never degenerated into those grotesque leapings and war cries, or cadenced groans, so often met with among savage native tribes" (p. 60).

While an explorer's theory eventually evolved into the "famous Hamite myth" of Central Africa (Rutake and Gahama 1998: 83), the myth itself ran into problems when it was applied to reality. Patrick Balfour's description of the Tutsi, in his book *Lords of the Equator: An African Journey* (1939), aptly indicates how efforts to align myth with reality were inherently problematic. His analysis of royal Tutsi culture is at once glowing and confused. "Frequently, in Ruanda-Urundi," Balfour noted, "I imagined myself in a smaller and more civilized Abyssinia." Almost immediately, however, differences between Tutsi and Ethiopians sprout. "The height, the features, the clothes, the hair of the Watussi" seemed similar to the Ethiopian Amhara, as did the geography in which they lived. But Balfour also observed that the Tutsi spoke a Bantu language with no connection to Amharic, lacked a written alphabet of any kind, Amharic or otherwise, and even "the elegance of his manners and the grace of his smile [of] the Watussi was a contrast to the rough and querulous Amhara." By the end of his description, Balfour shifts his Tutsi comparison from Ethiopians to Egyptians, citing how "the [Tutsi] royal family claims celestial origin, as the Pharaohs did" (Balfour 1939: 202). Duke Mecklenburg's speculations on Tutsi origins ranged even further, connecting them through the Maasai people of East Africa to Egyptians and even Arabs (1910: 47).

Almost inevitably, European discussions of Tutsi difference returned to the shape of their noses. A Belgian colonial document reported that the Tutsi nose, which was "very high and relatively narrow ... made such an impression on the first [European] observers that, referring unconsciously to the European physique, they described thin lips to them as well" (Belgian Congo and Ruanda-Urundi Information and Public Relations Office 1960: 19). Though the text then explains that the Tutsi did not have thin lips at all (the Twa, in fact, "had by far the thinnest lips" [ibid.]), the comment betrays the European tendency to compare the Tutsi not to reality but to themselves. The mythology had assumed a life of its own, and through repetition it "took on the appearance of truth" (Taylor 1997: 4).

In the end, Ruanda-Urundi's colonial overlords—first the Germans beginning in approximately 1899 and then the Belgians in

1925–transformed latent "genetico-status group[s]" (Weinstein and Schrire 1976) into racial stereotypes that facilitated the governing and guiding of colonial society. As a result, while the Tutsi benefited from the colonial system, the Hutu suffered a general loss of political, social, and economic power. Living in this new colonial world, Rwandans and Burundians soon came to see each other through their overlords' stereotyping lenses. The Tutsi among them became a kind of African master race; dark, tall, elegant, wily people who naturally lorded over the brown, squat, strong, dim Hutu, all of whom were seen as suited for physical work. Prunier labeled this outcome "a racialisation of consciousness" which created a "Tutsi 'superior race'" amidst Hutu "inferiors" (Prunier 1995: 38–39). As a result,

> through the actions, both intellectual and material, of the white foreigners, myths had been synthesized into a new reality. And that new reality had become operational, with its heroes [the Tutsi], its tillers of the soil [the Hutu] and its clowns [the Twa]. Feelings and social actions would henceforth take place in relation to this reconstructed reality because by then it would have become the only one. The time-bomb had been set and it was now only a question of when it would go off. (Ibid.: 39)

Prunier's ethnic time bomb has in fact exploded many times, and is a critical underlying source of the cultural fear explored in this book. John, William, and James were well aware of the destructive potential of the fear they shared with Rwandans and other Burundians, for that fear, when appropriately manipulated, had regularly been the collective wick that sparked explosions of extraordinary violence in Rwanda and Burundi. The fear itself had grown out of the gap between pristine stereotypes and fuzzy realities. People could never be sure who was who: those who appeared Hutu-like could actually be Tutsi, and vice versa. When violence between Tutsi and Hutu arose, such elemental uncertainty only fed a person's terror. And for John, William, James, and other second generation survivors of the 1972 genocide in Burundi, the gap was a place where their cultural fear thrived. Present only in the harrowing stories of genocidal destruction they had heard, over and again, while growing up in the refugee camps, the Tutsi were an idea as much as a group of people. This had the effect of enhancing suspicions about the underlying truth of another's identity and motivations, supporting individual refugee fears that Tanzanian neighbors or fellow Burundi refugees were actually Tutsi accomplices–or, perhaps, real Tutsi.

1972

During the violence in Burundi in 1972 and 1973, as many as 250,000 Burundians died (Weinstein 1976) while another 200,000 became refugees (Clark 1987). This violence actually took place in two very separate acts. The first was an isolated revolt arising in southern Burundi. It was largely carried out by Hutu farmers and was the most severe of a series of protests arising from what has been described as a "peasant protest culture" in Burundi (Weinstein and Schrire 1976: 48). The second was completely different: a massive operation, organized by the government, carried out by the army (with considerable assistance from Tutsi civilians) aimed at creating nothing less than a completely transformed society. The "selective genocide"[3] did not specifically target those who caused the initial uprising—mainly poorly educated Hutu farmers—as much as the entire membership of what was perceived as the Hutu elite. The attack illuminates the breadth of the acting Central African definition of "elite," which includes not just politicians, soldiers and urban professionals but nurses, priests, and secondary schoolchildren as well; or what Weinstein and Schrire considered in Burundi in 1972 "a general hunt for Hutu with any degree of westernization" (1976: 52). Burundi refugee elites in Dar es Salaam who had survived the massacres explained that a Hutu could even be killed if they wore glasses, since anyone who wore glasses would be considered an "intellectual." Makinson's analysis suggests that most of those killed during this operation were men (1993: 170).

The work of Weinstein and Schrire (1976) remains one of the most authoritative and detailed analyses of the 1972 events in Burundi. Their interpretation considers a number of issues that were substantiated in research with Burundi refugees in Dar es Salaam, including the striking difference in Hutu political perspectives according to class. They also considered why peasants largely from the Imbo and Mosso regions—in the southern cone of the country, from the lowland areas around Lake Tanganyika across to the Tanzania border along the Muragarazi River—revolted while Hutu in other parts of Burundi generally did not. Most of the refugees who later entered Tanzania came from areas of Burundi which had rebelled against centralizing control for decades. Relatively few were elites.

Weinstein and Schrire argue that, like previous outbreaks of peasant violence in Burundi, the 1972 revolt was "conservative in nature" and "essentially a response to the encroachment of alien life

PHOTOGRAPH 2.1 New Glasses

In Burundi and Rwanda, eyeglasses are thought to suggest sophistication, accomplishment, and a social position in the upper class. They also symbolize that the person is an intellectual. Many Burundian Hutu wearing glasses during the 1972 genocide were targets for elimination. In this photograph, a Rwandan refugee child wears a pair of homemade glasses in an attempt to enhance his image. Photograph: Marc Sommers.

MAP 2.1 Map of Burundi

Adapted from the United Nations map of Burundi. Two of the primary sites where the initial uprising and violent repression took place in 1972 are underlined.

Source: United Nations Department of Public Information Cartographic Section, Map No. 3753 Rev. 2, December 1997.

patterns on the local way of life" (Weinstein and Schrire 1976: 43). Ethnic animosities, they argued, were not the driving force of this violent trend. Lemarchand, among others, viewed these events somewhat differently. In Lemarchand's analysis, the uprising appears to have been planned with "Mulelist" rebels from Zaire, whose motives were not entirely clear, and speculates on the involvement of a number of other parties; Hutu politicians, students, and military officers among them.

In any event, Weinstein and Schrire also noted a "strong influence of cult ritualists" (ibid.: 45) from Buha, the home of the Ha people, who live across the Tanzanian border from southern Burundi and have a culture and language similar to those of its Burundian neighbors. Together with Lemarchand, Weinstein and Schrire further found that, although most of the victims were Tutsi, many Hutu were killed as well. Yet while Lemarchand took a largely ethnic tack in this regard–Hutu killing, for the most part, Tutsi–Weinstein and Schrire argued that, in its essence, the revolt "was an attack on the symbols of authority, and those groups that enjoyed the fruits of independence at the peasant's expense" (ibid.: 40). The fact that most of those enjoying such fruits were Tutsi was a secondary concern. At the same time, the revolt was timed to take place, in part, when members of the Tutsi leadership were in conflict, largely pitting the lower status Tutsi-Hima, who had ascended into power after first dominating the national army, against the higher status Tutsi-Banyaruguru, who had lost power and, not coincidentally, had generally disdained military careers. During the subsequent genocide, thousands of Tutsi-Banyaruguru were among those targeted for elimination by the ruling Tutsi-Hima elite.

The 1972 revolt and subsequent genocide thus brings together a number of threads that have been woven into Burundi refugee lives since their flight into Tanzania in 1972–73: the significant involvement of Burundian Hutu from the Imbo region in the initial revolt; the victimization of Tutsi-Banyaruguru as well as Hutu; the cultural and linguistic connections between southern Burundians and the Ha across the border in Tanzania; and, as will be considered shortly, the very different perspectives and experiences between non-elite Hutu in southern Burundi and their elite ethnic brethren.

The 1972 uprising began on April 29. The genocidal operation mainly aimed at Hutu elites began soon after that, and, like the Rwandan genocide twenty-two years later, lasted about three months. In fact, the similarities between these two genocides are striking. Both genocides were "final solution" operations. In Burundi, the *genocidaires* strove to eliminate all Hutu–and some Tutsi–elites, while in Rwanda the genocidal operation sought to kill all Tutsi and many politically moderate Hutu.[4] Many of the victims of both genocides responded to their imminent deaths without a fight. Commenting on Burundian Hutu facing death in 1972, Lemarchand was struck by how "extraordinary was the apparent placidity with which innocent Hutu went to their graves" (Lemarchand 1996b: 97), while several observers, including members of the Physicians for Human Rights, noted similar responses among Tutsi victims in Rwanda. Lists of those who were to be executed were used in both genocides, and in Burundi in 1972 many of those on lists were children in secondary school. In both genocides, radio was employed as a weapon of war, and references to the stereotyped ranking of Tutsi as higher status and Hutu as lower status were commonplace. While Greenland noted that Burundian government radio urged people to "hunt down the python in the grass," which gave Tutsi "license to exterminate all educated Hutu" (Greenland 1976: 120), the Rwandan Hutu extremist Radio Television Libre des Milles Collines repeatedly reminded listeners in 1994 to "reach for the top part of the house" and exterminate all Tutsi (Prunier 1995: 211). Yet another similarity between the two genocides is found in the involvement of outside supporters–notably the French–as accomplices to mass slaughter. While Prunier detailed France's complicity in the Rwandan genocide in his book *The Rwanda Crisis* (1995), Greenland noted how French military pilots kept "Burundi's planes on a steady course while [Burundi] soldiers machine-gun[ned] Hutu rebels out of the side windows" (Greenland 1973: 450).

Amidst all these similarities were two notable differences. Rwanda's genocide received considerable international attention while Burundi's genocide did not. Weinstein was one of a handful of observers at the time to chastise the slight attention the Burundian genocide received in the media and by Burundi scholars (Weinstein 1972). But more important were the outcomes for each band of *genocidaires*. The extremist Hutu organizers of the Rwandan genocide succeeded in carrying out a devastating genocide, but in the process were driven from the country by the advancing Tutsi army, the Rwandan Patriotic Front. In Burundi in 1972, the result was the opposite, with the perpetuation of fear the *genocidaires'* objective. Afraid of "Hutu numerical superiority" themselves, Weinstein and Schrire observed, Tutsi government organizers of the genocide sought to instill fear in all Burundian Hutu by "execut[ing] a repression so pervasive in its brutality that Hutu would be stunned into submission" (Weinstein and Schrire 1976: 51).

They succeeded. Carrying out such an activity made the stereotype of the Tutsi as fundamentally superior to Burundian Hutu more concrete. "Never before," Lemarchand observed, "had the Hutu as a group been so thoroughly reduced to the status of an underclass" (Lemarchand 1996b: 103). The psychological effect of this on Hutu inside Burundi and among Burundi refugees has been lasting. Educated Burundi refugees were well aware of their status as the only surviving Burundian Hutu elites, and it accorded them a special status in refugee society. With the later generations of Burundi refugees, including the generation of John, William, and James, the ultimate aim of the planners of the 1972 genocide has been confirmed. For these refugees, Tutsi evil, superiority, and determination to destroy their Hutu enemies were facts of life. Cultural fear, and the role of senior refugees in cultivating it, kept these beliefs alive. As Lemarchand explained, the Tutsi organizers of the genocide "aimed not only to decapitate a potential counterelite but to spread terror throughout the entire Hutu community and thus create an enduring sense of fear and submission among the living and the unborn—in short, to teach a lesson that would be remembered by generations to come" (Lemarchand 1996b: 102). Findings gathered for this book only underscore how well later generations learned this lesson.

Historians and Their Followers

Claiming Constituencies

If refugees from Burundi proved unable to dislodge the lasting sense of fear that the 1972 genocide created, it was not for lack of trying. The history they developed, which Malkki has called their "mythico-history" (1995), proved more successful at addressing submission to the Tutsi than their fear of them. This mythico-history, Malkki has argued, preached that Burundian Hutu victims of Tutsi oppression constituted a moral community with a national past, making the refugee camp "the most central place from which to imagine a 'pure' Hutu national identity" (ibid.: 3). The significance of this research is considerable, and Malkki's thesis, and her methods, will be examined shortly, but an important contextual concern will considered here first. Malkki's focus on historical imagining as the collective practice of Burundi refugees from Mishamo settlement (or "camp") obscures how that history was created, transmitted and promoted. Here, it will be argued that the mythico-history had specific authors and keepers of the flame. John, William, James, and other Burundi refugees of their generation who had grown up in the refugee settlements were well aware of these people: educated, elite men, often with a strong political bent, who imparted the experience of surviving ethnic genocide to young refugees. These men will here be called *refugee historians.*

The refugee historians became critical players in the lives of young refugees for two reasons. First, they created a picture of the Burundian past that the younger generation of refugees could internalize. This was the "official" history that established the refugees' connections to, and claims upon, their Burundian homeland. The second reason arose from the convergence between cultural history and political utility. Burundi refugee leaders sought to hide the fact that refugee camp communities were sharply divided into two groups—Imbo and Banyaruguru—because they wished to be seen as the representatives of all Burundi refugees. Emphasizing ethnic solidarity promised to greatly enhance their power base. To promote the outward perception that all Burundi refugees were Hutu refugees and nothing more, they outlawed public discussion of the Imbo-Banyaruguru division. As a result, regardless of whether the refugee historians supported the leaders' political agendas or not, the refugee historians' promotion of mythico-history through its retelling to refugee children and youth supported the leaders' political aims.

The significance of the separation between Burundi refugee elites such as refugee historians, some of whom were politicized refugee leaders, and their non-elite Burundian Hutu brethren, has roots in history. Evidence suggests that Burundian Hutu elites have often shared little with the masses of Hutu peasants (Horner 1967; Weinstein and Schrire 1976). High-status Hutu in pre-colonial times shared class interests with high-status Tutsi. During the colonial era, most of the Westernized Hutu elites distanced themselves from protests involving rural Hutu. Following independence, Hutu elites vied for power against Tutsi elites and ultimately lost, and only then "did they seek to associate themselves with the Hutu peasantry" (Weinstein and Schrire: 37). During those years, Weinstein and Schrire described how educated Hutu men claimed a constituency for themselves that constituted every Hutu in the country, or approximately 85 percent of the entire population.

Yet a fundamental difference between the aims of Hutu elites and non-elites remained. In the abortive 1965 revolt, for example, "the peasants attacked a system," Weinstein and Schrire wrote, while "the Hutu elite wanted to gain control over it" (ibid.: 37). Such differences in perspective continued to echo across Burundi refugee society. During my 1990–92 field research period, for example, elite refugees stated that they wanted free and fair elections in Burundi before they repatriated, while members of the non-elite majority stated clearly that changing the ethnic composition of the Tutsi-dominated army, which had carried out much of the 1972 genocide, was far more important to them. As many non-elite refugees pointed out, "The army *is* the government."[5]

Even in a region of the world where people value education highly, education for refugee survivors of Burundi's 1972 massacre is particularly significant. This, again, arises in large part from Burundi's past. Colonial administrators elevated Tutsi men for advanced training and education and excluded the Hutu almost completely. Aspiring Hutu found access mainly in missionary schools and seminaries, which spawned an educated and resentful Hutu counter-elite (Greenland 1976: 110). Following the 1972 genocide, when the Tutsi government used the peasant revolt as an excuse to "decimate all potential leadership elements among the Hutu" (Weinstein and Schrire 1976: 51), educated Hutu who managed to escape the army's clutches began to perceive themselves as leaders of Burundi refugees.

In the settlements, very few refugees continued education beyond primary school. As Malkki explained, refugees perceived Tanzanian authorities as carrying out a Tutsi-like policy of excluding Burundian Hutu refugees from higher education (1995). University-educated refugees seemed to have attained an unusually high social stature in refugee society. Few in number, and holding the education that caused Hutu with similar backgrounds to become Tutsi victims in 1972, they stood as symbolic survivors of Tutsi oppression for Burundi's refugees.

Some of the elite refugees living in Dar es Salaam fled Burundi after the 1972 genocide, when the combination of Hutu ethnicity and secondary or university education made them justifiably fear for their lives. Most of them lived in Dar es Salaam with UNHCR recognition, although very few received financial support from UNHCR. Still, their legal residence meant that they did not have to lead clandestine lives, and could be far more outspoken with their views. Although still careful of attracting attention, they had the luxury of relative safety in Dar es Salaam, and their symbolic stature in refugee society lent their views importance. Quite often, these men would send word through other refugees that they wanted to speak with me.

One of these meetings dramatized this relationship between refugee historians and the younger refugee generation. Pastor Albert had arranged for John and Marko to accompany the two of us to our audience with an especially esteemed refugee historian.

We met in an unfinished concrete house in a peri-urban section of Dar es Salaam. When we arrived, the two young tailors were told to sit on concrete blocks and listen while the historian directed his historical descriptions to me. As with all meetings with refugee historians, I was first quizzed on Burundian Hutu history. The refugee historians wanted to see whether I agreed that the Hutu had occupied Burundi first. The issue of original occupancy was critical to them, as it supported Hutu claims to power as the original, authentic Burundians and the Tutsi as foreign interlopers.[6]

During the meeting with the refugee historian, John and Marko were silent, their eyes downcast. After they returned to the privacy of their quarters behind the tailoring shop, they explained how all refugee children must periodically come before historians in the settlements and listen to stories of the genocide and Tutsi oppression of the Hutu in Burundi—stories to which their parents would then continually refer. Both John and Marko said that they had heard nothing new during our meeting with the historian. They had found his descriptions of violence and oppression unsettling, but somewhat boring too, because he touched on themes and passages that they had heard many times before. John argued that Pastor Albert was still treating them like boys who still needed to learn about their history, while they clearly saw themselves as men who already knew enough about the Hutu's violent past.

Although this particular refugee historian was not a political party member, many of them were. The dominant refugee political party at the time of field research was Palipehutu (Parti pour la libération du peuple Hutu, or Party for the Liberation of the Hutu People). In the hands of party leaders, stories of Tutsi repression were inflected with clear political meanings. Tutsi leaders were not only evil but politically illegitimate. Palipehutu leaders were the rightful leaders of Burundi. Their claims to be leaders of the entire Burundian Hutu constituency mirrored the claims of pre-independence Hutu leaders as unelected representatives of the Hutu majority. But they also borrowed from the Burundian Tutsi leaders who outlawed public mention of Hutu and Tutsi following the 1972 genocide by prohibiting mention of Imbo and Banyaruguru in the refugee settlements.

The mere suggestion of this division could rankle such leaders. They shot down questions of Imbo and Banyaruguru factions in refugee society with disparaging remarks for those refugees relating such information to me. They called my sources *wahuni* (ignorant people), but more often *Watu wa Chinichini* (the Very Low People). John, among other refugees, later related that refugee leaders, and not just Palipehutu members, considered themselves the *Watu wa Juu* (the High People). Subsequent research with non-elite Rwandan Hutu refugees on definitions of these categories revealed similar results: that the *Watu wa Juu* represented those with power, while *Watu wa Chinichini* described those that were affected by power.[7] This Central African dichotomy did not apply elsewhere—many Tanzanians applied *Watu wa Chinichini* to people working "underground" and outside of the social and political mainstream.

The mythico-history that Malkki recorded from her field research in Mishamo camp (1995), which elaborated on many of the historical depictions that refugee historians described to me, is the most thoroughly documented example of ethnic Hutu history found anywhere. Though many of its themes have been trumpeted in Rwandan and Burundian Hutu-dominated political pronouncements, Malkki's version is especially coherent and thorough. Her analysis and conceptual framework are also compelling. The author defined her mythico-history concept in the following way: the "Hutu history" that "camp" refugees (that is, refugees living in Mishamo Settlement, where she conducted half of her field research) described did not simply record events but instead was "a subversive recasting and reinterpretation of [Hutu history] in fundamentally moral terms." Since the result "cannot be accurately described as either history or myth," Malkki labeled it mythico-history (Malkki 1995: 54).

Malkki found that the historical narratives of these camp refugees "emerged" from conversations with refugees in Mishamo and usually "led to broader, historicizing reflections" (Malkki 1995: 49). These reflections were remarkably similar; "almost formulaic" (p. 56), but nevertheless, Malkki argued that "people commonly arranged memories or experiences into mythico-historical configurations" and "standard versions of [historical] events routinely produced themselves" (Malkki 1995: 58). Living together in an isolated space, the refugee camp "fixed and objectified" the refugees as "'the Hutu' and as 'the refugees'" (Malkki 1995: 234), and became the site for the creation of a people—the Hutu—as a nation in exile.

Malkki's findings depicted a Burundi refugee world in Tanzania that contained two distinctly different types of experiences. In addition to the "camp" refugees, there were "town" refugees who lived in Kigoma, located near the Burundi border. This set of refugees lived separately from the camp refugees and developed their own culture and survival strategies. They also employed "strategies of invisibility" to shield their refugee identity from others. Refugees accordingly presented themselves as different kinds of Tanzanian citizen; a Waha from the Burundian border area, a Burundian immigrant from colonial times, or a Muslim. Malkki found that fear, while present in their lives, was unremarkable for these Burundi refugees. The town refugees of Kigoma may have had a "generalized fear of conspicuousness" (Malkki 1995: 157), but it hardly seemed unusual. Instead of a "knee-jerk reaction of fear," Malkki characterized it as merely "a specific form of a much more general kind of strategy employed by urbanites throughout the region" (ibid.). Malkki notes that the Burundi refugees in Kigoma town oriented their lives around practical, day-to-day concerns and "construed their [future] paths as *individuals*," the opposite of "the collective path of the Hutu refugees [that is, those living in refugee camps] as 'a people'" (Malkki 1995: 184).

The Burundi refugees described here constitute a hybrid of Malkki's dichotomy: camp refugees who migrated to town. The youth that dominate Burundi refugee society in Dar es Salaam absorbed the refugee camp culture Malkki depicted and transported it into the city. There, John, William, and James employed strategies of invisibility just as their Kigoma brethren did, but their cultural fear, emanating in large part from stories of genocidal violence contained in the mythico-history, made them far more fearful than the Kigoma refugees Malkki described.

Field research for this book confirms the existence and power of Malkki's findings on the mythico-history of Burundi refugees. The differences between findings from the two research endeavors on the issue of ethnic history center not on content but context. To explore these differences, a comparison between the two methodological approaches is useful.

Malkki employed an experimental technique to represent the "variations on a single, shared grand narrative" that she recorded from refugees she interviewed in Mishamo camp (Malkki 1995: 57). She used a series of "panels," which she described as "extended narrative passages clearly demarcated and set apart of the rest of the text" (ibid.: 56). To gather the narratives from many refugees that she then collectively represented in panels, Malkki placed considerable emphasis on listening. "The success of the fieldwork," Malkki wrote, "hinged not so much on a determination to ferret out 'the facts' as on a willingness to leave some stones unturned, to listen to what my informants deemed important, and to demonstrate my trustworthiness by not prying where I was not wanted" (ibid.: 51). Noting that the "difficult and politically charged nature of the

field work setting made such attempts at delicacy a simple necessity," Malkki further argued that "It may be precisely by giving up
the scientific detective's urge to know 'everything' that we gain
access to those very partial vistas that our informants may desire to
share with us" (Malkki 1995: 51). She then stated that "there may
be a greater wisdom in refraining from the blind accumulation of
'data' and the extraction of truth for its own sake" (ibid.).

The evidence from research presented here on Hutu, Imbo, and
Banyaruguru histories strongly suggest that Malkki accomplished
her goal of recording the "very partial vistas" that informants
wanted to share with a foreign researcher. Malkki was able to detail
the mythico-history while avoiding the difficulties created by working in a politically charged environment. Her technique produced
a startling achievement and a methodological safeguard against, in
all probability, resistance from the refugee political leadership both
for Malkki and her informants had she attempted to dig deeper.

But during Malkki's research period, Mishamo settlement also
contained political activists for the then-dominant Burundian Hutu
political party, Palipehutu. For such a liberation movement, a
mythico-history is clearly useful; indeed, its retelling to a foreign
researcher would seem to help broadcast arguments for Hutu legit-
imacy and the Palipehutu movement simultaneously. Malkki did
not directly examine the political implications of her mythico-history, and has been questioned on this. Research conducted with a
more recently arriving Burundi refugee population in Tanzania by
Turner, for example, led him to argue that "whereas mythico-histo-
ries seem to simply 'emerge' in [Malkki's] analysis, I believe that
these histories are actively used and manipulated for political
means" (Turner 1998: 23). Turner then proceeds to note that the
"beautiful and dangerous" mythico-history (ibid.: 28) has direct
connections to Palipehutu ideology and intentions. Gourevitch,
after observing that visits to several refugee camps containing
Rwandan or Burundian Hutu refugees revealed how "virtually
everybody I met told me an almost identical version of the history
of Hutu-Tutsi relations," concluded that "much of what Malkki was
told at Mishamo was probably propaganda fed to her informants
and to herself by Palipehutu activists" (1996: 62).

Research with Burundi refugees in Dar es Salaam indicates that
both sets of analyses—Malkki's argument that the mythico-history
"was a powerful device for the creation of a cosmological and moral
order" (Malkki 1996: 79) and the political tracts and manipulations
that Turner and Gourevitch describe, existed in the refugee camps

at the same time. The mythico-history's concern "with the ordering and reordering of social and political categories" (ibid.: 55) certainly invited manipulation by politicians. But this did not reduce the mythico-history to a mere political tract. It was far more than that. The stories told by refugee historians anchored the Hutu identities of the generation of John, William, and James. Still, it appears that political censorship in the refugee settlements would have prevented refugee informants from describing to Malkki how using history and group victimization to 'purify' the refugees as ethnic Hutu, which Malkki recorded, also created a divisive internal debate over which refugee group—Imbo or Banyaruguru—represented the purest Hutu.

Gathering information on sub-ethnicities, in methodological terms, was easier in Dar es Salaam than in the refugee settlements. Hiding in town, refugees were distanced from the kinds of social pressures they reported as existing in the settlements. John consistently related how he could never have described the Imbo-Banyaruguru rivalry to me if we were in the camps instead of in Dar es Salaam. Other young refugees confirmed John's assertion. Social divisions, they all said, were to remain hidden. As one refugee historian inquired in response to an initial question about Imbo and Banyaruguru refugees, "Who told you our secret?"

Descriptions of refugee political operatives censoring discussions with non-refugees about social fractures also summoned a lament from refugee elites that the Hutu were unable to work together against the Tutsi. One of the first historians that I interviewed commented: "Naturally, the Hutu don't cooperate. That's why we can't overthrow the [Burundian Tutsi] regime. There are so many of us, but we can't unite." This expression of frustration at the 'natural' divisiveness among Hutu was a painful reality to many refugee elites, and the source of often extraordinary tension among non-elite refugees.

Refugees as Hutu: The Unity Described

The themes that arose throughout the refugee historians' descriptions of history and current social tensions resonated to the young tailors in this story. Through these themes, their own identification as Imbo or Banyaruguru, Hutu, and refugee was connected to vulnerability and victimization. Regardless of the group they specified—Hutu versus Tutsi, Imbo versus Banyaruguru, or Tanzanian versus refugee—they perceived their own group as innocent of any wrongdoing, while their opposition were seen as potential perpetrators of crimes against them. The lesson to be learned was that they were persecuted by opposing groups because of their identity. Ultimately the opposing force was connected back to the Tutsi, who either directly committed the offense or persuaded others to do their dirty work for them.

The purpose of this section is to reveal in the refugee historians' version of history and social conflict some common themes that refugees collectively considered factual. Two of the three themes described here–Tutsi power, and the Tutsi's determination to exclude Hutu from educational opportunities–expand on findings Malkki has identified (1995). The subsequent section will focus on the aspects of refugee history that separated Burundi refugees into opposing Imbo and Banyaruguru camps. To gather versions of history that both united and divided Burundi refugees, I interviewed more than thirty educated refugee men, many of them several times. I had originally received most of their names from either UNHCR or the Ministry of Home Affairs. These names comprised the list of all those Burundi refugees who had received permission to reside in Dar es Salaam–the official extent of knowledge on the Burundi refugee population in the capital. Significantly, the only elites I managed to interview at length were men. I tried but failed to elicit details from women. Even university-educated women handed over the role of historian to male associates.[8]

"The Tutsi have all the power" The fact that the Hutu resided in Burundi before the Tutsi arrived, and continued to comprise an overwhelming majority of the population, summoned the perplexing question of why Burundian Hutu had yet to gain power over the Tutsi minority. Refugee historians contended that the Tutsi came to power long before the age of European colonization. During the colonial era, however, the Europeans solidified and institutionalized Tutsi power. As one refugee historian explained, "the Hutu were like slaves before the Tutsi," and it eventually allowed the Tutsi to establish a post-colonial system that resembled South Africa's apartheid system. The fact that the Tutsi could dominate the Hutu in Burundi for so long, while Rwandan Hutu were able to instigate what they considered a "revolution" in 1959 and overcome Tutsi domination, signified to the refugee historians that the Burundian Tutsi were unusually clever and powerful.

Refugee historians found it difficult to describe differences between Hutu and Tutsi ethnicity, a problem that is reflected in the actual historical record. Some refugees claimed that the Tutsi looked just like Somalis, but others strongly disagreed. Yet all refugee historians could define the Tutsi in metaphysical terms. As one concluded, "The Tutsi aren't human."

The conception of Tutsi as depraved, devil-like beings helped refugees define Hutu as well as Tutsi identities. The extent of their killing in Burundi in 1972 seemed frankly incomprehensible. For many, especially refugees who were born in Tanzania or arrived at a young age, the Tutsi were simply those people in Burundi who perpetrated evil upon innocent victims. Their victims, in turn, were all defined as Hutu. Tutsi and Hutu identities were thus defined in terms of their mutual opposition: the Hutu became the good victims, and the Tutsi became their bad assassins.

The Tutsi's hatred of the Hutu, the historians contended, was unchangeable and unquenchable. Even Tutsi who were outwardly pleasant to Hutu, one refugee historian whispered to me, "would rather see the Hutu dead." Refugees, most of whom were already unsure how to identify a Tutsi physically, assumed that the Tutsi had hired masses of spies, particularly Tanzanians, to inform on and harass refugees on their behalf. As a result, anyone who opposed refugees was seen to be working for the Tutsi. As one refugee historian explained: "The Burundi government is using Tanzanians to eliminate Burundians." This theme deeply affected the refugees' perceptions of their social surroundings and fused the identities of refugee and ethnic Hutu together. One refugee historian concluded that "All who died [in 1972] were Hutu, and all refugees are Hutu."

Refugee historians portrayed Burundi's Hutu as victims of extravagant evil which the outside world had chosen to ignore. They repeatedly expressed their conviction that "nobody cares about the Hutu." The outside world, symbolized by the UNHCR, simply looked the other way. As a consequence, refugees were powerless to present their plight to the world. They could neither speak for nor represent themselves, and nobody spoke for them. Their tragedy had been forgotten, and this allowed, in their collective view, the Tutsi to continue their hidden reign of terror against them.[9]

"The Tutsi stop us from becoming educated" Refugee historians generally contended that the long arm of Tutsi oppression asserted direct control over refugee lives by preventing them from attaining post-primary education. The education programs sponsored by UNHCR and administrated in part by Tanzania's Ministry of Home Affairs were seen to favor other refugee populations over Burundi refugees. Despite the fact that Tanzania's refugee population was dominated by Burundi refugees during my field research period (1990–92), the Tutsi managed, refugee historians asserted, to

allow few Burundi refugees access to secondary, vocational and university education.

The connection between education and power flowed through the historians' discourse on Burundi's history. They accurately described how the Belgians favored ethnic Tutsi over Hutu for access to education in colonial Burundi. The educated Tutsi were those who helped the Belgians rule the country. Thus, from early in the colonial period, formal education was equated with power. As one refugee historian commented, "The Tutsi were so near the [colonial] government, they were so clever, they were favored and [were the] first to go to school." The root of Tutsi power was their domination of access to higher education in the colony: "They succeed because they were favored in receiving education [from the Belgians]."

In the view of refugee historians, the Tutsi could maintain their power in Burundi by preventing Hutu from accessing higher education. Evidence that the Burundian army's retaliation in 1972 was aimed at eliminating educated Hutu helped create a sense among educated refugee men that their high level of education directly threatened Tutsi power in Burundi and automatically accorded them power and prominence within refugee society. Refugee historians concluded that the Burundi government had "a plan ... to keep [Burundi refugees] from getting education. If they do get it, they can to lead the Hutu against those in power in Burundi." The Tutsi government would thus perceive any refugees with education as dangerous because they qualified to be leaders of Burundian Hutu among refugee communities and inside Burundi itself.

"The Tutsi plan to exterminate us" Many of the refugee historians related a Burundian Tutsi plot to eliminate the Hutu. The 1972 genocide was merely the first step in their determination to continue eradicating Burundian Hutu until they no longer comprised the majority of the country's population. Every violent incident that had occurred in Burundi since 1972 was considered part of this Tutsi master plan. Once the Tutsi accomplished their goal, the historians explained, they could not be threatened by free elections or fear being overwhelmed by Hutu. As one refugee put it, if the refugees repatriated *en masse*, the Burundi authorities would "close the door" on the rest of the world and massacre the refugees in isolation.[10] Just as Burundi refugees foretold, Tutsi extremists in the army closed the door on the outside world and sealed Burundi's borders after assassinating Burundian President Ndadaye, a democratically elected Hutu, in October, 1993. Since that point, it must be said, full-blown civil war has erupted, pitting,

most of the time, Tutsi militias and the national army on one side against Hutu militias, including Palipehutu's, on the other. Both sides usually target and kill civilians from the opposite ethnic group. Tens of thousands of Burundians have perished, and hundreds of thousands have been displaced. As this book goes to press, the savage war continues.

Refugees as Tutsi: Beneath Hutu Solidarity

Much of the literature on Burundi's refugees implicitly assumes that the large and dispersed Burundi refugee society is not particularly divided. In many ways Burundi refugees appear to be united, and so are often spoken of as a single unit that tied Burundi refugee identity and Hutu ethnicity together. In the hands of refugee historians, such perceptions were often strengthened.

Most refugee historians, however, also used history to emphasize either Imbo or Banyaruguru superiority. Characterizing Burundi refugees as Hutu was part of the process of becoming a refugee, though even then there were conflicting versions of history. Imbo and Banyaruguru refugee historians illuminated this conflict by providing different interpretations of Burundi's history which, they argued, confirmed their own group's comparative purity as Hutu. This potent refugee rift was not only social and cultural, but political as well. The largest refugee party at the time of this research was Palipehutu, whose members appeared to be dominated by Banyaruguru refugees. A second, competing political party, Ubumwe ("Unity," also known, particularly in Burundi, as Frolina, or Front de Libération National), seemed to be entirely composed of Imbo refugees.

The area of the Imbo, the homeland of William's family, is a lowland region beginning above Bujumbura, in the northwestern province of Burundi known as Cibitoke (pronounced "Chee-be-toe-kay"), and then stretching along nearly all of Burundi's Lake Tanganyika coastline. At the end of the nineteenth century much of the area was on the periphery of the Rundi state. The inhabitants were known as Babo (Weinstein 1976: 148). It is the site of the only intensive cassava production in the country, and has been a prime area for rural migrations to eastern Congo and Tanzania. The warm, humid climate also makes it the only part of Burundi where malaria, bilharzia, and onchocersis all thrive. "Imboland" is Burundi's natural center for fishing but is not particularly hospitable to cattle. This is an issue of great significance to the forthcoming

MAP 2.2 Burundi: The Four Primary Natural Regions

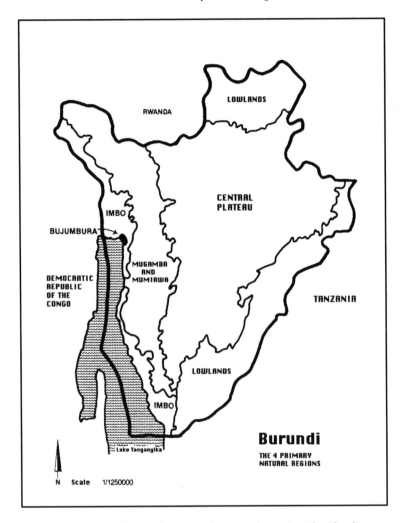

The Imbo area, here designated as a specific geographic region, identifies the homeland for Imbo refugees.

Source: Adapted from Segamba, Ndikumasabo, Makinson, and Ayad 1988: xix.

debate, for it implies that the Imbo lived separately from the Tutsi, who are known for their devotion to cattle herding. The southern Imbo area, particularly the town of Nyanza-Lac, was the center of intense fighting during the uprising and repression of 1972. Weinstein has reported that "nearly all of the Hutu population was killed or fled" from the Imbo area. Beginning in 1973, "Tutsi began to resettle the region" (ibid.: 149).

Imbo people seem to be united in large part by their historic distance from pre-colonial Rundi authority, their familiarity with foreigners (Muslim as well as those from the western side of Lake Tanganyika), and a rural lifestyle centered on cassava and fish production that set them apart from mainstream Burundian culture. They view their historic, cultural, economic, geographic and climactic differences from the rest of Burundi as significant, and these differences alone can challenge conceptions of refugee solidarity. These differences are also reflected linguistically. All refugees in the settlements converse with each other in Kirundi, and many people, particularly older women, speak scarcely any Kiswahili at all (Daley 1991a). At the same time, most of the Imbo I met in Tanzania spoke both Swahili and Kirundi with an accent that was noticeably different from the accent of Banyaruguru refugees. In the tailoring shop, John, a Banyaruguru, after detecting the identity of a visiting Burundi refugee to the shop by his dialect, would write "Imbo" or "Ban" (short for Banyaruguru) in chalk on his work desk so I could see it. Then he would quickly erase it.

The self-appointed name for refugees such as John and James, who both came from the mountainous highlands in southern Burundi, was Banyaruguru. John translated the name for me as *Watu wa Juu*, which he said meant "The People from Up," or the highland people. These two titles were borrowed from other sources. Highland refugees had lifted their self-appointed title from the Banyaruguru Tutsi, who, according to Lemarchand and other commentators, arrived in Burundi before the upstart Hima Tutsi who eventually came to dominate Burundian government. Despite their fall from political influence, these Banyaruguru retained their standing as the higher-caste, higher status Burundian Tutsi group. There was also a regional difference: the Hima's base is in the south (centered around the town of Bururi), while the Banyaruguru are based in the central and northern highlands of the country. Some Banyaruguru were also murdered by government forces during the 1972 genocide.

The *Watu wa Juu* title also borrowed the conception of being both high status and powerful from its more common Central

African application, as discussed previously. By applying these two titles to themselves, highland refugees had consciously staked a symbolic claim over the Imbo, both as the Hutu who had first arrived in Burundi (and were thus the more purely ethnic Hutu), and as the higher status Hutu group. These two issues lay at the core of the Imbo-Banyaruguru debate.

While Imbo refugees were connected to the specific lowland culture and geography of lakeland Burundi, Banyaruguru refugees were not. Their connection to highland culture was less direct because it contained a pastiche of localities and identities under one grouping. Banyaruguru refugees largely came from the southern highland area; from Bururi in the southeast to the Burundi-Tanzania border in the southwest. This border area includes Bukemba, located just south of the city of Rutana in southeastern Burundi. Many Banyaruguru I interviewed, John and James among them, also called themselves *Wakemba* (Kemba people), who comprised a significant segment of highland people in the refugee camps.

Until they became refugees, most lowland and highland Burundians had never lived together. They constituted disparate peoples who, when forced to live together as refugees, discovered a shared solidarity as Hutu victims of Tutsi oppression as well as significant differences. The Imbo-Banyaruguru division arose only after Burundians arrived in Tanzanian refugee settlements. The subsequent Imbo-Banyaruguru dispute was not over each side's claim to being Hutu. As Malkki has detailed, every Burundi refugee had been victimized by Tutsi violence, an experience which certified, and linked, their collective identities as refugee and as Hutu. Instead, the dispute centered on comparative degrees of ethnic purity. Tensions arising from Imbo and Banyaruguru refugees in Dar es Salaam tailoring shops focused on the degree to which they were on the same side. Everyone agreed that they were all Burundian Hutu refugees. But were those refugees sitting across the Imbo-Banyaruguru divide really trustworthy?

Imbo Claims to Hutu Purity

Much of the debate over which group represented a higher form of Hutu hinged on the Imbo's geographic separation from the rest of the country. Banyaruguru and Imbo refugees both cited the significance of the Imbo's different dialect, diet, and the absence of Tutsi in Imboland. The Imbo used these three issues to assert that

Banyaruguru refugees and the Tutsi were united against them. As one Imbo historian explained: "The Banyaruguru think we are different from them. We *are* different: the Tutsi don't herd near us, but up there in the hills with the Banyaruguru they do, and so the two groups–Tutsi and Banyaruguru–mix." For the Imbo, the age-old proximity between highland Hutu and Tutsi seemed to have exacerbated difficulties in separating Hutu from Tutsi. While both sides admitted that some Banyaruguru had intermarried with the Tutsi, the Imbo claimed that the two highland groups formed a single mixture. The following commentary typified their views: "The difference [between Imbo and Banyaruguru] is that the Banyaruguru have mixed with the Tutsi in the hills [of Burundi], they have intermarried, traded cows for wives, and they live with each other. The two [Banyaruguru and Tutsi] are different from us, but not different from each other. *They* have caused the problems!" Ultimately, Imbo self-perceptions placed them as the most victimized of Burundi refugees, and the only pure Hutu people; the only Hutu in Burundi who had not been "contaminated" by Tutsi culture and, most significantly, "Tutsi blood."

The Imbo historians' claim of separate development from the rest of Burundi provided the basis for their claims of ethnic purity. The Tutsi chose to stay away from the lakeland region because the highlands provided better pastureland for their cattle.[11] This allowed the Imbo to develop "their own culture and dialect." This separation enabled Imbo society to retain a "pure" Hutu culture, which is indicated by the different dialect of Kirundi they speak: "The real Kirundi language is from Imbo because we were not mixed [with the Tutsi]."

To mix with the Tutsi, the Imbo's argument implies, is to lose part of one's Hutu identity. "The Tutsi," one Imbo historian explained, "so dominated the [highland] Hutu that [they] had to sell their being to be called a Tutsi." The Imbo version posits that while the Banyaruguru's proximity to the Tutsi enabled some highland Hutu to receive secondary and university education (while the Imbo were excluded), the Banyaruguru refugees' separate Hutu culture and identity receded. In highland culture, Banyaruguru Hutu assumed subordinate roles to their Tutsi relatives. Banyaruguru land, in addition, was comparatively poorer than Imboland. Thus, over time, highland Hutu became economically as well as culturally impoverished.

Imbo historians did not contend that the Imbo were able to overpower the Tutsi. Instead, they claimed to have retained the purity of their Hutu ethnicity simply because the Tutsi chose to settle in the hills. The Tutsi were too powerful, too clever even for the Imbo to overwhelm. Imbo historians were fond of describing their people's triumph despite their lack of access to education. They asserted that only those Hutu of "mixed background" (that is, Banyaruguru) entered secondary school. Yet the absence of Tutsi people and culture from "Imboland," together with the fertility of the lowland soils, created a land of "civilized" people. "Even without education, the [Imbo] were civilized," said one. Another claimed that "The Imbo area is a favorable area. It's a good area to live. This [area] is the most civilized [in Burundi]."

The sharp differences separating Imbo from Banyaruguru were summed up by the Imbo historians' collective depiction of Imbo and Banyaruguru groups upon their arrival in Tanzania as refugees. They explained that the Banyaruguru arrived wearing the garb of the "primitive": animal skins. Meanwhile, the Imbo announced their "civilized" upbringing by wearing European-style clothes into Tanzania. Once in Tanzania, Banyaruguru refugees initiated the conflict with Imbo refugees, many Imbo claimed. They were jealous of the Imbo's sophistication. As one Imbo historian explained,

> The [Imbo's] land is more productive than in Bukemba. So when we arrived here [in Tanzania] we were already civilized and rich people. Themselves they were wearing skins, very poor, but we, we were smart. So [Banyaruguru] people were admiring us and saying "Who are these clean people? Maybe these are the real Rundis [Burundians]." So the difference [between Banyaruguru and Imbo] started to be created.

When the refugees arrived, another Imbo historian summed up, the Banyaruguru "were still ignorant.... So they came to feel inferior to the Imbo." And from their "inferiority complex," he claimed, arose the divisive separation between Imbo and Banyaruguru.

Banyaruguru Claims to Hutu Superiority

Banyaruguru historians related that the Imbo people constituted a small proportion of the refugee population who were wealthy and arrogant. They did not dispute two critical components of the Imbo's argument: that the Imbo lived separately from all other Burundians and had not intermarried with the Tutsi. Intermarriage, indeed, seemed to symbolize Banyaruguru victimization, and thus strengthened their claims to ethnic Hutu purity. Those Hutu who married Tutsi, the historians explained, only did so through coercion. The purity of one's Hutu ethnicity, they argued, centered less on the ethnic purity of one's blood than the struggle that was required to retain it. The Imbo's separation from a history of contact with and domination by the Tutsi, Banyaruguru historians claimed, distanced them from the identities not only of ethnic Hutu but Burundian national as well. This was demonstrated, they asserted, by the Imbo's perception of themselves as the only Hutu people. As one explained, "The Imbo think the Tutsi and the [highland] Hutu are all the same."

In response, some Banyaruguru historians claimed that the Imbo were not truly Burundian. "The Imbo are the people who came from the Zaire side of Lake Tanganyika–the Bo people," one explained, and in 1950 "they came from Zaire [to Burundi]." The Imbo's newcomer status, according to this view, was indicated by their different dialect and their preference for different foods. Their position as a kind of new Hutu also distanced them from the center of Burundian culture. As one Banyaruguru historian explained, "The culture of Burundi is centered on the 'cow culture.' That is, in the highland areas, non-Imbo [Hutu] and Tutsi, they have the cow culture ... [there] the Hutu live like Tutsi.... The Hutu in the low regions have no influence of the cow culture. They have a fish culture." In strong contrast to Imbo claims, the Banyaruguru directly linked their proximity to the Tutsi to their identities as both ethnic Hutu and Burundian national: centuries of intimate domination by Tutsi neighbors certified their purity as Hutu, while their connection to "cow culture" certified them as Burundians. The Imbo, on the other hand, were undoubtedly Hutu because they also suffered at the hands of the Tutsi in 1972. But some Banyaruguru historians also claimed that the Imbo's suffering had not been nearly as difficult. The lakeland Imbo were able to flee Burundi in their boats and thus enter Tanzania with their wealth intact, while the Banyaruguru were forced to flee overland, unable to carry their most important source of wealth: cattle.

The Conspiracy: Fearing Tutsi Spies

In the competition for the mantle of the purest Hutu, Imbo and Banyaruguru each claimed greater degrees of victimization and powerlessness as refugees. To defend their positions, Imbo and Banyaruguru employed the same argument: their opposition group had obtained greater access to education and capital because of their secret intimacy with the Tutsi. This claim conveniently implicated their refugee opposition as Tutsi allies, for in Burundi the Tutsi dominated access to higher education and controlled the lion's share of Burundi's wealth. One Banyaruguru historian told me that "those [Burundi refugees] who get the [university] scholarships are the Imbo." Imbo refugees, he told me, were selected for the few UNHCR-sponsored slots that Burundi refugees had qualified for, and their Burundian Tutsi allies had made this possible. At the same time, Imbo historians told me that Banyaruguru refugees received assistance for their educational goals from Tutsi relatives back in Burundi. As one explained: "Since the Banyaruguru and the Tutsi have the same blood ... [and] their Tutsi relatives back home have wealth, [the Tutsi relatives] can send money to Banyaruguru refugees in the settlements no problem.... Where do they get the money? They must get it from [them]."

Imbo refugees, who were numerically outnumbered in the refugee settlements by their Banyaruguru counterparts, often expressed their views with the bitterness of a minority. Here is a statement characteristic of Imbo historians: "The Banyaruguru, they are often illiterate, and these people believe these kinds of things [that the Imbo are their enemies]. The Banyaruguru can turn us in [to the authorities] and cause me to lose my job, and anything else! Just to cause me trouble! Just because I am an Imbo!"

Imbo and Banyaruguru historians both contended that some members in the opposing refugee group worked as Tutsi spies, and decried the disunity in refugee society. They saw members of their opponents as instruments of discord, bribed by the Burundian government to accentuate the differences that separated them. The Tutsi's intention, both Imbo and Banyaruguru refugees told me, was to insure that refugees fought among themselves and remained unable to unite together as ethnic Hutu against the Tutsi. "Some Imbo wanted to separate [from us]," a Banyaruguru historian told me, "because they were bribed with money from the Burundi government to ... be spies." The Imbo's distinctiveness, when combined with their standing as a minority group in both refugee and Burundian society, signified to Banyaruguru historians that the Imbo alone "can't threaten the Tutsi." They were too small to overcome them. Owing to their isolated lakeland experience, the Imbo also lacked sufficient knowledge of the Tutsi to plot a viable strategy to beat them. This laid the groundwork for the allegation that the Tutsi government had co-opted the Imbo. To the Banyaruguru, Imbo spies had caused many of their troubles as refugees. And to the Imbo, the Banyaruguru's blood and cultural ties to the Tutsi supported their contention that some Banyaruguru were Tutsi spies who worked against them.

Suspicions that other refugees worked as spies for the evil Tutsi tightened the psychological noose around all Burundi refugees and became fertile ground for enhancing their fear of being over-whelmed by enemies. All refugees might be seen as Hutu because all refugees had survived the genocide. Refugee camps may have also become sites for the creation of a purified Hutu people who formed a nation in exile, as Malkki has argued. But all Hutu refugees were not equally Hutu. Degrees of ethnic purity were debatable, and engaging in the debate was a matter not only of identity refinement but probably one of survival, too. Different degrees of ethnic purity had created new opponents, and it was easy enough to perceive the new adversaries as likely Tutsi allies. The Imbo-Banyaruguru rivalry had made feelings of Hutu vulnerability to the Tutsi exceedingly intimate. There seemed to be nowhere for any Burundi refugee to hide.

Tortured Violence

To this day, Rwandan Tutsi call the waves of massacres that began in their country in 1959 and ultimately took the lives of approximately ten thousand Rwandans (most of them Tutsi) and sent 120,000 more Tutsi into neighboring countries as refugees (Waller 1996: 7) a genocide. To many Rwandan Hutu, these same events constitute a revolution that liberated them from Tutsi oppression. However one interprets the desperate violence that sent tremors of terror across Rwanda and Burundi, it was uncommonly brutal, extraordinarily lasting and psychologically lacerating. It also inspired a particular kind of tortured violence wherein ethnic victims were not simply killed but violated. Corpses disfigured by the hacking of machetes has become a trademark of Central African violence, with the impaled pregnant woman, together with her fetus cut into pieces nearby, the most horrific example of this tendency. Such violence allows the African Rights observation that the 1994 genocide in Rwanda "appeared not only intended to kill the Tutsis, but to destroy their humanity, too" (1995: 624) to apply equally to the Tutsi genocide of Hutu in Burundi in 1972.

Evidence of ethnic stereotypes informing the killers' methods have also been present in virtually every episode of mass violence in Central Africa since 1959. In one example, Hutu cut off the feet of Tutsi victims to make them "short like a Hutu" (Greenland 1976: 113). Targeting schoolchildren for slaughter has proven to be an unusually powerful and recurring strategy, either because Hutu view Tutsi as inherently superior (illuminated by a Rwandan Hutu youth explaining that a Tutsi schoolboy must be killed "otherwise he will be ruling over us when he is older" [African Rights 1995: 626]), or, alternatively, because Tutsi view educated Hutu as a moral and mortal threat to their superiority (underscored by an apparently widespread Burundian Hutu belief that, following the 1972 genocide, educating Hutu children would "prove to be the mark of Cain" [Greenland 1980: 103] whenever ethnic violence returned).

The power of ethnic stereotypes to instill terror and incite violence is matched by their ability to explain reality. Since Hutu and Tutsi share the same culture and language and are difficult to tell apart physically, character stereotypes become the critical interpretive tools. As the refugee historians demonstrate, applying unseen motivations to explain violent actions appears to work extremely well, as each side can claim victims of countless instances of predatory, even sadistic, behavior since 1959, if not before.

One does not have to be Rwandan or Burundian to see the inherent utility of this approach. "The Tutsi tribe," a European priest of the White Fathers Catholic mission explained to me in 1996, "they are very gifted, there's no doubt about that." Fluent in Kirundi and Kinyarwanda, and having lived more than four decades among Rwandans and Burundians, the priest was well schooled in the heritage of Hutu and Tutsi stereotyping. "When the Europeans came [to Central Africa]," he explained, "they were amazed by the Tutsi's gifts in school. Tutsi feelings were like ours [that is, Europeans], and they could guess our feelings, so they adapted themselves to us." As a result, "the Europeans favored the Tutsi." The priest also described the opposing natures of Hutu and Tutsi. The Aryan-like Tutsi, he explained, were "clever," "prudent," and "careful." But they also lied a lot, and were not trustworthy. The Hutu, on the other hand, were almost childlike in their simplicity. "I would believe a Hutu more quickly than a Tutsi," the priest explained, "because what [the Hutu] says is not as deep, not as far-fetched." The Hutu, in addition, though as violent as the Tutsi, are clumsier by nature: "When Hutus are killing, they do it in front of everybody," the priest explained. "They look stupid. They don't hide anything." On the other hand, "When Tutsis kill people, nobody knows."

Like a receding glacier, terror and extreme violence between Rwandan and Burundian Tutsi and Hutu has carved the region's psychological landscape. Devoid of consistently verifiable differences, Hutu and Tutsi identities are circumscribed by the virtual realities each stereotype has created. But in their essence, it is violence, and fear of violence, which define the essential difference between Hutu and Tutsi. One identity cannot exist without the other. Each side has dealt an array of unusually violent episodes to their ethnic adversaries. These can be held up to prove the opposite group's predatory nature while certifying their own group's victimization. And it is fear of being overwhelmed by their ethnic adversary—Hutu sabotaged by a "superior" Tutsi minority or Tutsi overwhelmed by an "inferior" Hutu majority—which has become the grease that keeps the cycle of violence turning.

As the mutually perceived inferior of the two, the Hutu's collective psychological burden has proven particularly heavy. Lemarchand witnessed Hutu attacks on Tutsi in Rwanda in 1960, and experienced "what can only be described as a sense of cultural shock in the face of wanton killings" (1970: ix). These massacres, which had begun in 1959, continued in sporadic and terrifying fashion into 1964. Grappling to understand what had taken place, Lemarchand argued that the "popular [Hutu] participation in violence created a kind of collective catharsis through which years of pent-up hatred suddenly seemed to find an outlet" (ibid.: 224). At the same time, he believed that the behavior of the Rwandan Hutu killers "can only be regarded as an extreme example of pathological behaviour, as the blind reaction of a people traumatized by a deep and lasting sense of inferiority" (ibid.: 44). John, William, and James, in addition to the refugee historians and many other refugees interviewed, echoed Lemarchand's sentiment, repeatedly lamenting "the badness with our [Hutu] people" or the Tutsi's elemental ability to dupe the Hutu.

In a strange way, the Imbo-Banyaruguru rivalry, which weakened Hutu solidarity by debating degrees of ethnic purity, also strengthened the connection between Hutu identity and victimization. Perceiving some refugees as conspiratorial, lesser Hutu made the case for Tutsi superiority seem undeniable. Leaving the refugee camps, where the sub-ethnic rivalry had emerged, didn't help much because the Tutsi had left no stone unturned. Refugees might succeed in hiding their identities from the Tanzanian authorities, but protecting oneself from the Tutsi was something altogether different. If Tanzanians might not be able to track you down, other refugees, who knew your whereabouts and true identity, were undoubted Tutsi allies. The Imbo-Banyaruguru fracture in refugee society turned non-Tutsi Hutu into nearly Tutsi Hutu, which colored Hutu identity with a dark sense of impending doom. Being Hutu meant being forever surrounded by an unseen Tutsi trap.

"Home Is Home"

> I love the refugees. They cultivate the country for me. But I have no money. You bring in the money.
>
> –Julius Nyerere, to the former UN High Commissioner for Refugees, Poul Hartling (Lamb 1982: 199)

The Tanzanian government settled Burundi refugees in vast, remote settlements in western and central Tanzania. In the 1890s, the combination of extensive plagues of rinderpest, smallpox, sand fleas, and locusts created an "ecological catastrophe" (Iliffe 1979:163) and famine across colonial Tanganyika. People starved or fled the hinterlands, leaving behind untended farmland that grew into woodland. Many of these forests still remain, and it is in these nearly deserted woods that all three settlements for Burundi refugees from the 1972 genocide came into being.

The first Burundi refugee settlement was Ulyankulu, a swampy, wooded, malarial, and tsetse-infested flatland eighty-five kilometers northwest of Tabora. Ulyankulu was originally considered suitable for eighteen thousand refugees (Christensen 1985), but held sixty thousand refugees by 1976. A second settlement, Katumba, arose northeast of Mpanda, and a third, Mishamo, was established in 1978 to accommodate some of Ulyankulu's population overflow. In terms of land mass, these three refugee settlements are among Africa's largest. Ulyankulu covers one thousand square kilometers–nearly the size of Zanzibar Island or Luxembourg. Katumba, with an estimated population of at least seventy-four thousand refugees but, considering its longstanding "exploding" population growth (Clark 1987a: 33) and informal estimates of it actually containing well over one hundred thousand refugees, is nearing the size of Burundi's capital city, Bujumbura. Even when guided by official numbers, refugees in Mishamo and Katumba settlements, both located in Mpanda District, outnumber Tanzanian nationals living there. Regular bus service connects Ulyankulu to Tabora, and the train line between Mpanda and Tabora runs straight through Katumba Settlement. Mishamo is the remotest settlement.

MAP 2.3 Map of Tanzania

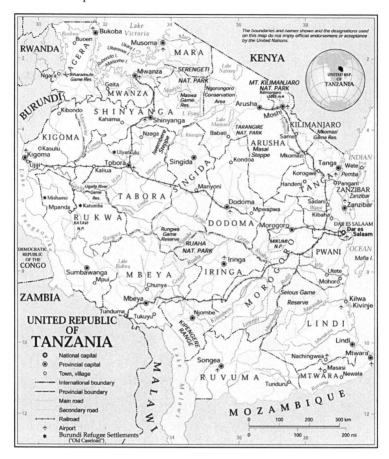

Adapted from the United Nations map of Tanzania. Refugee settlement locations are approximate.

Source: United Nations Department of Public Information Cartographic Section, Map No. 3667 Rev. 2, October 1999.

Since "self-reliance" has been an objective both of the Tanzanian state for Tanzanians and the UNHCR for refugees, the literature about Burundi refugees from the 1972 genocide has often focused on this issue, examining the extent of the Burundi refugees' integration into Tanzania's economy and, to a lesser extent, local society (Armstrong 1986, 1987b, 1988; Armstong and Garry 1988; Ayok and Mbago 1987; Christensen 1985; Daley

1991a; Gasarasi 1987). However, despite references to the difficulties that Tanzanian authorities, and especially the Settlement Commandant, have caused for Burundi refugees in each settlement (Armstrong 1988; Ayok and Mbago 1987; Christensen 1985; Daley 1991a, 1991b; Malkki 1995), there has been a tendency to overlook the explicit influence of the Tanzanian state over refugee lives.

Most refugees in Tanzania must live in settlements, an option that refugees have long disliked (Ayok and Mbago 1987; Lugusha 1981; Ogbru 1983). The settlements themselves follow Tanzania's Villages and Ujamaa Villages Act, but are overlaid with an additional internal settlement administration. The settlements, Katumba and Mishamo in particular, conform to Ujamaa specifications: the "villages" form a grid-like pattern with no center and a civic structure matching Tanzanian rural villages (Christensen 1985). Yet at the same time, the Tanzanian constitution prohibits refugees from voting or forming political associations themselves. These and other conditions are enforced by the settlement administration, which reports to the Ministry for Home Affairs. The Settlement Commandant also controls access to a *kibali* (exit permit), which is required to leave the settlement legally.

Men Go to Town, Women Stay Home

For John, William, James, and many other Burundi refugee men, movement meant empowerment. Tanzanian laws governing refugees may have restricted movement, but they did not make movement impossible. A person needed determination, guile, and probably some assistance from a friend or patron to get out—the very same qualities that success in Bongoland demanded.

Burundian men have been migrating to work in other places for decades. In colonial Burundi, Albert has noted, "Men [were] rarely at home" (Albert 1963: 199). Significant numbers of young Burundian men were accustomed to working for others to raise money for a bride price. It was commonplace to find these men working in colonial Tanganyika. Migration out of the refugee settlements, in this context, represented an extension of this tradition. For younger generation refugees such as John, William, and James, the refugee settlements represented their "Burundi," and migrating beyond their borders appears to have been a widely popular aspiration for members of their peer group. Christensen has suggested (1985) that refugees evaluated their situation with reference to their former lives in Burundi and not to Tanzanians residing nearby. This is significant, because although standards of living were generally lower for refugees than for their Tanzanian neighbors (Armstrong 1988), they may have seemed even lower when compared to their former living standards, actual or imagined, in Burundi. The bride price motivation also remained a part of this aspiration, though its cultural significance appeared to have declined over time. Still, Luka, John, and several other young refugee men interviewed all explained that they had sought work in Dar es Salaam partly to save money for their bride price.

An additional motive can be derived by noting the omission of religion from surveys of Burundi refugee economic activity in Tanzania. Daley asserted that tobacco was "the most profitable of the crops grown in [Katumba] settlement" (1991a: 258). Christensen's findings indicated that every household in Ulyankulu was involved in raising cash crops (tobacco or peanuts), but Armstrong cited religious preference as a factor in the choice of crops. "The predominance of Pentecostalism in the settlements," he explained, "which discourages the growing of tobacco, partly explains the relative insignificance of tobacco production …" (1988: 61). At the very least, one might suspect that the Pentecostal refugees, who comprise more than a third of Ulyankulu's entire population (Christensen 1985) and an equivalent or perhaps even larger proportion in Katumba and Mishamo, were among those refugees who were not raising this relatively lucrative cash crop. This may help explain the preponderance of Pentecostal refugees in Dar es Salaam, who may have been more motivated to search for other sources of household income than non-Pentecostal refugees who could grow tobacco in the settlements.

Regardless of the reasons that motivated migration, researchers have agreed that most refugees in the settlements have consistently lacked sufficient sources of cash to accommodate basic needs: "… the level of monetary income of the majority of the sampled households appears too low to meet even essential cash requirements to cope with daily basic spending and to insure a steady income for the following year" (Christensen 1985: 108). Because most refugee families have been able to raise sufficient levels of food for household consumption, their major cash requirements have centered on purchasing clothing and other non-food necessities. Restrictions on refugee settlement residents, however, have made it difficult for most to earn cash. Scarcity of money in the settlements was one of the primary motivating factors that compelled refugee families to send household members to cities.

Migrating from the refugee settlements was risky because it was rarely permitted. In 1965, the Tanzanian government passed the Refugee Control Act. The Act required nearly all refugees to live in settlements which they could only leave if Tanzanian authorities gave them a pass. Most passes did not extend beyond two weeks' time, and permitted refugees to use only specified kinds of transportation along specified roads. Refugees were not allowed to organize political parties or public meetings unless they first received citizenship, which they might qualify for after seven years' residence within Tanzania.[12] Refugees were also restricted from residing in Dar es Salaam (with few exceptions) without first proving that they were legally employed and economically self-sufficient. Yet migrating to Dar es Salaam was illegal. Thus, many refugees in town who were economically self-sufficient in legally licensed work continued to avoid detection by authorities because they had entered the city clandestinely. A Ministry of Home Affairs official explained the apparent legal contradiction by stating that refugees in this situation would have to return to the settlements with documents to prove that they had a legal occupation in the capital, and present their case to the Settlement Commandant. I never heard of any refugee following this recommendation, which ran counter to refugee efforts to keep a low profile before all of the Tanzanian authorities.

The Settlement Commandants for Mishamo, Katumba, and Ulyankulu were among the most prominent and powerful figures for refugees living under their authority. As Armstrong surmised:

> … the restricted rights of refugees under the 1965 Refugee Control Act together with the vesting of significant power into the hands of the Government's Settlement Commandant have encouraged, in the words of one UNHCR report (1974), "an almost military leadership structure." The authoritarian attitudes of a centralized administration concerned with imposing order have, not infrequently, led to abuses of power and the imposition of restrictions.… (Armstrong 1988: 67)

Armstrong also related the refugee leaders' feelings of "victimization, powerlessness and exploitation" to Tanzanian authorities' acts of "suppression, maltreatment and wrongful arrest, and even violations of and fears for their security and physical safety" (ibid.). This image of refugees as exploited, powerless victims is supported by other authors, notably Daley. Yet the relationship did not seem to overwhelm refugee life. Christensen, for example, notes that "In Ulyankulu [the refugees] could be sure of what they had and could

rely on it, even though it might be very little. The settlement provided a secure corner in which to pursue a livelihood and where
they felt sheltered. They were uncertain of finding any improvement should they leave Ulyankulu" (Christensen 1985: 123). The
difference of perspective between authors who viewed Burundi
refugees as feeling isolated instead of sheltered and unstable
instead of secure may not necessarily represent contradictory
claims about the actual conditions of refugee settlement existence.
As survivors of a genocide, isolation in settlements may have summoned feelings of relative safety from their ultimate oppressors,
Burundi's Tutsi-dominated army. Furthermore, although Tanzanian authorities in the settlements could descend on a refugee at any
time, refugees were also aware that they could not be evicted from
the settlement. Burundi refugees, in short, seemed quite aware that
their situation, while in many respects difficult and unappealing,
could certainly have been much worse. Danger and fear were present in their lives, but they were not as palpable as they no doubt
would have been in Burundi. Christensen's description indicates
that refugees had accepted and made the best out of their settlement existence.

Refugee settlement life, then, though far from serene or even
easy, was at least familiar. If Tanzanian state authorities were harsh,
they were also known quantities, and refugees did not necessarily
follow their rules in any case. The Settlement Commandant may
have played an invasive role in refugee settlement life but his
power was hardly absolute. Tanzanian and UNHCR officials, as
well as refugees, complained that Commandants were too often
corrupt, but this also suggested that it was possible to purchase
exceptions to his rules.

Though some refugees reacted against the Tanzanian power
structure by migrating from the settlements, gender roles facilitated
male mobility while keeping most women homebound in the settlements. Daley observed that "most men migrate to find employment" (1991a: 254) during dry seasons. Some of this movement was
clearly legal: donor officials encouraged refugee men to "work as
casual wage laborers on nearby commodity producing agricultural
schemes" (ibid.: 257). However, much of the migration was clearly
not permitted. In addition to migration to Dar es Salaam and other
urban areas, men were observed going to Arusha for wheat flour
(Daley 1991a) and even to Burundi every year to check on their
property and maintain links with their home area (Christensen
1985:124). Indeed, half of the refugees in Christensen's sample

maintained regular contact with relatives, friends and neighbors in Burundi, who cared for their property and updated them on local conditions there.[13]

The situation for Burundi refugee women in settlements was entirely different. Sixty-seven percent of the women in Daley's sample did not speak Kiswahili, and, as a rule, never left the settlement. A small number of younger women migrated as well, but only those who had learned Swahili at settlement primary schools and "[had] greater experience of the host country and life outside the settlement" (Daley 1991a:264) than their mother's generation. This exception to the social rule aligns with indications that a woman's mobility has generally been "constrained by social and cultural constructions of gender" in developing countries (Chant and Radcliffe 1992: 7), although there are indications that young Burundi refugee women may be part of a shift in women's roles to increase their mobility in East Africa and beyond (Nelson 1992). Nevertheless, the avenue for exiting the Burundi refugee settlements had been established, and was familiar and well used, by men. Their numbers in Dar es Salaam simply demonstrated this tendency.

John, William, and James would have added another reason for leaving the settlements: life there was boring. In addition to the presence of a corrupt Commandant and aggressive Tanzanian soldiers in their midst, the continual scarcity of cash, and the hardships, living in the refugee settlements was unrelentingly dull. They wanted to migrate to Dar es Salaam to assist their struggling families, but they also knew plenty of other refugees and Tanzanians who had gone to Bongoland and returned with shillings in their pockets and stories of high adventure. Like so many other young Burundi refugee men, they had set their sights on leaving their settlement limbo to pursue a life of excitement in Bongoland.

Notes

1. Chrétien, indeed, opens one essay with the following: "The existence of the Hutu and Tutsi ethnic groups in Rwanda and Burundi come to us from a different source of evidence. Here, we are faced with ethnic groups that do not differ from each other, either by their language, their culture, their history, nor by the geographical space that they occupy" (Chrétien 1985: 129, in translation).

2. Lemarchand's *Rwanda and Burundi* (1970) remains among the most detailed sources on the intricacies of Tutsi migration.

3. This phrase was coined by Lemarchand and Martin (1974).

4. Prunier's reckonings suggest that the organizers came very close to achieving this goal, having estimated that 800,000 out of 930,000 Rwandan Tutsi were murdered, or 86 percent of that population (1995: 265).

5. See Sommers 1993 and 1995 for more information.

6. Overlooked in this Hutu-Tutsi history competition is the fact that neither ethnic group occupied Burundi first. The Twa were in Burundi before either the Hutu or Tutsi arrived.

7. See Sommers 1998b and 1995 for more information.

8. Malkki has also recorded how her "efforts to work with women were frustrated" (1995: 50).

9. Refugees of every age and educational level also believed that their experience in 1972 was a silent tragedy. The Tutsi-dominated government, they contended, tried to cover up the truth. Historical evidence aligns with this assessment.

10. A group of refugees told me of another plan to reduce the Hutu population—to sterilize all Hutu in Burundi. This plan was organized in 1969, I was told, by Burundi's UN ambassador but never carried out. I treated this information as an unsubstantiated rumor, having found no proof whatsoever to support this claim.

11. Watson supports their claims, but also shows how the Tutsi settled in that area after the Imbo/Hutu fled into Tanzania: "The flat, fertile, palm-oil producing strip of lake shore south of Bujumbura had previously been home to very few Tutsi. Most Tutsi preferred to live in the cool hills where their cattle could thrive … [But] with the death and flight of so many Hutu [in 1972–73], Tutsi rushed to occupy the lucrative palm plots" (Watson 1993: 11).

12. A revised law took effect several years after the field research period. It will be discussed in the final chapter.

13. Though Christensen's findings applied to conditions in Burundi before President Ndadaye's assassination on October 21, 1993, more recent findings indicate that this tradition has continued (see Sommers 1998a).

3

Bongoland Adventures

One who has ever lived in Dar-Es-Salaam would be familiar with the completely overcrowded and infrequent ... buses bulging with chickens, bags of *mchicha* (spinach), *mihogo* (cassava), and *mapapai* (pawpaws), and commuters from the suburban areas around Dar-Es-Salaam. One would also be familiar with frequent water cuts which sometimes leave areas dry for more than a week, frequent electricity blackouts, telephones which maintain an eerie silence, inadequate parking spaces, overflowing sewage, lack of traffic regulation, hospitals without medicine (but with fly-infested garbage), pick-pocketing, and armed robbery.

—Dr. Joe Lugalla (1995: 96)

One dusty, sweaty day at Pastor Albert's tailoring shop, I asked some of the refugee tailors about seeing young men frying chicken heads and feet in pots of fat and selling them. They ventured daily to large poultry factories to buy the heads and feet, which they sold with salt and spices for five shillings apiece (two cents). I mentioned that I had seen these *wauzaji* (vendors) in other Dar es Salaam neighborhoods, but never in their own. The refugees responded with pride. You cannot find that food in our neighborhood, they all agreed, because our neighborhood is not poor. In the poor neighborhoods, yes, they eat those foods, but never here.

The refugees' perception of their neighborhood as less poor than many other Dar es Salaam communities was accurate. Their community was in one of the city's planned housing districts, built by the National Housing Corporation. The rows of identical government-made houses indicated a community with relative financial stability, unlike, in general, the many unplanned areas of urban residence. Houses here were supplied with running water and electricity and laid out in an ordered fashion. In nearby communities, as in many other parts of the city, houses were built in a haphazard fashion, with narrow footpaths winding between cement block houses and roads made of sand.

The pastor's tailoring shop sat on a large main road with a ragtag bus stand across the street. During my fieldwork period, most of Dar es Salaam's roads were so potholed that it seemed the city had recently been victimized by meteors. This included the street outside Pastor Albert's house, until my stay in town had nearly ended. Then, reconstruction by a foreign company began (part of an enormous World Bank-funded project). Their workers gradually filled in the crater-like potholes and paved the street. Albert's shop was located near a large market, but more significant was the tailoring shop located across the street. The pastor strongly recommended that I not visit there, as it contained Burundi refugees who worked for the breakaway Pentecostal church, an issue that will be examined in Chapter 6. The two members of rival Pentecostal churches were not on speaking terms.

Hulks of car frames lay near the sides of the street between the two tailoring shops. Schoolboys played soccer on dusty sidewalks. A couple of small goods stores stood across the street alongside an outdoor restaurant specializing in fried chips. There was a milling service nearby, where the tailors took their maize to be ground into flour to make *ugali*, the stiff porridge that is the staple food for most East Africans. There were very few trees on the street, the hedges in front of many of the houses were worn and irregular, and there was no grass anywhere. Like most of the city, at night the neighborhood was almost completely dark, for the street lights had either been stolen or no longer worked. The water tap near the pastor's house had a runoff ditch that was usually blocked. Between the pastor's and his neighbor's courtyard walls was a small strip of land with a palm tree, two garbage piles and a small garden plot. On the tamped down dirt under the tree were cinder blocks reserved for a future construction plan. It was relatively cool and shady there, and often the Pastor's children lay a straw mat there to nap, chat, or complete their homework. Chickens clucked by, neighbors chatted while fetching water at the outdoor tap, and the street was in plain view. One would hardly suspect that illegal refugees would be hiding at such a public location.

This chapter will focus on how Burundi refugees have migrated to Dar es Salaam and what they have found on arriving there. Although John and Luka are often featured, the chapter will focus on what is perhaps Dar es Salaam's central paradox: that young men—refugees and non-refugees alike—are drawn to a city which has considered them a serious problem for decades. Out of this paradox has arisen a vital Swahili vocabulary that expresses urban youth alienation and fascination with city life, as well as a legacy of attacks on young men who work in the city's enormous "shadow economy" (Kerner 1988a). Into this volatile urban soup have come young Burundi refugee men, burdened by fears yet determined to save money from their tailoring work and savor some of Bongoland's urban delights.

Refugees on the Move

Moving a Society

The migration of peoples across vast distances is a characteristic of African history. Kopytoff (1987) used this phenomenon to frame his discussion of the re-creation of African political cultures in new territories. His concept is distinctly Durkheimian: people carry their society's "*conscience collective*" with them (Durkheim, from Bohannan 1960: 77), and utilize it to re-create the old socio-cultural model in a new location: "[T]he continuous [re-creation] of the frontier has maintained an African frontier-conditioned ideology in the political consciousness of African metropolitan societies" (Kopytoff 1987: 7). Kopytoff examined the genesis of socio-cultural creation by examining "ethnically ambiguous marginal societies," refugee groups among them, instead of those that have already developed into stable societies. Yet the culture and society reconstituted in Burundi refugee settlements was more different from than similar to the social order they were forced to flee. Indeed, the model of "legitimate social order" that Kopytoff argued is portable (1987: 17), was considered quite illegitimate by Burundi refugees. To John, William, James, and other refugees, the old system featured an evil, oppressive Tutsi minority that exploited the Hutu majority. Fleeing ethnic genocide changed how refugees thought about themselves. Burundi refugee society consequently represented a social and cultural transformation of the past, not a re-creation.

Two studies on the impact of migration indicate how the difference between chosen and forced migration produce strikingly different outcomes. Aronson's study of ethnic Ijebu Yoruba who chose to become urban migrants argued that they maintained their "cultural stability" even during "profound" social change (Aronson 1980: 188). So little cultural change was observable after the dramatic shift from rural to urban life that Aronson could declare that "these same people pursue goals and behave in full continuity with the ideals of social life of precolonial days" (ibid.).

The same cannot be said for Colson's Gwembe Tonga. Their forced resettlement to make way for the huge Kariba Dam project was initially destructive but eventually transformative. Over time, Colson found that Gwembe society adjusted. People created "new formal structures," which may have resulted "when people ponder why their traditional order failed them in their need, or when ... it no longer accounts for the realities they now face" (Colson 1971: 2). Such an account differs radically from Kopytoff's formulation.[1] Colson's analysis ends with a consideration of "The increasing role of God" (1971: 250) in the lives of the resettled, and mentions that "messianic and other revitalization movements" may arise to replace the fallen "traditional order" (ibid.: 2).

As involuntary migrants who became voluntary migrants, John, William, and James embodied a combination of the findings in the works of Colson and Aronson. The initial hardship of Burundi refugees in settlements, described in detail by Christensen (1985) and others, resemble Colson's descriptions. Yet after the refugee tailors migrated to Dar es Salaam, they began to resemble Aronson's Yoruba, carrying stable cultural forms, such as a shared cultural fear of Tutsi enemies, from their refugee past to their new lives in Dar es Salaam.

Fathers and Their Sons

The decision for a young man to enter Dar es Salaam was generally made by his parents, who usually sent their eldest son to the capital to earn money for the family. The family could use this additional cash to buy soap, sugar, clothing, school uniforms and supplies, and other essentials.

John, William, and James all reported that there was usually enough to eat at their settlement homes but money was hard to find. Among the reasons for this, the refugees said, were the Tanzanian authorities' intentionally low prices for purchasing surplus crops from the refugees. The refugees reported that the Tanzanians carried out this policy to exploit them. It was more likely that the Burundi refugees had personalized government restrictions that were also used with Tanzanian farmers. They were also reluctant to describe how refugees sold produce to private Tanzanian buyers for higher prices whenever the opportunity arose. This was but one example of how refugees and Tanzanians would contend that they had no alternative to breaking government restrictions; what Tripp referred to as "quiet strategies of resistance in the form of economic noncompliance" (1997: 8). For young Burundi refugees and, to a lesser extent, Tanzanian urban migrants, such noncompliance included migrating to Dar es Salaam, a potentially dangerous but justifiable effort to "survive."

Still, the young Burundi refugees' role in becoming urban migrants was largely passive. James's urban situation had been arranged by his father in Katumba settlement and his uncle in Dar es Salaam: "My father is just a farmer. He told [his children] we can't go to [secondary] school; he can't afford the fees.... So he paid for me to tailor instead. This is how I got here for tailoring. My father worked it out with Amosi to be taught at his shop." John's father also arranged for his placement in a Dar es Salaam tailoring shop. Although he had no relatives in the capital, his uncle had a connection:

> My father wanted me to get education.... He tried hard to get me something for the future, but [secondary school] was too expensive for him. Then he wanted me to go to be a fisherman in Mwanza, but I refused. [Fishermen] never stop working, and you can fall into the water, especially if you look at it too long.
>
> So his little brother [John's uncle] ... had a business [trading] in other cities, and he knew Yona.... [My uncle asked Yona] to help his nephew, and Yona said there was room at his tailoring shop for an apprentice.

The next time John's uncle visited Dar es Salaam on business, John's uncle paid a fee to Yona and Pastor Albert and returned to the settlement. He gave John a small amount of money and a ticket, and John went to the capital for a year's apprenticeship.

William's route to the tailoring shop was different, as he had already learned the tailoring trade in the Ulyankulu refugee settlement before coming to Dar es Salaam. For him, working in the capital meant the chance to make a larger, and more reliable, salary.

His father had paid a tailor in his settlement to allow him to apprentice there. William remained for eight months but did not learn to make trousers–the main job that tailors in Tanzania are hired to do–just blouses, skirts, and shirts. He claimed to have taught himself to make trousers by watching other tailors do it while he apprenticed. Later, he bought a piece of material to practice making a suitcoat on his own. After watching other tailors make coats, his first attempt had only "small mistakes." Soon thereafter, William rented a sewing machine from another refugee tailor and set up shop outdoors, in the settlement market.

The details of William's route were sketchy because he volunteered few specific details about his past. He explained that he ventured to Kigoma to tailor but refused to describe how he got work there. After about a year in Kigoma, a friend of William's in Dar es Salaam "called me to tailor here [in Dar es Salaam]." After a few months tailoring in a different section of the city, Pastor Albert hired William to work in the shop. Excepting sporadic return trips to Ulyankulu settlement to visit his wife and children, William remained in the Pastor's shop for four years.

All of the refugees who had helped John, William, and James migrate to the Tanzanian capital were Pentecostals. As has already been documented for Pentecostal migrants in Latin America (Martin 1990), members of Pentecostal congregations often develop networks that facilitate urban migration for its members. Yet once the refugee tailors arrived in Dar es Salaam, their Pentecostal identification changed in meaning. Unlike refugee settlement society, where there were Catholics, Anglicans, and a variety of other churches, almost every Burundi refugee that they would encounter in town were Pentecostals. And yet John, William, and (to a lesser extent) James became friendly with few of these urban refugees. Part of the reason for this was a product of the Pentecostals' separation into two rival church associations. Most Banyaruguru refugees attended churches affiliated with the mainstream Pentecostal mission, while most Imbo refugees worshipped at the outcast church. Being a Pentecostal refugee in Dar es Salaam was less meaningful than which kind of Pentecostal they were.[2]

The Pull of Bongoland

Several times, John described how young men in his settlement regularly spoke about Dar es Salaam. Exchanging the settlement's boredom, its hard physical labor, and pall of entrapment for a chance to enter Bongoland was the goal of countless numbers of the tailors' peers back home in the settlements. They all picked up some words in *Kidar* (Dar es Salaam Language, also known as, among other names, the *Lugha ya Wahuni*, or Language of the Ignorant)—a limited, ever-changing vocabulary that young men and women all over rural Tanzania try to master—as well. Being able to speak *Kidar* signaled a young person's interest in urban excitement and their aspirations to migrate to town. But Tanzanians and refugees usually needed a relative or friend with urban connections to assist them, since openings in tailoring shops, on fishing boats, or even with coffee vendors, were scarce. Competition between refugee families for available openings was reportedly fierce.

Dar es Salaam—Bongoland—was known to rural Tanzanian and refugee youth as a place of fabulous wealth. John once told me that young refugees in the settlements had all heard that Bongoland was so wealthy that everybody there wore shoes. Arriving in town, he found that it was true. Successful migrant refugees brought thousands of Tanzanians shillings and gifts to their siblings and parents on return visits to the settlements. These returnees described Dar es Salaam as a place where buildings had many stories and vehicles clogged the roadways. A tailor's monthly salary was often more than twice the amount offered to tailors in the settlements or the largest towns near the settlements (Kigoma, Mpanda, and Tabora).

John himself seemed especially impressed by Dar es Salaam's tall buildings.[3] The feel of city life, its energy and variety, endlessly fascinated him. He had made a collage in the back room from newspaper and magazine pictures, a private altar to the wonders of urban life. Most prominently, it contained pictures of traffic jams in Western cities and a series of magazine pictures of a white woman eating an apple. Having grown up in a settlement where there were few bicycles and fewer cars, John equated traffic jams with bounty. It epitomized his ideal of urban wealth. Yet even the traffic in Dar es Salaam seemed minuscule when compared to his picture of gridlock in New York City. That picture of lines of cars between amazingly tall buildings, he told me, showed him how much richer America was than Tanzania. At the center of this picture, John had written *toun.*

John's collage also included drawings of African women dancing, taken from local newspaper advertisements for discos. The African women in these pictures were drawn as large and bountiful, with exaggerated buttocks called *wowowo*—the kind of urban woman, in short, that young men were attracted to. For John, the

women and the traffic together indicated the city's extravagant pos-
sibilities. These urban attractions captivated him, and residing in
Dar es Salaam made him the envy of his friends back in Katumba
settlement. "Making it" meant owning an urban address and earning, by refugee standards, *pesa nyingi* (lots of money). John had both.

The Initiation into Hiding

For all young refugees heading to the capital, their parents or relatives had to save enough money to purchase a train ticket. Wishing
to maintain a low profile and not expecting a positive response, it
was probable that aspiring young migrants did not even try to get
an exit permit from the Settlement Commandant. Even so, it was
possible to leave without one, as Tanzanian authorities did not
make efforts to leave the settlements particularly difficult. Still, from
the moment they boarded the train or bus for Dar es Salaam, the
refugees began to fear that Tanzanian passengers would discover
their refugee identity. And so, on the train the young refugee men
traveled alone and began to study Tanzanian passengers in order to
speak Swahili like them. Suddenly, refugees had an accent to hide.
They were now amongst ethnic Ha and other Tanzanians, and the
Ha–whose Kiha language is related to the refugees' Kirundi, and
whose home area is located along the Burundian border–had the
ability to detect their accent and identify them as Burundians.

John told me that refugees making the trip between Dar es
Salaam and their settlement homes could be discovered, arrested
by Tanzanian authorities, and jailed for six months, though this last
seems to have been an exaggeration. Tabora was the terminus for
refugees from Katumba and Ulyankulu settlements, for they all had
to catch the Dar es Salaam train from there. But the Tabora police,
John explained, knew all about "the people of '72." John described
how policemen at the Tabora station always asked to see their
papers. His reply to them was always the same: that "they were
lost"[4] and that he was "from Mpanda." He hoped that they would
consider him a Tanzanian Ha from Mpanda town and leave him
alone. Usually he would be told to hand over one hundred shillings
(about three U.S. dollars), which he soon learned had become the
established fee that all refugees expected to pay when traveling
through Tabora. Marko later mentioned that during his first trip
from Katumba to Dar es Salaam he had to pay 1,400 shillings to
policemen in Tabora. This was unusual, he explained. The police
usually had an amount in mind that they would expect to collect

FIGURE 3.1 "Wowowo!"

The complete title of this Dar es Salaam comic book cover, written and drawn by Ibra Washokera, translates as "Wo Wo Wo: The Scud of Books." The style and natural beauty of the dancing woman (especially her dramatic use of her "wowowo" buttocks) at the center of the cover picture has created an intentional sensation on the beach. The picture is in part a statement about the outcast nature of urban youth culture in Dar es Salaam.

Source: Washokera 1992.

from refugees in a day. John had paid a fraction of the amount Marko handed over because he was traveling with many other refugees. Marko also told me that refugees usually had to stay overnight in Tabora before catching the train to Dar es Salaam. The managers of the hotels that the refugees frequented were required by law to ask their guests for proper identification. In order to keep the hotel manager from reporting the presence of refugees without papers to the police, Marko explained, the refugees had to pay hotel managers the same standard rate: one hundred shillings.

Luka's Poch

The young refugee tailors I met in Dar es Salaam were fortunate. Their families may have been poor, but they were not among the poorest refugees. They had enough money to make arrangements with urban refugee employers as well as gather enough money to pay for transport and an apprenticeship for their sons. Refugee families with fewer economic resources either had no chance of arranging an urban situation or had to accept unskilled, lower paying, and far more unstable positions in town, such as selling coffee.

The refugee migrants had to build a "*poch*" while working in town. The *poch* (taken from the English word pouch), or *paspot* (passport) both referred to a lump amount of savings. Luka would consistently tell me that the only reason he was in "Bongo" was to gather a *poch* for his family. His father had died during his family's struggle to escape Burundi in 1972, and as the oldest child he had become the family breadwinner:

> If I return with 5,600 shillings, I will pay for clothes for my younger siblings, their pants, notebooks, etc., for schooling and school fees. I don't keep any of the money that I earn in Dar es Salaam. It's only for them. My family needs the cash to buy these things and we cannot get the money in the settlements. Mama cannot pay for anything, so I have to pay instead. I have no father.

Luka then touched on another reason for his presence in Dar es Salaam. "I don't like living [in Katumba] very much," he said, "because everybody wants to be changed by their environment." The sentence is typically in the passive tense, a characteristic indication of how refugees perceived life events. As *Watu was Chini-chini*, tailors evoked the sense that their lives had been altered by events to which they could only react. The tailors' very identity as refugees arose from this: they believed that their families had lived peacefully in Burundi until violent events occurred to them and compelled them to flee.

While refugees consistently described major moments in their lives as events which had changed them, their actions often told a different story. Luka exemplified this tendency. He loved to relate how popular he was back in his village. Providing for his family made him important. Luka also spoke of his *poch*, and the opportunities it could provide, more openly than any of the other tailors. He intended to work in Dar es Salaam until all of his siblings completed primary school, at which time, he claimed, he would save to pay the bride price for a wife. Then he would move back to the settlement and farm.

Having proved his abilities as a family provider, Luka was approaching the refugees' shared definition of true manhood. He would truly become a man when, like William, he had married, had children, and was able to support them. But his sense of accomplishment did not make him popular with his work mates, whom he refused to consider his peers. Luka would not sweep out the shop or prepare tea, the morning's shared tasks, for example, and his cheerful arrogance frequently aligned John and William against him. Still, ever confident and extraordinarily independent and proud, John and William's resentments never seemed to bother Luka.

The Illegals

> I'm telling you all this to demonstrate to you the extent of my parents' disappointment when I married a woman who did not know even how to wield a hoe. But since I convinced myself I would never become a farmer, [i]t never bothered me whether my wife knew farmwork or not.
>
> —Agoro Anduru (in "Loyalty to My Friend" 1982: 75)

At the outset of Tanzanian independence, Dar es Salaam was a small capital city in a nation with an overwhelmingly rural population. Since that time, the city has become the focal point of Tanzania's demographic transformation. Just before independence, in 1957, Dar es Salaam claimed less than 130,000 residents. There are close to 2 million residents now.

In the official conception of the post-colonial Tanzanian state, this never should have happened. Julius K. Nyerere, Tanzania's

PHOTOGRAPH 3.1 At Home

Despite the efforts of the Tanzanian government, the flow of migrant youth into Dar es Salaam could not be stopped. Here, young men live in makeshift houses on a beach near the downtown harbor. Photograph: Marc Sommers.

"Father of the Nation," had conceived of a country populated primarily by farmers in rural areas. He wrote that this idea was rooted in Africa's past. Accordingly, he advanced the idea that education should prepare young Tanzanians to be successful, content farmers who were productive in Tanzania's brand of "happy society" (Nyerere 1966: 170).

The dramatic drift away from Tanzanian state principles by young Tanzanians has been demonstrated by their overwhelming of Dar es Salaam; an endless stream of unemployed, unskilled, poorly educated rural-urban migrants entering the capital. The eager and energetic young Burundi refugees, who had grown up in Tanzanian settlements, attended primary schools with Tanzanian curriculums, and then joined Tanzanian youth in becoming urban migrants, highlight the lure of urban life in Tanzania, for if any group should be deterred from urban migration, it should be refugees. Restrictions designed to contain them in rural settlements were strict, and difficult circumstances await them on arrival in Dar es Salaam. Their drive toward the capital dramatically demonstrates how increasing numbers of African refugees, like other African populations, seek to become urbanized.

Totalizing the African

> Life was easy.
>
> –Julius K. Nyerere, on pre-colonial life in Africa (1968: 137)

In a sense, Julius K. Nyerere, Tanzania's first President and the country's dominant political figure since independence, was a revivalist. His concept of *Ujamaa* attempted to wipe away the capitalist, class-oriented values that European colonialists had invaded Tanzania with and return to a specific notion of pre-colonial Africa. It was a conservative social perspective:

> We, in Africa, have no more need of being 'converted' to socialism than we have of being 'taught' democracy. Both are rooted in our own past–in the traditional society which produced us. Modern African socialism can draw from its traditional heritage the recognition of 'society' as an extension of the basic family unit. (Nyerere 1966: 170)

Ujamaa, which literally translates as "familyhood" or "communityhood," became Tanzania's code word for change: Ujamaa meant that African Socialism and history would become the foundation for a new nationalist ideology.

Ujamaa called for Tanzanians to create a modern version of the good old days, where capitalist-inspired behavior had no place. The countryside had been infected with colonialism's capitalist principles, and this had to be eradicated. In stating his case, Nyerere spoke on behalf of all Africans:

> In the old days the African had never aspired to the possession of personal wealth for the purpose of dominating any of his fellows.... But then came the foreign capitalists. They were wealthy. They were powerful. And the African naturally started wanting to be wealthy too ... some of us would lie to use, or exploit, our brothers for the purpose of building up our own personal power and prestige. This is completely foreign to us, and it is incompatible with the socialist society we want to build here. (Nyerere 1966: 166)

Nyerere's socialist vision of pre-colonial Africa, involving societies where everyone worked for the good of the collective body and nobody exploited anyone else, necessarily excluded another capitalist offspring from the traditional African mix: people who did not work. Throughout his career, Nyerere condemned those who, simply by not working, threatened the Ujamaa idea of pitching in for the common good, and were, together with capitalist exploiters, enemies of the Tanzanian state:

> When I say that in traditional African society everybody was a worker, I do not use the word 'worker' simply as opposed to 'employer' but also as opposed to 'loiterer' or 'idler'. One of the most socialistic achievements of our society was the sense of security it gave to its members, and the universal hospitality on which they could rely. But it is too often forgotten, nowadays, that the basis of this great socialistic achievement was this: that it was taken for granted that every member of society—barring only the children and the infirm—contributed his fair share of effort towards the production of its wealth. Not only was the capitalist, or the landed exploiter, unknown to traditional African society, but we did not have that other form of modern parasite—the loiterer, or idler, who accepts the hospitality of society as his 'right' but gives nothing in return! Capitalistic exploitation was impossible. Loitering was an unthinkable disgrace. (Nyerere 1966: 165)

Nyerere added that "There is no such thing as socialism without work" (ibid.: 165), and the urban campaigns of the 1970s and 1980s demonstrated how strongly he believed this. The capitalist and the loiterer eventually had to be dealt with jointly as dual examples of Ujamaa's worst enemy: the "parasite."

Traditional African society revolved around farming, Nyerere believed, and so the modern Tanzanian state should contain farmers in overwhelming numbers. The education system should thus prepare young Tanzanians to farm, not migrate:

> In the past there was a tendency for young people—and even their parents—to assume that having an education meant leaving the land and taking wage employment.... Unfortunately, too many of our people still have this attitude. It is time that we dropped it, and realized that this is an independent country, with no room for colonial attitudes of the mind. (Nyerere 1968: 71)

Working for a wage, usually in town, represented the very sort of colonial attitude that Nyerere sought to transform, and primary schooling became the foundation for changing his predominantly rural vision for Tanzania into a reality. "Our young people are not disqualified from being farmers," he intoned. "They are qualified to be better farmers, and better citizens" (Nyerere 1968: 72).

This new purpose for education—preparing young Tanzanians to be "better farmers"—meant reforming the education system to support the idea that most Tanzanians should farm. This is clearly explained in Nyerere's famous essay, "Education for Self-Reliance." Tanzanian education, he argued, needed to be reformed to eradicate its inherent colonial frame of reference. The old British system set a high "emphasis on subservient attitudes and on white-collar skills." British colonial education deliberately inculcated "Tanzanian society" with "induced attitudes of human inequality" (ibid.: 269). The new education system needed to "prepare young people for the work they will be called upon to do in the society which exists in Tanzania—a rural society where improvement will depend largely upon the efforts of the people in agriculture and in village development" (ibid.: 274). Primary education would become the focus, "a complete education in itself" (ibid.: 280). The new system would eradicate the colonial concept that "a man is too precious for the rough and hard life which the masses of our people still live" (ibid.: 277). Instead, primary education would prepare Tanzanians to improve the lot of their individual, community, and ultimately, national situation—by farming.

Complementing this emphatically rural orientation of the new national education system was the equally emphatic diversion of resources away from Dar es Salaam to rural Tanzania and the towns designed to serve rural people:

> The "Arusha Declaration" emphasizes the necessity to give priority to the development of the agricultural sector of the economy and demands the diversion of capital, formerly earmarked for Dar es Salaam, to other regions of Tanzania. (Grohs 1972: 157)

The message to Tanzania's youth was clear: they should farm, and be content doing so.

The State Responds

> One of the consequences of [Tanzania's] state-centric approach to governance was the need to keep expanding state control over society, usually at the expense of society.
>
> —Aili Mari Tripp (1989a: 20)

> We must not allow the growth of parasites here in Tanganyika.
>
> —Nyerere (1966: 167)

The relationship between the state and urban migrants has produced three themes which connect urban migration to crime in Tanzanian history. The first relates directly to Nyerere's interpretation of urban migration to Dar es Salaam as a form of rebellion against the emphatically rural emphasis in Ujamaa. The second theme holds that urban migrants were the cause of urban crime, an impression that newspaper reporters and politicians frequently conveyed. The third theme makes unemployment by urban migrants a crime. In Tanzania, those with unlicensed and unregistered employment work illegally, and so are legally unemployed. This section examines these three themes.

Much of the suspicion and tension that proliferates among Dar es Salaam's huge urban migrant population arises from their awareness that they are not supposed to be there. Since the British colonial era, government authorities have been trying to expel underemployed urbanites from the capital and repatriate them to the rural areas. In the era of British rule, urban newcomers needed employment licenses and permission to reside in Dar es Salaam. Despite this, migrants lacking the proper papers thronged the streets in ever-growing numbers. Most migrants knew that they were in some way breaking the law simply by being in the city or by not working in a licensed workplace. Situated outside the law, they have routinely been considered the perpetrators of urban crime.

The British began to note serious problems in rural-urban migration to Dar es Salaam in the early 1950s. Yet their exertions to restrict migration and register urban dwellers—requiring everyone to carry an identity card—were comparatively mild: "the degree of control exerted over mobility and urban residence was markedly less strict and authoritarian than in most neighboring colonies" (Armstrong 1987a: 13). The independent Tanzanian administration extended British urban policies into the post-colonial era. The Tanzanian government also has required registration cards (*kitambulisho*) for urban residence, but their actions against the urban unemployed has been sporadic. Major campaigns launched in 1964, 1968, 1970, and, with great fanfare, 1976, rounded up thousands of the unemployed lacking identity cards for urban residence or employ. These campaigns had little lasting effect, barely slowing rural-urban migration to the capital. Government officials repeatedly attempted to "repatriate" migrants to their home villages or assign them for re-settlement in newly created farming villages. As soon as migrants were deposited in the countryside, however, many returned to the capital. One permanent result in many African cities has been the "steady intensification of population density and land use around the towns as a form of African urban sprawl" (Armstrong 1987a: 22). Dar es Salaam is no exception. By farming on the urban fringe, some migrants sustain a rural residence within reach of the town's magnetic attractions.[5]

While Armstrong claimed that "employment absorption of the urban workforce kept pace with the influx until the mid-1970s" (1987a: 23), by 1983 Dar es Salaam's Regional Commissioner declared that the city contained 168,000 workers and 400,000 jobless in a population of 1.3 million (ibid.: 26). By 1993, the Minister for Labour and Youth Development, Hassan Diria, estimated that only three youths in a hundred were employed, causing increases in "loitering and juvenile delinquency" (Maunya 1993: 1).

It must be noted that the employment Minister Diria mentioned pertained exclusively to the formal sector. Beneath this, the urban economies of the informal sector and the "shadow economy" (Kerner 1988b) operate. The necessity of these illegal economic avenues was borne out by the simple fact that formal sector wage scales were minuscule in comparison to the cost of urban living. This fact did not simply make payment of bribes, or "fees," to government officials increasingly common. It also rendered the possibility of surviving on a formal sector wage increasingly difficult. Tripp observed that "the average-sized household of six could not be fed for more than three days of the month on what many workers earned. For the rest of the month, expenses would have to be met from other sources" (1989b: 602). One study claimed that informal sector work drew an average monthly earning that was almost twice the government's minimum wage in urban areas.[6]

Tanzanians throughout the social and economic strata have been somehow engaged in the transfer of goods and services from the strictly legal and recognized economy (formal sector) to the sometimes illegal informal sector.[7] The vast economic area that reaches beyond the formal economic sector has been given a number of names, among them the black market, second economy, parallel economy, and the hidden sector (Tripp 1997: 18). Kerner has defined the informal sector in most African countries as "those traders and service workers from whom the state receives no revenue" who are "tolerated during times of prosperity and harassed and restricted when the economy is depressed" (Kerner 1988b: 48). Other researchers corroborate Kerner's claims of the pervasiveness of illegal economic activities in urban Tanzania. Kaluba, for example, has noted that even urban residents earning a "regular salary or wage" commonly gather "supplementary income[s] from other economic activities–especially petty trade ..." (1989: 212), which is entirely unregulated.

Kerner has made a distinction between two levels of informal economic activity: black market import smuggling (most commonly referred to in Tanzania as *magendo*) and the shadow economy. This last concept goes beyond traditional concepts of informal economic activities to, in this case, implicate just about every Tanzanian in some sort of illegal or semi-illegal activity (the boundaries have been irregular and changing in Tanzania for decades). The shadow economy, Kerner argued, is a "Tanzanian distribution sphere ... that can only be termed an essential survival strategy adopted by everyone from the highest level bureaucrat to the poorest peasant and worker" (Kerner 1988b: 48). In her view, "Anyone who could manage to divert some essential goods or services from legal channels would do so" (ibid.). Furthermore, the legality of various economic activities and transactions vacillated constantly: "The shadow economy is sometimes illegal, sometimes legal, and sometimes only hazily so," concluding that "It is this distribution realm which dominates the practical strategies of every day life for Tanzanians ..." (ibid.: 49).[8]

Perhaps the most significant outcome of the pervasive shadow economy is that it wrapped virtually everyone in the cloak of illegality. This created an atmosphere of fluctuating uncertainty, anxiety, and tension in Dar es Salaam, where such economic activities proliferate. All had to be careful to preserve their private operations. They were also preoccupied with quietly noting how others managed to succeed economically. As Kerner noted: "Tanzanians who know that illegal strategies are part and parcel of survival will profess ignorance or confusion about how one individual or another manages to get by. Yet people are constantly observing one another, piecing together the frameworks of their respective strategies" (1988a: 51). In the Tanzania that John, William, and James inhabited, uncertainty and tension went hand in hand, creating a pervasive, secret, silent world where people were constantly aware of the illegality of their activities and fearful of being caught. Kerner explained this situation well:

> Part of the reason why such things are not spoken of is that they are illegal–illegal to do and illegal to acknowledge. Another reason is that the rules (often laws) are frequently changed and even changed retroactively, making what a person did yesterday (when it was legal or semilegal) illegal today.... In a situation where the rules concerning what is correct are so often in flux, people must constantly ascertain how much leeway is available to manipulate the rules so as to avoid jeopardy. (Ibid.: 51–52)

And while most all Tanzanians, in Kerner's view, entered the realm of apparent illegality as a survival strategy, Nyerere, who developed a reputation for incorruptibility, looked down on them disapprovingly.[9]

Campaigning for "Hard Work"

> One major weakness of the *Nguvu-Kazi* operation is its perception of the broader issue of unemployment in Tanzania. Because land is abundant, the government and party leaders can't seem to understand why the unemployment exists. They argue that anybody who is unemployed in the urban areas could be gainfully employed in the agricultural sector. It is on the basis of this false assumption that the urban unemployed are given several insulting names like loiterers, exploiters, and lazy.
>
> –Dr. Joe Lugalla (1995: 176)

Tanzania's difficulties with villagization campaigns and rural stagnation during the mid- and late 1970s coincided with the explosion of migrant populations in urban areas. Beginning in 1976, Tanzania's "year of campaigns" (Armstrong 1987a: 17), the Tanzanian government led highly publicized actions that vilified and attacked the urban jobless. Urban campaigns began, in fact, during the colonial era and continued under Nyerere. But it was with the "*Nguvu Kazi*" (Hard Work) campaign, begun at the end of 1983, that Nyerere's ideology of a rural farming society was directly connected to those labeled as the system's recalcitrants: the loitering, idling parasites–the urban jobless. Nguvu Kazi represented a state campaign determined to align ideology with reality, for it had "the simple aim of relocating the urban unemployed back to the rural sector where they could be gainfully engaged in agricultural production" (Kerner 1988a: 303–304).

Those identified as "jobless loiterers" (ibid.: 305) often had jobs, but they were not legally licensed ones: "loitering and joblessness were defined by the absence of a government-issued identity card (*kitambulisho*) which designated both legal address and registered employment status" (ibid.: 306). Street vendors, casual laborers, traders, and other young men in public view became easy targets. Men were hardly the only targets. Women in Dar es Salaam, perhaps 66 percent of whom were self-employed in the informal sector, were also required to produce their marriage licenses as proof that they were not engaged in prostitution or informal sector activity (Kerner 1988b). Government officials targeted these kinds of urban migrants, repatriated them to rural areas, and registered them as rural dwellers.

Armstrong (1987a), Kerner (1988a, 1988b), Lugalla (1995), Sawers (1989) and Tripp (1997) have all commented on the difficulties of repatriating migrants to rural locations. Such campaigns against urbanites lacking official employment were also economically counterproductive. Sawers has noted that "The deportations of Dar es Salaam's unemployed wasted scarce transportation resources without affecting the city's population growth" (1989: 854–855). Ultimately, the campaign failed because Dar es Salaam's residents depended on unlicensed economic activities to sustain themselves, ignoring the restrictions *en masse* "because their survival depended on doing so" (Tripp 1989b: 619). *Nguvu Kazi*, as Lugalla explained, was doomed to fail:

> By imposing strict regulations in licensing informal petty business in urban areas, the *Nguvu-Kazi* exercise has been exacerbating the very problem it aimed to solve.... By forcing the unemployed to become

peasants, the act ... denie[d] the fact that life in the rural areas has become unbearable to many. By so doing, the act has been treating the symptoms rather than the cause of the so-called urban cancer. (1995: 177)

Although Nyerere had claimed that his *Ujamaa* ideology was tied to a purely African, pre-colonial socialism, he defined work just as the British colonialists had:

... the definition of work centered primarily on peasant cash crop production [which] has precedent in Tanzanian's colonial history.... In this colonial ideology, those who refuse to, or only lackadaisically engage in, commercial agriculture should be redefined as parasitical at best and troublesome, even criminal, at worst. (Kerner 1988b: 42)

For decades, leaving the rural areas was one of the strategies that agrarian Tanzanians have quietly implemented in resistance to state methods of control and agricultural surplus extraction.[10] Colonial and post-colonial policies of social coercion and surplus extraction contributed to an agricultural crisis.[11] At the same time, the availability of consumer goods and government subsidies of food prices and social services in urban areas, and, critically, the continuing expansion of government bureaucracy "ensured that the lion's share of [rural-urban] migration would go to the capital city" (Sawers 1989: 854).

The Legacy of Urban Campaigns

> ... informal sector activities have expanded very rapidly not only without government support, but despite frequent government harassment.
>
> –Dr. Joe Lugalla (1995: 188)

Urban campaigns have failed to stem the tide of urban migrants into Dar es Salaam. Instead, they have filled urban life with suspicion and tension. If a migrant seeks work in Dar es Salaam, it usually means working along (or beyond) the legal margins of the economy. Most migrants enter the sprawling informal or shadow economies in Dar es Salaam as a matter of course, as they lack the qualifications or connections to obtain the relatively few opportunities in the formal sector. Ishumi's study on the urban jobless (that is, those urbanites without legally recognized jobs) in East Africa indicated that men "mostly in their young ages" (Ishumi 1984: 36) comprised nearly three quarters of this population. Despite the economic might and pervasiveness of women in urban Tanzania (Tripp 1989b), the likelihood for urban Africa to contain more males than females is borne out in Dar es Salaam (Barke and Sowden 1992).

An interesting example of migrant conditions and concerns arose from analyses of the 1988 population census of Tanzania. The data showed a significant drop-off in the rate of Dar es Salaam's population growth. The census counted 1,369,850 residents of Dar es Salaam in 1988, notably lower than the projected population of 1,723,000. Barke and Sowden hailed this finding as evidence running "counter to the 'conventional wisdom' of increasing urban primacy in poor Third World countries" (1992: 14). Briggs, however, countered that Barke and Sowden were taking at face value a census containing "data of dubious reliability and accuracy, especially with regard to Dar es Salaam itself" (1993: 117). Briggs argued that the expanse and density of the capital had increased dramatically since the last national census in 1978. Why, then, was the 1988 census figure so inaccurate?

Briggs illuminated three reasons, each addressing different areas of urban difficulty in Dar es Salaam. The first concerned simple logistics. The delay in receiving sufficient supplies of blank census forms meant that enumerators ran out of forms before noon each day. Morale was already poor, due to low wages, and it was exacerbated because the census coincided with a period of heavy rain, which made much of the city's fragile road system virtually impassable. Many of the newly settled areas were "effectively cut off" (Briggs 1993: 118) from surrounding areas. Second, rapid urban expansion meant that "large areas of the city ... had not been properly or fully mapped" (ibid.). Thus, census workers could not accurately locate their enumeration districts with any accuracy. Proper coverage of the city became impossible to assure.

Beneath these logistical concerns lay a third reason. The 1988 census occurred when "many people were still extremely wary and suspicious of activities associated with the government" (ibid.). The government had expended considerable resources in attempts to persuade people to participate in the census. This made many people nervous. Briggs plainly stated that living in Dar es Salaam without an identity card (*kitambulisho*), obtainable only through a formal sector employer or at the government's party offices (*Chama Cha Mapinduzi*, or C.C.M., the sole legal party in Tanzania until 1992), was "strictly illegal." Those working beyond the formal market consequently feared another cleansing campaign aimed against the illegals who were enumerated in the census. These illegals thus went underground during the census operation (Briggs 1993: 118) and studiously avoided participating.

Dar es Salaam can thus be seen as a city filled with young men who, if they worked with any regularity, did so without a license—shining shoes, hawking produce or cassette tapes, running small outdoor stalls, and so on. They continued in their endeavors fully aware that they were prime targets for government initiatives against urban blight. As in other African capitals, young men in repose or at work are visible throughout Dar es Salaam. Living on the economic margins but in full public view, they remain potential targets for sweeps against unlicensed workers or residents—or criminals, as most are believed to arise from their numbers. Castigated and periodically chased by authorities, forever wary of sudden inquiries about the legality of their work or residence, or of suddenly becoming a crime suspect, the young men of Dar es Salaam are filled with endemic anxiety and suspicion of others.

To Live and Work in "Bongo"

The physical condition of Dar es Salaam afflicts all of its residents. With few exceptions, the tropical air is interminably hot and excessively humid. Despite a vigorous recent campaign to improve the city's road network, many remain in poor condition. Garbage collection is infrequent at best for most residents, and electric power and water supplies are sporadic. Fumes from burning garbage and dust from passing traffic regularly drift through public spaces and private homes. During the two annual rainy seasons, many roadways become bogs, with interlaced ponds gradually spawning malarial mosquitoes and filling with garbage. AIDS (*ukimwi*), malaria, and other diseases proliferate, and patients requiring assistance overwhelm the country's primary medical center, Muhimbili, located in the capital. Even the poorest households in town are terrified of crime. Dar es Salaam, in short, is expanding at a pace far beyond the government's capacity to provide basic services and support, a situation only exacerbated by their difficulties with tax collection (Kaluba 1989).

Clearly, Dar es Salaam can be a difficult and exasperating place to make a living and establish oneself.[12] The dismal state of the city was a common topic of complaint among its inhabitants and the gulf between urban aspirations and urban realities have found regular expression in popular culture. The wonders of urban ideals and Western technology and cultural imports constantly confront everyday difficulties and disappointments.

Dar es Salaam is largely comprised of migrants, and this fact has greatly affected its social and cultural life. The Zaramo and Shomvi, the original inhabitants of the area, and the Nyamwezi, long familiar with Dar es Salaam because of their history of working as porters for Arab slave and ivory caravans, have been superseded by other ethnic groups such as the Chagga and Haya.[13] The city has become a diverse ethnic soup, which nonetheless has allowed established forms of urban society and culture to continue into the present. In 1912, early in the German colonial era, when Dar es Salaam first became the capital, the Germans divided the town into three racial zones (that is, White, Asian, and African).[14] The Africans' commercial center was Kariakoo, an Africanized name for the Germans' African "Carrier Corps" residing there. Kariakoo soon became the "core of the African town and the nearest thing Tanganyika had to a territorial focus" (Iliffe 1979: 385). Kariakoo remains the central commercial area for most African consumers.

FIGURE 3.2 "Dar Is Worst!"

An editorial cartoonist draws from a Muslim schoolchildren's chant ("East, West, East is best!") to comment on the state of Dar es Salaam. The message on the boards nailed across the public toilets on the right translates as "Rotten Toilets (by order of the city)."

Source: Mwapembwa 1991: 3.

Among the evolving types of African townsmen were those who, from early in Dar es Salaam's growth, "accepted no authority at all" (ibid.: 388). These people lived an existence detached from local institutions, and lived unplanned, hand-to-mouth lives. Many were teenaged boys who searched for work, such as selling scrap or working as day laborers. Some seemed to roam in gangs. This urban lifestyle of tenuousness, poverty, and alienation has included growing numbers of young men (as well as women) in Dar es Salaam.

Tripp has commented that the difference between the kinds of informal enterprises in Dar es Salaam differ by gender, in large part because women have limited access to capital. As a consequence,

> Women were primarily involved in making and selling pastries, fried fish, porridge, beans, tea, soup, retail charcoal, firewood, kerosene, and flour ... [while] men tended to be the tailors, masons, carpenters, launderers, mechanics, and shoemakers ... their starting capital was four times higher than women and ... on the whole they had been twice as long in business, and had 5.4 times higher returns. (Tripp 1989b: 610)

Women also participated in prostitution and brewing and selling beer, activities common to women in other parts of urban Africa (Rogge 1985a). It should also be noted that participation in the informal sector has exploded since the 1980s, when a sharp decline in living standards pressed regular wage earners increasingly into informal activities (Kaluba 1989) and led to the increased participation of other household members in income generation (Tripp 1989b). Young migrants, many of whom join together to share crowded rented rooms instead of living with relatives, create small microenterprises as well, selling coffee or fruits, or working for others in fishing, road, or construction crews. Vacancies in the industrial sector often remain open, apparently because unskilled workers expect a higher return, as well as more independence, from informal sector work.

How Are Your Anxieties?

> Tamar committed the bizarre crime in a borrowed room in a squalid building in one of the mushrooming slums of the city of Dar es Salaam.
>
> —Agoro Anduru (opening to "This is Living" 1982: 75)

PHOTOGRAPH 3.2 Kariakoo Scene

On the outskirts of Kariakoo, Dar es Salaam. Photograph: Marc Sommers

"*Bongoland*" symbolized the multitude of difficulties and challenges that await young urban migrants in Tanzania's capital. The steamy heat and constant threat of crime, the overcrowded housing, poor medical facilities, and overburdened infrastructure, all conspire to make "Bongo" an especially difficult and stressful place to live. The rush of youths to embrace "toun life" has made it dense with economic competition between the unskilled. Yet this challenge can actually become a point of departure. Gathering tips as they go, urban newcomers seek to shed characteristics that would classify them as "confused" and "bushy." They quickly learn that real young urbanites consider themselves "modern," "fit," "top," and "fashion design." To make this change, migrating rural youth must figure out how to exchange their *mshamba* (farm person, or "country hick") image for something new. For migrating Burundi refugee youth, the image they cultivated had to be not just urban—it had to be Tanzanian, too.

Although Burundi refugee tailors strove to convince others that they were fellow Tanzanians, invention and experimentation were part and parcel of urban youth living more generally. And perhaps nowhere was urban inventiveness more apparent than in the urban vocabulary known across Tanzania as *Kidar* (Dar es Salaam Language). The language of Kidar was referred to as the *Lugha ya Vijana* (Language of the Young), *Lugha ya Mtaani* (the Community Language), or *Kiswahili Kali* (Angry Swahili) by youths in the capital. The language was considered disrespectful and improper by many in the city's older generation, who called it the *Lugha ya Wahuni* (The Language of the Ignorant). For practicing fundamentalist Christians, the slang words were sinful.

Given its widespread use, written references to Bongoland and the urban youth *Lugha* are curiously rare outside the city's popular culture. Bongoland is rarely mentioned either in the media or academic works. Meanwhile, the word, and the myths attached to it, are known by youths across the country. Young people in rural Tanzania speak a localized version of *Kidar* to indicate their connection to Dar es Salaam's modern urban lifestyle and their striving for upward mobility.[15]

Perhaps the greatest *Kidar* popularizer is a musician and songwriter based in Dar es Salaam named Dr. Remmy Ongala. Many of his songs describe the difficulties and changes in urban life, and some of these condemn or praise individuals (as in his song "Mrema," about Augustine Mrema, a former Minister of Home Affairs). One of Dr. Remmy's hits was "*Mambo Kwa Soks*" (Issues

PHOTOGRAPH 3.3 The Aquarium

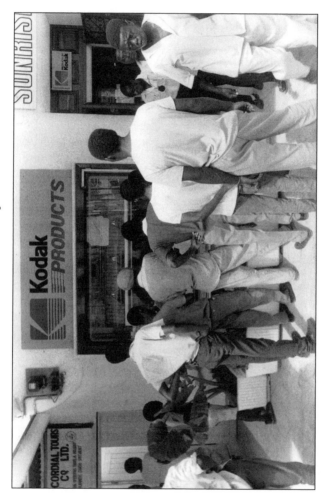

The finding of work and intellectual stimulation are dual problems in Dar es Salaam. Here, young men take time out from their days looking for work to gaze at an aquarium in the window of a photography store. Photograph: Marc Sommers.

with Socks), about the need to wear condoms (*Soks*) nowadays, because of the dangers of *ukimwi* (AIDS). The song's influence on youth behavior extended far beyond public health awareness, as it helped spread a new greeting between youths. Using the thumb's up sign with the words "*Kwa Soks!*" signaled not only that the respondent was practicing safe sex but that he was "up to date" with the latest urban expressions.

The Young People's language is the language of young urban migrants and those rural youth who strive to experience "*toun life.*" The language incorporates invented words and phrases to describe the difficulties they face in Dar es Salaam. Greetings between young people may begin with "*Habari ya mihangaiko?*" (How are your anxieties?) There are also verbs to describe one's activities of the day, including two meaning "I've been going here or there." One such verb connotes aimless or hopeful wanderings (*kuzururazurura*), while another implies the active or even desperate pursuit of money (*kuhangaika,* taken from the verb "to be anxious"). The thumb's up signal may refer to condom use, but might also be used with "*dole tupu*" (thumb alone). With this phrase, the thumb may simply mean "cool," or "A-OK," but it may also mean "Hey, I'm circumcised too!" signaling togetherness between young men from different ethnic groups that both practice circumcision. In the fierce competition for limited opportunities in Bongoland, young men may envision themselves as allies against uncircumcised youth, or even the *Rasta.*

Although English is the second of Tanzania's two national languages (Swahili being the first), relatively few Tanzanians know more than a handful of words or phrases in English and only a small fraction of the total population speaks it proficiently. Youths, however, consider English "very modern" and a tool for understanding global culture, and a way to confer heightened social status on the speaker. As a result, using English words in Swahili conversations has become increasingly common. At the same time, English words that have been lifted into Swahili take on new meanings in part because the speakers usually don't understand their original meanings. It is in this way that "fashion design" came to mean "I'm doing well."

Important themes in urban migrant lives are often applied to foreign words. The most important theme is the concept of being an underdog battling against an unjust and formidable system. The verb *kuyeya,* for example, translates as "to escape," and was used to warn others of impending trouble. A youth might use it to alert friends that a policeman was approaching (of course, they had to

PHOTOGRAPH 3.4 On the Street

Away from the heat of the midday sun, some young musicians relax. Photograph: Marc Sommers.

hope that the policeman didn't understand the signal). Many migrant youth had explained that *kuyeya* had been lifted from a movie starring Chuck Norris. They described how the bearded Norris, whom some youth described as a modern-day Jesus Christ figure, gathered his fellow American prisoner of war camp inmates around him to explain his plan for escape. Following his explanation, all the American men said "Yeah!" in unison. Using *kuyeya* thus indicates that young people are leaving behind advancing authorities and going to join colleagues who also use the word "Yeah!"

A similar meaning was attached to another word after the Gulf War began in January, 1991. Stories of the war in newspapers and national radio broadcasts hailed the audacity and daring of the underdog, Saddam Hussein, and his Iraqi army. Suddenly "Scud," or "Scudi," which referred to the missiles the Iraqis employed against the mighty U.S.-led coalition, became visible all over town—written into the caked dirt on city buses or trucks or as graffiti. Urban youth had added a new word to their lexicon which heroized their view of themselves as formidable underdogs or outcasts. Like Saddam, the forces against them might ultimately overwhelm them. But they were ready to put up a good fight.

The "Anti-Socials"

The *Lugha ya Wahuni*, even though many of its words have been absorbed into spoken Swahili, has been thoroughly denigrated by urban residents who consider its adherents to be the scourge of urban life: young men engaged in illegal economic activities and outright crime. It is commonly believed that these people are not merely acting cheeky when they use this language—they are signifying their presence beyond the bounds of established urban society. And their presence is threatening.

Many connect the presence of large numbers of young men in town to the city's state of disrepair. Newspaper reports in the *Daily News* of Tanzania, the government-run English language daily, indicated the growing frustration with the ever-rising tide of migrant youth. One article, for example, connected the city's problems directly to the presence of young men selling their wares at *kiosks*, or outdoor stalls:

> Dar es Salaam used to be a planned city with open spaces, parking areas and the few roads that ran through the city centre were immaculate and shop pavements well kept....

Dar es Salaam today looks like a ghetto. The natural appearance is gone, as kiosks mushroom every day at the most unexpected spots....

Now, one can hardly find space in the down-centre Dar es Salaam except where the area has been fenced off. This invasion of space has created problems not only for city planners and health officers, but also to shopkeepers and residents in the area. (Masamba 1993: 5)

The author, Nyambona Masamba, asked why so many young men had fallen into running kiosks, and discovered that they were primary and secondary school leavers who "could not find paid employment." Surveying this population, the author described lives colored with anxiety and insecurity: "they are always worried of ambushes from the City Council because their licenses to trade in the area were only temporary." The author wondered "what [can] be done to save Dar es Salaam from destruction," since city authorities seem unable to solve the problem. Lacking answers, the author concluded: "Does it mean Dar–The Haven of Peace–is a doomed City?" (ibid.).

Such ruminations about Dar es Salaam's troubles, and their connection to the urban overflow of young men, are not unusual. In 1993, the Minister for Labour and Youth Development, Hassan Diria, commented that only 171,000 Tanzanian youth out of more than five million searching for work had obtained employment in the formal sector. "This means that 96.65 per cent of youths in the country could not get employment in the formal sector," he added (Maunya 1993: 1). As a result, "cases of loitering, robbery, drug abuse and armed banditry were on the increase, a situation compounded by the poor upbringing of the anti-socials" (ibid.). Then former President Ali Hassan Mwinyi, in a speech urging the expansion of vocational training, announced that "between 600,000 and 700,000 primary school leavers were produced each year who flocked into urban areas to become a potential force for crime, due to lack of vocations" (Daily News 1993a: 1). In a shift from former President Nyerere's drive to keep most young people in the countryside as farmers, his successor, President Mwinyi, seemed to have accepted urban migration by Tanzania's youth population as a fact of urban life. Despite the startling suggestion by government leaders that most of the nation's youth were unemployable, and hundreds of thousands annually descended on urban Tanzania, the government's response was limited. One such response occurred in September, 1993. City Council Officers had ordered local police to remove youths hawking goods at illegal stalls (or kiosks) from the

PHOTOGRAPH 3.5 Selling Sodas

In Dar es Salaam, vendors seem to be everywhere. Here, a young man sells sodas in a parking lot. Photograph: Marc Sommers.

city's center and the predominant market area, Kariakoo, and shifted them to Jangwani, one of the few remaining open spaces in the city. Jangwani instantly became the newest of Dar es Salaam's squatter settlements and informal marketplaces.

A senior environmentalist of the government's National Environmental Management Council (NEMC) immediately condemned the hastily planned undertaking for inviting "imminent disaster" to the local environment and public health (Masendo 1993a: 1). This public attack on a government initiative seemed to have fueled the subsequent rioting in Kariakoo by street vendors the following day, when police ordered further removals of their kiosks and later charged sixteen people for "allegedly conducting business in the streets illegally" (Daily News 1993c: 1)–a charge that could have applied to thousands of street vendors in town. An additional cause of the rioting was raised by Thompson Nseka, Wholesale Co-operative Society Publicity Secretary, who alleged that government officials were demanding bribes from the vendors (who, of course, lacked official business licenses) "so that vendors [could] continue to conduct business in the areas" (Masendo 1993b: 1).

In characteristic fashion, city officials resolved the crisis by treating it as an isolated incident. They requested formal applications for street vending plots in Kariakoo, thereby making a small section of the city's street vending population part of the licensed, formal economy. Vendors would also be offered other city sites to work in, where, presumably, they would not need licenses. The city government's hasty response to overcrowding in Dar es Salaam's central marketplace did not generate any attempt to address the larger problems of unregulated trading and settlement that plagued Dar es Salaam.

Hidden Observers

> Corruption has become the way of life in Tanzania at present, and its negative effects are not hard to see.... In reality, it means that in a situation where corruption is dominant, public policies and laws enforcing individual rights, collective rights and freedom cannot be implemented.
>
> –Dr. Joe Lugalla (1995: 148)

Crossing into the shadow economy may have been common in Dar es Salaam, but it was still illegal. Despite the economic necessities behind much of this activity, Tanzanian policemen could harass, fine or arrest those engaged in illegal work at any time. Given the legacy of campaigns aimed at them, and constant suspicions that they were criminals, this was especially true for young men. Still, the general uncertainty caused tension, secrecy, and anxiety to become an accepted part of Dar es Salaam life. One final factor, however, cemented anxiety to urban living: surveillance.

Written information about surveillance in Tanzania is scarce. Yet Kerner attests to the remarkable reach of the government's intelligence activities: "Almost every Tanzanian I encountered ventured to guess that up to 50% of the population operates at least part-time in an intelligence-gathering capacity for the state" (Kerner 1988a: ix). This situation had made it difficult for Dar es Salaam residents to trust others and easy for them to be fearful and anxious, especially when the range of actors involved in some sort of illegal or semi-illegal activity had become so wide.[16] Everyone is vulnerable, and self-censorship frequently applies. Lamb has argued that Nyerere "tolerate[d] no dissent and … closed all avenues of opposition and free expression" (1982: 67). This situation has since been relaxed, but state controls continue to affect public life in Tanzania. The institution of Ten Cell Leaders (*Kumikumi*) for every ten households ("cells") in the country, established decades ago, remained a strong influence on public discourse and action during the fieldwork period. Ten Cell Leaders have been called "The eyes of the party," and appeared to be the central point of state intelligence-gathering on citizens. This role expanded with the introduction of the *sungusungu*. This institution, which first arose to stop cattle rustling (Abrahams 1987; Kerner 1988a), became a national night guard activity supervised by the Ten Cell Leaders in 1990. Throughout Tanzania, the *Kumikumi* assigned "volunteers" from each of his ten households different nights of the week to stand guard. Typically, these *sungusungu* were comprised of the households' young men.[17]

"Toun Life"

Bongoland Days

A typical work day in the two tailoring shops I regularly visited, from Monday through Saturday, required tailors to awake at dawn, have tea and sweep the shop, and open by 7:30 A.M. The head tailor rarely swept or cooked. For most of the year, the intense heat baked the shops' low corrugated metal roofs, which, together with drifting dust, made working strenuous and uncomfortable. Yet the tailors, all seated behind their sewing machines, worked steadily until closing at 7:00 or 8:00 at night, excepting an hour's break for lunch. Tailors alternated performing the cooking chores, which usually consisted of *ugali* (stiff porridge made from maize four) with greens, beans, or fish.

James's shop was a prime neighborhood gathering place for young Pentecostals from his church. The visitors sat on the bench just outside the shop's front door, or in one of the two chairs located just inside. When the radio worked, it was tuned to the national Swahili language station, the Voice of Tanzania (VOT). The atmosphere was often festive and always relaxed, and neighborhood gossip, jokes and local issues flowed across conversations. Refugees were often among the shop's visitors, although they joined Tanzanians in emphasizing their identity as fellow saved Christians.

James thrived in this environment. Many of his fellow church choir members were regular visitors to the shop. He also usually kept near his sewing machine the choir's songbook, a worn ledger book which contained handwritten hymns. Choir members had written most of the songs.

The atmosphere in the Pastor's shop was different. Pastor Albert and his wife forbade radio playing, because stations regularly broadcast popular Swahili music, the kind heard in the city's nightclubs. The pastor considered this music spiritually dangerous, as it could inspire listeners to sin. The tension this issue aroused was exacerbated by the presence of a nightclub nearby which nightly boomed "sinful" music into Pastor Albert's household and shop. Albert's wife often responded by playing a cassette of choir music (some of which was produced in Burundi refugee recording studios in Ulyankulu settlement) and turning up the volume. Day and night, John, William, and Luka endured what Pastor Albert believed was a musical battle for influence over their souls. Needless to say, the atmosphere in their tailoring shop was tense.

After working nearly a year without a radio, John asserted his independence by purchasing a small transistor radio and listening at low volume, but only while he worked alone. He kept it hidden in a drawer at his work area, and usually tuned into soccer broadcasts, a consuming passion for most young men in Dar es Salaam, instead of music shows. Even as he defied Pastor Albert, John maintained the caution that characterized Burundi refugee actions in Dar es Salaam.

The Business of Tailoring

All tailoring shops in Dar es Salaam had layers of material hung on rungs along the walls. The colors were sedate: dark browns, blues, greens, and black. The most popular material was polyester, as it was seen to be lightweight, durable and could hold a crease best. Each piece of material was one and a quarter meters long: the length required to make a pair of pants, the mainstay of tailoring shop business.

The central economic niche that local tailoring shops filled—making trousers—was created by the nature of clothing merchandising in Dar es Salaam. There were three types of clothes one could purchase: *mitumba, redimed* (ready-made or factory-made), or custom work performed by one of the myriad of tailoring shops in the city. These shops broke down into three categories: the large downtown shops, usually owned and managed by Asians and containing as many as fifteen tailors; the small neighborhood tailoring shops such as those that John, William, and James worked in; and individual tailors with one machine, located outdoors either in markets or on neighborhood verandahs.

Mitumba clothing was the cheapest and commonest clothing in Dar es Salaam. It arrived in Tanzania either as donated clothing or as discounted used clothing. *Mitumba* was bought by the bale and sold in markets throughout the town. A pair of pants might cost as little as five hundred shillings (less than two U.S. dollars), and slightly more for higher quality. These pants were always used and often in need of repair.

Redimed referred to factory-made clothes, usually from Asia. They cost significantly more than *mitumba*, perhaps the equivalent of twelve U.S. dollars, or more than a month's salary for most people. *Redimed* trousers, as William and John described to me, almost never fit right and so usually required additional tailoring after purchase, and were not especially durable. The best pants to buy were custom-made by tailors. These cost the equivalent of eighteen to twenty U.S. dollars for materials and labor. The tailors' work thus consisted primarily of making pants and repairing or fitting *mitumba* and *redimed* clothing.

Mitumba shirts, especially T-shirts from the U.S. containing the widest range of possible emblems, were the commonest shirts in town, costing the equivalent of one U.S. dollar each. *Redimed* shirts, with collars and long sleeves, were for formal occasions like Sunday church. They competed in price with tailored shirts (about ten to twelve U.S. dollars). Tailors rarely made shirts, as *redimed* style and quality were considered unbeatable.

Tailors made dresses and skirts more often, but this was still fairly rare. The city's tailors were almost all male, and they considered women's clothing easier to make than men's trousers. Women tended to buy either *mitumba* or *redimed* clothing. Watching James or William measure a woman customer was quite a spectacle. Visitors to the shops would stare at the fidgeting, blushing woman standing before them, who anxiously waited for the tailor to finish measuring her.

Clothing styles for men and women in Dar es Salaam were restrictive. Most women wore dresses, and used colorful printed materials called *khangas* to shade their head, carry a child on their back or wear around their waist. Men wore slacks and shirts. Skirts for girls and shorts for boys were worn by schoolchildren. Muslim men wore *koffia* caps, and some also wore a *khanzu*, a men's gown. Some Muslim women wore the *buibui* veil, but it was a rare sight. Western, "modern" fashions predominated in Dar es Salaam. Indeed, all clothing that the tailors made was designed to emulate *redimed* styles. The finest clothing a person could have would be *redimed*, but only *redimed* produced by a European or American company. Factory-made clothing from Europe or the West was the model and standard for most clothing in Dar es Salaam, but it was expensive. Some men chose to emulate Western styles by paying extra to have a *lebo*, a locally made label, sewn over the back pants pocket. Van Heusen (often spelled as Van Husen) was one of the *lebos* of choice.

The following list suggests the hierarchy of eight major tailoring skills, listed in order of difficulty (with number one being the easiest), that tailors were required to perform:

1. Sewing edges for *khangas*
2. Mending clothes
3. Tailoring *mitumba* or *redimed* clothes
4. Making dresses and skirts
5. Making pants
6. Making shirts (a rare occurrence)
7. Making Kaunda suitcoats (the short-sleeved suitcoat popularized by Zambia's former President, Kenneth Kaunda)
8. Making long-sleeved Western style suitcoats

Tailors entering as apprentices learned to perform the first three tasks immediately. The focus, however, was on making pants.

Accomplishing this skill marked the point when a person truly became a tailor. From that point, the goal was to make a suitcoat, which was very difficult. Mastery of this skill, however, could enable a tailor to one day manage a shop or start his own. Amosi, James's cousin and boss, explained the process for new tailors this way:

> After doing [the initial tasks listed above] for a while, a long time, they can learn to make a *koti* [suitcoat]. That's hard, let me tell you. After one year or so ... again, it depends on how fast they learn, and when they think they are ready, they then ask to learn to make a *koti*. At that point [after learning to make suitcoats] they are full tailors, and can make anything, and so are on their own....

Across more than a year's time that I spent with John and James, the two had only started learning to make a suitcoat. William, on the other hand, had already learned this skill in his settlement prior to working in Dar es Salaam.

Tailoring shops typically contained two to four manual sewing machines, plus a *zigzag*, another manual machine made by Singer Company which sewed the jagged line used for inseams. A shop lacking a *zigzag* had to pay a fee to another shop to use theirs. Shop space was reserved for ironing clothes. Behind most shops was a cramped bedroom where tailors shared a bed and cooked their meals. I noticed that tailors in both shops each received three nails to hang their belongings.

At work, each tailor sat behind their own sewing machine. The *zigzag* machine remained open for all to use. Sometimes the choice of sewing machines indicated their degree of interest in social interaction with customers and visitors. In Pastor Albert's shop, Luka always sat closest to the bench next to the front door, where visitors and customers sat. John eventually moved to the front machine across from the bench and next to the front window. William, on the other hand, always sat far in the back, his face partly hidden from view by low-hanging material samples.

The Pastor described the tailoring shop attached to his house as a church business, whose sole purpose was to employ congregation members. In 1983, the church received a government small industry loan to purchase three sewing machines for the shop. They also raised money from congregation members (called "shareholders") to make the building and buy materials. Within six years, Albert noted with pride, he repaid the government loan from shop profits.

The issue of profits was difficult to ascertain, as neither shop allowed me to look at their income and expenditure records. But the tailors told me that their salary, usually at around three to four thousand shillings a month (about twelve to sixteen U.S. dollars) plus room and board, was insufficient. And so, like most other adults in town, they tried to make additional money on the side. In all tailoring shops, custom tailoring work was noted in a large ledger book. The customer's measurements and style requests were recorded, as well as the agreed price for work. This was the money that the shop's manager could count. Small jobs went unrecorded and were easy to pocket.

John told me that he got his spending money by pocketing the cash for small repairs. He was secretly sharing the money with William, he said, adding that Luka had been frozen out of the arrangement because they didn't trust him. In response, Luka began selling maize as a sideline. This work arose when a trader in his church congregation asked if he would to sell his maize in town. Luka posted huge sacks of maize at the tailoring shop door until Albert forbade it. After this, Luka made verbal deals with customers by day and delivered their orders after work.

Urban Networks

The Burundi refugees' urban network configuration differs dramatically from those characterized in the literature. The use of networks has been critiqued as "a method ... and a concept that has more often than not been misapplied or used merely metaphorically" (Sanjek 1990:175). Sanjek also observed that the study of urban networks has begun to serve a different anthropological objective. Rather than focusing, for example, on the "characteristics of the linkages ... as a means of explaining the behaviour of the people involved in them" (Mitchell 1969: 4), Sanjek indicated how more recent studies, notably those by Finnegan (1989) and Hannerz (1980), considered urban networks as pathways that led anthropologists to situations worthy of study. In this sense, network analysis became a useful methodological tool in service to a separate objective; a social indicator, perhaps, leading to locations where culture was practiced.

Implicit in both of these conceptions is the assumption that networks are useful in large part because they are so expansive. Mitchell, for example, stated that among the critical characteristics of networks is their "multiplexity" (Mitchell 1987: 309). Finnegan's study of pathways (1989) suggested equally dense urban networks. Karadawi considered urban refugees exceptions to this rule, since their mobility created "changing and mostly transient social networks" (1987: 115). This study illuminates urban refugee networks that differ from both of those conceptions. The networks that John, William, and James belonged to were stable but hardly encompassing. Most urban refugees interviewed for this book ultimately trusted few other refugees, and consequently produced exclusive, individualized networks designed only to deliver them from the settlements into a prearranged living and work situation in town.

Nevertheless, regardless of their backgrounds and private fears, all Burundi refugees in Dar es Salaam maintained connections to other refugees living there. They created two networks that illuminated the inherent push-pull within their society between the ethnic Hutu identity that unified them and the Imbo and Banyaruguru identities that split them apart. Refugees simultaneously relied on a "Hutu Network" that included all Burundi refugees in town while also privately maintaining a much smaller network containing a finite set of people. Both networks operated out of necessity—one could not easily survive long in Bongoland in isolation—but served different practical yet complimentary purposes.

The Hutu Network applied to issues affecting Burundi refugees generally, notably the exchange of information and hand delivery of mail between the settlements and town. It recognized the need for all refugees to join with others to maintain individual connections to friends and family and become better informed about issues affecting all Burundi refugees. In this context, refugees exhibited their solidarity as ethnic Hutu. But this solidarity was still fairly tenuous and formalized, and much more common in Pastor Albert's shop than Amosi's. Albert frequently hosted visitors from the settlements, often Pentecostal traders visiting Dar es Salaam to sell surplus food crops grown in the refugee settlements. There were also student refugees with UNHCR scholarships moving between the settlements and their schools during school breaks. If they were Pentecostal, they might visit Pastor Albert while in town. Refugees living in other parts of the city also visited. John, William, and even Luka were cordial but distant with such people, exchanging settlement mail and sometimes, if only very briefly and with coded words, political news about Burundi or refugees in Tanzania. Occasionally a refugee tailor from the shop across the street (which was aligned with the rival Pentecostal church in town) would stop by to deliver mail from the settlements. James would exchange mail but avoided open conversations about anything related to Burundi or refugees. Surrounded by Tanzanians, he did not want to give his cover away.

Examples of interactions between members of the Hutu Network occurred frequently. Refugees who would normally distrust and be wary of each other, such as an educated Imbo and an uneducated Banyaruguru, could help each other at times. Their shared identity as Hutu and experience as settlement refugees provided them with a platform for exchanging information about, for instance, the March 1992 ultimatum issued by the Home Affairs Minister, Augustine Mrema, to Burundi refugees. Mrema had declared that all Burundi refugees would have three months to decide whether to repatriate to Burundi or become Tanzanian citizens. The Hutu Network flowered during this period, as Burundi refugees flush with excitement and often immense anxiety shared updates about recent events.[18]

In addition to the Hutu Network, refugees also maintained economic networks that were far more important to a refugee's survival in Dar es Salaam. Their general outlines were known to all, but the specific configuration of individual networks remained secret. For tailors, the pathway that led them to an urban apprenticeship usually involved their parents or guardian paying a trader to set up an urban apprenticeship for a son. Traders often had dynamic personalities and fairly extensive capital resources. They were accustomed to paying regular "fees" to Tanzanian officials to transport their goods between their settlement and the capital (as well as other Tanzanian towns). Their regular trips between destinations enabled them to fill openings in refugee-run urban businesses.

It is not hard to see why refugee entrepreneurs in the capital hoped to fill their businesses with young refugee men. In economic terms, they relied on each other. Often this bond was strengthened by their membership in the same Christian church. The urban refugee entrepreneur knew that the migrant refugees provided excellent, stable labor. Young men lucky enough to obtain an urban apprenticeship knew that they had been fortunate to get one. Yet migrant refugees lacked the ability to leave a business, because their survival in town depended on their patron's favor. Their labor was replaceable, given the substantial pool of available labor back in the settlements.

The other kind of economic network for Burundi refugees in Dar es Salaam applied to unskilled workers. Young men coming from families lacking the capital or connections to arrange an urban apprenticeship relied on friends or relatives already in town. Creating this kind of network was easier to do. News that an opening was available for a brother or specific friend could be related in a letter delivered by another urbanite visiting the settlement. The newcomer then ventured to Dar es Salaam alone, armed with a small amount of cash to pay for work tools, some payment toward the rent he would share, and living expenses. He would then enter a job that his friend/relative had arranged for him.

Portable Fears

While Burundi refugees understandably perceived Dar es Salaam as fraught with serious dangers and challenges, Tanzanian residents shared many of the same concerns. Many Tanzanians, young men in particular, migrated to their capital knowing that the government did not want them there. The youth's near-inevitable participation in illegal, or at the very least, not officially recognized, economic activities cemented their perception that they lived at the margins of urban life. While urban youth culture may have welcomed them, the larger urban social structure remained suspicious. Unlike Hannerz' idea that cities transmit "openness to the wider society" (1992: 206), Dar es Salaam was in many respects a closed city.

Burundi refugees in town clearly had grounds for additional concerns. It was not simply that government authorities disapproved of the rising tide of young migrants in Dar es Salaam. John, William, and James broke the law to live and work in Bongoland. Yet their culturally imbued perceptions of danger, which they imported from the refugee settlements into town, made their situation unique.

Douglas and Wildavsky have argued that "the selection of dangers and the choice of social organization run hand in hand" (1982: 186), and their conception of culture helps explain the impact of cultural fear on Burundi refugees in Dar es Salaam. They defined culture as "a middle area of shared beliefs and values" pitched between "private, subjective perception" and "public, physical science" (ibid.: 194), which might be construed as objectivity. As refugees moved from the private to the public, culture fueled their perceptions of apparent realities and gave cultural fear its power over refugee perceptions. Though cultural fear did not prevent urban migration, it did promote the sense that unseen Tutsi terrors could arise at any time, spurring refugees to be unusually careful and suspicious in Dar es Salaam, and fashion isolated networks for maintaining their urban residence. For unlike young Tanzanian migrant men, who knew that their presence in town could threaten others, John, William, James, and thousands of their young Burundi refugee peers in Dar es Salaam viewed this power relationship in reverse. The unknown Tanzanian outsiders, together with many Burundi refugee insiders, threatened them. Ultimately, it was cultural fear that set the young refugees apart.

Notes

1. It also contributed to the influential Scudder-Colson Model for the analysis of dislocated peoples (Scudder and Colson 1982).
2. Connections between religious affiliation and urban migration will be discussed in Chapter 6.
3. At the time of field research, Tanzania's tallest building was the NIC Investment House in downtown Dar es Salaam. It is thirteen stories high.
4. Refugees and Tanzanians alike commonly use the passive tense to indicate an action that might possibly get them in trouble. This is designed to distance them from any involvement in the act itself, and hopefully builds the impression that the speaker was victimized by others.
5. Briggs (1991) has observed that the use of agricultural land in the peri-urban zone surrounding urbanized Dar es Salaam moved from a survival strategy for growing food in the early 1980s, when incomes decreased drastically in real value, to the production of commercial crops in the late 1980s, following Tanzania's shift to economic liberalization in the post-Nyerere era.
6. The information was reported by Chemi Che-Mponda in the Daily News (Tanzania) on September 2, 1993, based on information from a draft report of "The Rural Informal Sector in Tanzania," by Prof. Mboya S. D. Bagwachwa.
7. This strict legal-illegal dichotomy appears to be evolving. The December 1993 National Workshop on Informal Sector Policy in Tanzania examined issues involved in incorporating that sector, which includes fully 56 percent of the urban labor force, into national development strategies. As one paper described, "The informal sector has become a key component of the choices open to Tanzanian development ... [which] is not the largest employer for school leavers" (Tueros and Mwaduma 1993: i). The Tanzanian government is officially recognizing the informal sector's existence: an Act for Microenterprise and Informal Sector Promotion has been proposed in the nation's Parliament. Only time will tell, however, if official recognition will significantly affect levels of urban anxiety and suspicion.
8. Kerner's description, despite the shift towards economic liberalization since Nyerere relinquished formal reins of power in 1985, nonetheless applies in Tanzania's post-Nyerere era.
9. Nyerere's presence in Tanzanian society remained strong until his death in 1999, long after relinquishing the presidency in 1985.
10. Strategies of peasant resistance have also been elaborated at length by Scott (1985, 1986), and documented about Tanzanian farmers by Hyden (1980).

11. In the view of some commentators this is rather an understatement. They contend that government policies were the primary reason for the agricultural crisis. Tripp, for example, argues that the government had acted coercively to extract the surplus in the agricultural sector: "a large portion of the [agricultural] surplus ... goes directly to the state" (1989a: 21).

12. Lamb was able to state, in 1982, that "... Dar es Salaam grows shabbier by the day, a listlessness engulfs the land and the people are perhaps the most dispirited and unmotivated on the entire continent" (1982:68). Lamb's view, to say the least, was unusually sharp, and did not account for the energies people utilize to create strategies for survival or enhancement outside of the formal market.

13. The Zaramo, the largest original group, was rapidly marginalized in its own town, "a fact," Iliffe notes, "which distinguished Dar es Salaam from East Africa's other capitals" (Iliffe 1979:388).

14. Although this study does not directly consider the activities of Asians, mention of their influence is necessary. The "Asians" from India and Pakistan began migrating during the colonial era. Many have become Tanzanian citizens, but others reside as residents. The Asians comprise a relatively small minority group holding tremendous economic sway in urban areas. Until recently, there was a strong Asian presence in informal sector banking, and their influence in large-scale retail remains formidable. Asians are often victims of discrimination, and were one of the groups targeted by the Tanzanian state during its many urban campaigns. Yet many Asians continue to wield substantial levels of economic influence and control.

15. Kerner, indeed, has connected this striving for social mobility to contemporary folklore characters (1988a).

16. Indeed, it is difficult to converse with many Tanzanians at any length without somehow returning to the issue of strategies for making money. Out of necessity, it has become a consuming interest.

17. Augustine Mrema became Minister for Home Affairs in November 1990 and immediately ordered the creation of *sungusungu* night guards throughout the country. This led to "an immediate drop in crime incidents" (Daily News 1993b: 5). The move gained him instant popularity, particularly in Dar es Salaam, and fueled Mrema's ascendancy as a populist phenomenon.

18. A more complete description of this issue lies in Chapter 7.

4

Suspicious Lives

Directly or indirectly, John, William, and James frequently alluded to the internalized fears that so often governed their perceptions. The term they most often used was *kuogopa*, which translates as being afraid, startled, or terrified (Rechenbach 1967). In one way or another, they constantly reminded me that they had much to fear. John was fond of giving me signals when suspicious characters entered the shop. James made it clear that we must never refer to Burundi in his shop, because he was surrounded by Tanzanians who might become suspicious of him. William's concerns that Tanzanian visitors to the tailoring shop could be spies frequently led him to withdraw into the safety of silence.

This chapter will examine aspects of the refugee tailors' experience that, together with the cultural fears they brought with them from their settlement homes, described their particular view of urban danger. The realities behind the refugees' perspective will also be examined, because John, William, and James perceived danger at levels difficult for an outsider to understand. Strapped with the heritage of surviving a genocide, it was not often clear where their actual dangers ended and their visions of predators began.

It is not unusual for refugees to dramatize their undeniable difficulties. They live exiled lives, detached from their roots, adrift in uncertainty. If one has never experienced exile created by violence, it can be difficult to grasp why refugees may seem jittery and uncertain. The dangers that John, William, and James endlessly referred to were clearly rooted to their situation as clandestine residents of a city brimming with stress and difficulty. Yet the fears they expressed hardly paralyzed them, and over time many ventured beyond their narrowly constructed urban universe. They also had networks to depend on in Dar es Salaam, and most important, the refugee tailors knew how to manipulate the system to avoid trouble. Still, they maintained that they had much to fear. It was not merely the possibility of Burundian Tutsi or their spies coolly plotting their destruction. They also feared much more sudden violence against them carried out by their Tanzanian neighbors.

While I never heard about violence against Burundi refugees in Dar es Salaam, the refugees reported that Tanzanians had committed violent acts against Burundi refugees in Mpanda and Tabora. Dar es Salaam life existed in a suspended air of tension and potential violence, which made the capital feel especially dangerous. The cathartic release that citizens expressed while deluging an entrapped thief with blows and insults exemplified the city's open expressions of violence, and refugees perceived themselves as potential targets of such expressions. Yet it must be said that Tanzanians were also worried about urban violence. People were on the alert in the capital. This tense atmosphere seemed to catalyze refugee anxieties and perceptions into palpable feelings of fear and dread. Although refugees expressed understandable fears and insecurities, they sometimes felt helpless even while their actions created a different picture.

The Curse of Refugee Status

The two major complaints that Burundi refugees mentioned with regard to their treatment as refugees related to tax collection and education, issues that Malkki has also cited (1995). Significantly, freedom of movement to pursue economic opportunities was a secondary concern because Tanzanian authorities never really prevented refugees from pursuing economic opportunity—they only made it difficult to do. Indeed, the refugees' economic success was a prime example of refugee self-empowerment succeeding in the face of the systematic repression they alleged by the Tanzanian authorities. They believed they paid more taxes than Tanzanian citizens did simply because they were from Burundi. The limited number of secondary school openings reserved for them meant that few refugees could improve their family's prospects through education. Refugees believed that secondary education was a right that Tanzanians willfully denied them, and, without UNHCR's help, they had no recourse to this unfair treatment because they were refugees.

The Tax

According to refugees, the yearly tax that they were required to pay was the worst example of their ill treatment in the settlements, and a source a considerable bitterness. Luka told me that refugees had to pay the Tanzanian government six hundred shillings per person while Tanzanian citizens paid only two hundred and fifty shillings. Payment was especially difficult for Burundi refugees in light of their high population growth rate–a single household could contain ten or more people. Since money in the settlements was scarce, paying the tax was always difficult. Moreover, the way that Tanzanians were said to collect the tax embittered refugees. Here is a common description:

> The [Tanzanian] soldiers come during the night and demand the poll tax. If you don't pay they drag you [away] with your family. So you find out people flee to the bushes [in the forests beyond the settlement boundaries] and stay there for a long time.... This is why people decide to go back to Burundi and face what will happen there.

According to stories refugees related, the high poll tax, which they said they could not afford, and the methods of extraction, which deeply offended them, were sufficient reasons to leave the settlements. John claimed that the poll tax forced his older brother to risk returning to Burundi with his family. Luka said that the night raids for tax money "makes people want to go home. I can never be a Tanzanian [because of this]!" Pastor Albert explained that harassment from the poll tax was the reason young men "escape from the refugee settlements and stay in these towns."

There were two notable exceptions to the tax stories mentioned above. William, characteristically, refused to discuss settlement life in detail, commenting that "home" was good in many ways–there just was no money there: "I only come here [to Dar es Salaam] because of poverty. Otherwise, if I had enough money to buy my own [sewing] machine, I would stay there. It is better [in Ulyankulu settlement]."

James's description of the poll tax issue was unique. In one conversation he implied that I had been hearing inaccurate information about the settlements. The refugee settlements, instead of being areas designated exclusively for Hutu survivors of Burundi's genocide, were home not just to Burundian Hutu, but to Tutsi from Burundi and Tanzanians, too:

> There are Tutsi in Katumba [settlement]. Yes! If they married a Hutu in Burundi, they had to run with their families. But we're all the same there. We study, play and talk together! There is no difference between us…. You know, many Tanzanians live in the camps too. Many! They are from all over: Waha, Wafipa, Wachagga … many![1] They are [our Primary School] teachers, they work for the government, even as farmers! They go to school with us. Everything! It is fine. The government doesn't care. As long as they pay tax, [there are] no problems.

In James's version, only those who do not pay their taxes were harassed, and this harassment could apply to Tanzanians, Tutsi and Hutu alike.

In all probability, both perspectives of settlement life were accurate. Tanzanians, after all, did live within settlement confines. The families of Tanzanian teachers and government officials had homes and grew crops within the settlement boundaries. Given the enormous size of the refugee settlements, it is not unlikely that Tanzanians would have lived along the fringes, as well. Some may also have married Burundi refugees. Yet most refugees in this study did not include Tanzanians in descriptions of their settlement homes: they defined settlement existence according to those who had suffered as they had.

Access to Education

For the purposes of this discussion, I shall use the term "educated" as refugees did: to refer to people who had at least some secondary school education–a fragment of the entire population. Most informants had completed primary school and then left school forever (some, like William, never even finished primary school). None of the tailors had any secondary school experience, but lacking secondary education is a defining feature of all tailors, Tanzanian or refugee. It would have been highly unusual to find young men with secondary education working as tailors. Such work was seen to be beneath them. Someone with secondary education usually sought a higher status post, such as office or managerial work for a large company. But educated refugees related that these avenues were closed to them, since they would have had to show a proper identity card or proof of Tanzanian citizenship. Consequently, most educated refugees that I met in Dar es Salaam were unemployed.

Burundi refugees nonetheless believed that lacking access to secondary education limited their chances in life. From the tailors' perspective, this left them with three choices: farming, becoming an apprentice, or attending a vocational or trade school. Women and most primary-school-age siblings tended to the farming chores in the settlements while young men were seen to have the best chance of becoming wage earners. Families often gathered funds to get their eldest sons into any training possible. The best placement seemed to have been work in Dar es Salaam because the wage scale following the training period was about twice the amount offered in towns near the settlements.

Most Hutu in Burundi did not attend secondary school either, but refugees blamed UNHCR if they did not receive a secondary education in Tanzania. Just as the poll tax symbolized the refugees' vulnerability to Tanzanian settlement authorities, the education issue symbolized UNHCR's lack of commitment to them. Refugees who qualified for secondary or university education complained the loudest about this issue. They believed they lacked access to the University of Dar es Salaam because UNHCR refused to support them. In their view, UNHCR officials chose not to uphold their obligation to support education for Burundi refugees even though Burundi refugees comprised the largest proportion of refugees in Tanzania.

Educated refugees promoted the perception that Burundi refugees were vulnerable and powerless, and less-educated refugees heard their complaints about UNHCR. The educated refugees claimed that no one was on the side of Burundi refugees. Scholarships for secondary or advanced education that UNHCR should have given to Burundi refugees, they complained, were awarded to Ugandan, Somali, or other refugee candidates instead. Many explained this state of affairs was because "they [UNHCR] are against us." Cutbacks in UNHCR's scholarship program seemed only to confirm their suspicions.

Refugees further believed that they were excluded from educational opportunities because they were Hutu. One educated refugee commented that "UNHCR doesn't do its job.... The only problem is UNHCR. They are not working effectively in Tanzania. If you go to see them, they just say 'We'll see.' Why? [Because] they talked with the Burundi [Tutsi government] people, to prevent [us] from going to secondary school."

This same refugee then echoed the common refugee belief that Tutsi from all Central African countries were out to eradicate the Hutu everywhere, not just those in Burundi or in refugee settlements in Tanzania. During the Rwandan civil conflict between refugees from Uganda and the Hutu-led Rwandan government in 1990–92, he claimed that

> Museveni [the president of Uganda] is a Tutsi. He's killing more people [there] than Idi Amin. I told some Ugandan refugees: "you see what this Tutsi is doing here?" I can't understand how they [the Tutsi] are allowed [to do this]. When Saddam invaded [Kuwait], the U.S. said "No! You can't invade!" So they chased them [out of Kuwait]....
>
> [But] why does Uganda allow the Tutsi to fight the Rwandan [Hutu government] and no country has complained? [Because the Tutsi] are trying to unite the three countries [Uganda, Rwanda and Burundi].

He concluded by offering the reason why the Tutsi were so successful: because "they were favored in receiving education."

Here, the theme that access to post-primary education equates with power is made clear. Burundi refugees believed that the Tutsi used this tactic to maintain power in Burundi, and feared that they were influencing Tanzanian authorities, and even UNHCR officials, to continue to restrict their access to higher education. Such views supported the tailors' perspective that powerful people were after them.

Sensing Danger

Fearing Tanzanians

The refugee tailors perceived opposition and danger in every direction. The Tutsi wanted to kill them, UNHCR refused to support them, Tanzanian authorities sought to exploit them, and their Tanzanian neighbors simply hated them. The reasons behind their concerns were based not only on personal experiences, such as the poll tax stories in the settlements, but those of other refugees as well. The tailors assumed that any story of the oppression of a Burundi refugee was probably true. As John often said, "To be a refugee is trouble."

Refugee tailors, like other Burundi refugees in Dar es Salaam, feared that one of two types of Tanzanians would discover their refugee identity: the police, and their neighbors, customers, or other associates. The police might question their permission to reside in Dar es Salaam and simply return them to the settlements. It was also possible that they might seek out other refugees in the neighborhood, who could implicate them. Worse, the police's fingering of a refugee might inspire other Tanzanians to "*riot*," destroying his property and forcing him, once again, to flee.

But why should refugees fear the wrath of Tanzanian citizens? I learned of no actual attack by Tanzanians against any Burundi refugees in Dar es Salaam. Mathayo vaguely mentioned that in 1988 "we had problems, we were suspected that we were not *Waha* [from Tanzania]." John and Pastor Albert both spoke of a sweep through Kariakoo in 1991 that nabbed many of the refugee coffee vendors working without licenses. Yet James's comments exemplified how the fear of Tanzanian neighbors was far greater than their concern for Tanzanian authorities. His concern about the police, albeit colored with bravado, illuminated his belief that his presence in Dar es Salaam presented a fairly inconsequential problem for the government: "Hey, if they catch me working here, what are they going to do? Just send me home. And if they do, fine, I like to go home…. And if they send me to jail first? I am a little afraid, but not much. And my neighbors won't do anything, never." The following month, however, James's views about his neighbors had changed:

> If they [the Tanzanians] hear that I'm a refugee, they'll chase me. Yes! It's true! My neighbors. That's why I can't tell them. They'll tell the government, or tell somebody else who can tell the government, and then they will chase me….
>
> Tanzanians don't want any refugees here [in Dar es Salaam], do you see? If they hear our Kirundi language, or if they hear that we are refugees, we'll be chased—they want us all in the [refugee] camps, and nowhere else. I don't know why that's true [but it is].

In considering why James's opinions had changed, it is important to note that he had Tanzanian relatives and so felt less alien to Tanzanian life than John or William. Yet even he was convinced that his Tanzanian friends would turn on him if they learned of his refugee identity. He viewed his popularity among Tanzanians in his neighborhood as conditional. Despite strong Tanzanian connections, his hidden refugee identity remained dangerous.

Erving Goffman's analysis of social performance helps explain just why refugees were so afraid of Tanzanians. He suggested that enacting a role to shield hidden motivations from others gave them a way to secretly obtain their chosen ends. Urban refugee newcomers must perform the combined roles of tailoring apprentice, for example, and Tanzanian soon after they reach Dar es Salaam and then personalize them over time. The refugee's acts before Tanzanians were in a very real sense theatrical performances, and the tailoring shop where they worked became their stage. Eventually the tailors developed personas, or roles, as their strategy for getting ahead.

Goffman also described how the actor's efforts to create a successful "misrepresentation" (1959: 58) created the potential for a precipitous downfall, and here we can identify a source of the urban refugees' insecurity and anxiety in the clandestine life they had chosen. Goffman called those who engaged in misrepresentation "impostors and liars" (ibid.: 66) who invite danger upon themselves if discovered:

> … the more closely the impostor's performance approximates to the real thing, the more intensely we [or, in this case, Tanzanians] may be threatened, for a competent performance by someone who proves to be an impostor may weaken in [Tanzanian] minds the moral connection between legitimate authorization to play a part and the capacity to play it. (Goffman 1959: 59)

Tanzanians, as observers who discover that the actor is actually a Burundi refugee misrepresenting himself as a fellow Tanzanian, may actually feel freed from exhibiting proper moral behavior and perceive the refugee as threatening. They may consequently react strongly because the impostors who "misrepresent[ed] themselves for private psychological or material gain" (ibid.: 60) had tricked them and were profiting from their trickery.

Goffman's theory aids our understanding of why John, William, and James expressed such fear of being publicly exposed as refugees. Hiding a person's identity by, in a sense, becoming con men, raised the stakes against them if the ruse was ever discovered. In this context, their fears become easier to understand.

Goffman did not mention violent retribution, but if his ideas are applied to the context of Dar es Salaam, then a violent outcome becomes plausible. In Dar es Salaam, life for most people is tenuous and often created, necessarily or by choice, through illicit means. People struggled to construct order for lives seemingly surrounded by, if not danger, then at least considerable difficulty. Young men circulate through neighborhoods, most of which are informal settlements or outright slums (Oberai 1992). Theft is a constant possibility. There is often a sense that urban life pushes ahead on the cusp of violence. It is thus understandable for refugees to fear becoming targets of urban frustration, and this helps shed light on why the tailors were so meticulous in protecting their refugee identity.

And yet Goffman alone cannot explain the fear and dread that John, William, and James so often felt. Certainly the socializing experience of growing up within the confines of a refugee settlement fueled their concern over Tanzanian retribution. Previous research has suggested that Tanzanians living in areas surrounding the settlements resented refugees (Armstrong 1988; Ayok and Mbago 1987). Armstrong reported that Tanzanian officials believed that refugees living in settlements received disproportionate levels of attention and support from UNHCR and the Tanganyika Christian Refugee Service (TCRS). Ayok and Mbago's survey of local Tanzanians revealed their apprehension that if Burundi refugees became naturalized Tanzanian citizens the refugees would socially and economically dominate them. Such concerns were made plain to refugees when an order by the Tanzanian government commanded all refugees to exit the cities and return to the settlements. "This order," Ayok and Mbago reported, "was rigorously enforced in Tabora and Mpanda" (1987: 24). Daley pointed out that this procedure had become a regular anti-refugee campaign: "Annually, refugees residing in Mpanda and Tabora towns, are rounded-up and sent back to the settlements" (1991b: 189). Daley added that refugees were found to be conducting "criminal activities" (ibid.: 199)—presumably working in town without a permit. Stories of these humiliating campaigns against refugees seem to have created a strong distrust and fear of Tanzanians in refugees, and a conviction that Tanzanians not only despised refugees but would actively conspire to ruin them.

One refugee tailor, Mathayo, had first-hand experience of being run out of town. Two of the three major Burundi refugee settlements, Mishamo and Katumba, are located in Mpanda District. The predominant group of Tanzanians living there are ethnic Ha, whose Kiha language is similar to the refugees' Kirundi. This familiarity enables Ha people (*Waha*) to quickly identify a Burundian accent. Mathayo had set up a small tailoring shop in Mpanda town, acquiring a business license by claiming to be a Ha who came from Kigoma (near the Burundi border). By the mid-1980s, Mathayo stated, the refugees had established themselves in Mpanda: "We were the first people to start businesses [there]. We dominated the place, more than the citizens of [Mpanda]." Mathayo's story expressed the common view among Burundi refugees that the Ha hated them for being overly industrious: "Soon they discovered me after a vigorous investigation against refugees. The *Waha* business-men were the ones who forwarded the information to the government [that we were actually refugees, not *Waha*] because we *Warundi* are hard workers and make money fast." Tanzanian author-ities, he said, demanded 100,000 shillings to remain in Mpanda, a huge sum of money, or they would be forced out. Mathayo sold all of his property, returned to Katumba settlement for a while, and eventually moved to Dar es Salaam.

Mathayo added that *Waha* lived all around him in Dar es Salaam and he was convinced that they all hated the Burundi refugees. Having to present himself as a Ha created considerable apprehen-sion that a real ethnic Ha would detect his Kirundi accent and report his presence to Tanzanian immigration officials. The refugee tailors consequently rarely spoke in Kirundi, and many attempted to imitate a Ha's accent when using Swahili. Regardless of their efforts, however, a Tanzanian Ha visiting the shop might be able to identify a tailor's Burundian accent. Thus, although refugees believed that any Tanzanian might turn on them, the Ha were the most dangerous kind of Tanzanian.

Mathayo's contention that the Ha resented the refugees' strong work ethnic reflected a widely held view among the tailors that the refugee tailors made their Tanzanian counterparts look bad. Pride in their own work combined with disdain for Tanzanians in general. As John explained,

> Tanzanians are different [than Burundi refugees]. They don't want to work. If they are in villages, and if they don't want to work, their parents do nothing. So they steal, and when they are caught, they come to Dar es Salaam. That's how they are. They can't sew [i.e., tailor], either. They do poor work, and often put off deadlines. They just want to take money. You can't trust them.

John also expressed disgust for Tanzanians because they accepted bribes, described as "eating money" in Dar es Salaam. Take his example of Tanzania's education system: "... whatever you do, you pass automatically. This is no good. If you pay the teacher, you [pass]. They don't care. So you don't learn." Attached to this belief was the conviction that the education system was better in Burundi. Regardless of Tutsi domination, Burundian education was of higher quality: "... in Burundi, hey, it's good there. Most don't pass [from one grade to the next]. You are rewarded for good work and good character there. If you pass, good, [but] if you fail, you repeat. That is a better system. [In Burundi], the teaching is better." John's view revealed a perception common to many uneducated refugees. Provided you could get one, education in Burundi was just. The Tanzanian system, on the other hand, was comparatively benign, for a bribe could wash away any scholastic problems.

The refugees' perceptions of Tanzanians in Dar es Salaam formed two lines of thought. Tanzanians, especially the *Waha*, hated Burundi refugees because Burundi refugees embarrassed Tanzanians by working harder. This hatred could inspire them to seek violent retribution. On the other hand, refugees also contended that the discovery of the refugees' clandestine lives might inspire Tanzanians to use the information to supplement their income. In this scenario, should they overhear conversations that might identify the tailors as refugees, they could sell the information to the police or party officials for shillings. The police or party officials could then confront the refugees and demand either a large bribe not to arrest them, or arrest, detain, and return them to the settlements. Refugees based this perception in large part on their contention that every Tanzanian could be bribed.

Potentially Paranoid

The Burundi refugees in this study had come to perceive their urban surroundings as unusually dangerous. Yet their perceptions had acted only to restrict their actions and behavior in specific ways, not immobilize them. Murray Last's analysis of danger and risk in Kano, Nigeria (1991) helps illuminate why young Burundi refugee men migrate, where Burundi refugees ultimately perceive power and danger in their surroundings, and what the city looks like to them.

Beyond the pull factors that generally compel African youth to migrate, Last has noted not only that "Cultures determine what people consider … a danger or an acceptable risk; they also determine what categories of people these dangers most affect" (1991: 1). His description of Nigerian culture is similar to a common Burundi refugee belief that youths have the best chance of succeeding as urban migrants in spite of the special risks that accompany clandestine urban life: "Older youths go on to do the jobs that are seen to be the more risky ones" (ibid.: 10). Last also argued that the riskiness of migrating to a city is a culturally constructed social role for young men: "It is youths … who travel to distant places to work and see the world; indeed it is expected of them" (ibid.). Although Last spoke of "Kano culture" (1991: 7), it applies equally to Burundi refugee culture. "Travel," Last adds, "is young man's work" (ibid.: 17). The presence of John, William, James and thousands of other young Burundi refugee men in Dar es Salaam support his statement.

Another helpful aspect of Last's analysis concerns "the mental map of power in Kano" (ibid.: 15), for it provides an indication of how refugees perceived power and danger in others in Dar es Salaam. Last argued that "closely involved with ideas of danger … are a culture's concepts concerning power" (1991: 16). He says that "a corollary of hidden power" rendered darkness "more benign than the light of day," for "Escape is not upwards but outwards; shelter is within. Contrast the European obsession with the visibility of power and its symbols: the castle on its mound, or the church on its hilltop (and a spire to beckon the traveler);… and the notion that limelight is actually necessary for the powerful!" (ibid.). By applying Last's assertion that "Real power is inconspicuous, almost inaudible; indeed the ultimate attribute of great power is to be able to render itself invisible at will" (1991: 16) to the Burundi refugees in this study, a component of refugee self-empowerment is revealed. Hiding their refugee identities from Tanzanians, John, William, and James outfoxed strangers and, in doing so, felt superior to them. It also helps explain why they thought it best to talk openly only after nightfall, as if the sharp light of day threatened to reveal hidden truths.

Last's ideas can assist outsiders in seeing Dar es Salaam through a refugee's lens—as a place that "gives rise to anxieties" (ibid.: 8). His description of hidden power and the uncertainty it causes helps shed light on why John, William, and James believed that spies might be on their trail, a perception that greatly exaggerated their significance to Tanzanian authorities. Despite evidence of the general presence of surveillance in Dar es Salaam, government officials were not, during the field period, trying to track down refugees who were residing illegally in the capital. Privately, they indicated that they knew that some Burundi refugees were slipping out of the settlements, but it didn't seem to concern them.

And yet John, William, and James worried about spies and what Last would consider other "potential sources of misfortune" as well: "… the fleeting stares and the remarks that bode ill. They occur at home or outside—especially in places where dangerous people gather, unnoticed for what they are—in … certain markets, at crossroads. For the potentially paranoid, the urban scene is beset with possible danger" (Last 1991: 8–9). Given their exaggerated sense of danger, the refugee tailors would be considered members of this "potentially paranoid" category of city dweller.

Mapping the Town

When John was learning to drive my car on a flat field, he told me that everyone watching us was a spy. This included the young men resting under a nearby tree as well as the policeman gently leaning on his machine gun in the distance. I had not noticed the policeman until John pointed him out.

To refugees, Dar es Salaam teems with alert onlookers who might trace them to their residence and investigate their identity. There are also policemen prepared to demand proper identification. Although the tailors spent most of their time in the shop, they gradually explored other sections of town, visiting a friend or associate, perhaps at a distant refugee tailoring shop. In order to move to these islands of relative safety, however, they had to navigate the narrow pathways that carried them there. Their object, always, was to travel without attracting the attention of others while moving about in public. The best way to achieve this was to walk alone on foot along busy thoroughfares to specific destinations. They tried to appear as ordinary as possible.

Another method of traversing Dar es Salaam safely was to avoid unknown parts of town. Although Dar es Salaam is a coastal city, John, William, and James saw the ocean for the first time when I drove them there. One tailor, who lived only a few hundred yards from a beach, had never ventured to the water's edge. "I am afraid to go to any new places," he related, adding that beaches were one of those areas that refugees couldn't visit because they were thought to be havens for spies and policemen. The tailors also believed that any area housing important Tanzanian officials was loaded with policeman guarding their residences, and officials dressed as ordinary citizens who searched for thieves and aliens. Other sections of Dar es Salaam that must never be visited were neighborhoods located near military or police residential blocks and the University of Dar es Salaam campus.

Intruders

The refugee tailors were suspicious of most people, myself included, and sensed danger from many sources. Their interactions with me revealed details about their perceptions of danger in Dar es Salaam. What follows are examples of precautions that two refugees undertook to prevent their discovery as refugees.

John John was relieved when I told him, only weeks before my departure, that my license plates did not identify me as an official who assisted refugees. He had been afraid that anyone interacting with me could be fingered as a refugee by Tanzanian authorities, as I had told him that I had leased my car from a refugee agency. John admitted that "I have been thinking since long ago that your license plate was for [people who dealt with] refugees." I then had to explain that the specific vehicle number bore no direct relation to refugee agencies–the "TX" on the plate simply indicated that a "Tanzanian Expatriate" owned the car.

Once John and I were returning in my car from a Sunday interview conducted in another part of town. While driving past a market near his shop, he asked me to immediately stop talking. Tanzanians in the streets knew him from the shop, and John was afraid that if they heard any conversation between us about refugees "there will be trouble." He said that even the appearance of conversation from afar might also cause other refugees to ask him questions later. "People" would be wondering just what he talking to that white man about.

John protected himself from other refugees. Teaching him to drive became our cover whenever refugees or Tanzanians asked him where he had gone with me. John instructed me never to tell the other tailors that we had gone elsewhere to talk. If they discovered the truth, John was afraid that they would attack him as a traitor and brand me a spy. Should this occur, he described the following scenario: he would be reported to the Burundi government by Imbo refugees who spy for them, who would then inform the Tanzanian government of his illegal presence in Dar es Salaam. The Tanzanian authorities would then force him back to the settlement, and he would have to surrender all of his belongings and savings gained in town. If his Tanzanian neighbors found out as well, they might attack and destroy the entire tailoring enterprise, and then John could never return to Dar es Salaam.

Although John's scenario illuminated his perception of urban danger, he nonetheless continued to insist on speaking with me. He told me that his father had once worked as a driver in Burundi and he aspired to become one, too. John was an avid learner and a careful driver, and our conversations in the car were frequently compelling. In the end, I got the information I sought, and John had a learner's permit to drive cars and get a Tanzanian license. From his perspective, our meetings were well worth the risks because they helped him get ahead.

Mama Pastor Albert's wife was always aloof with me, and near the end of my research period she began to pressure the tailors to restrict their interactions. She forbid my presence in the back room of the shop when it was closed, such as at lunch time or when the tailors continued to work after closing up at 7:00 P.M. She also frowned on any conversations between the tailors and myself outside of the shop. I assumed she feared that even if I was not a spy, I had no business learning the refugees' secrets. She had always refused to talk to me about Burundi. During those final weeks, her restrictions made my work difficult. In accordance with her wishes, I reduced my visits to Albert's shop and increased visits to Amosi's shop, where they were always welcomed.

If at all possible, residences in Dar es Salaam were never vacated. Residents feared that any piece of property, no matter how insignificant, could be stolen. Mama rarely went to church, remaining home to guard the house and tailoring shop while the rest of the family worshipped. The tailors were expected to attend as well. Mama consequently spied on John, who rarely attended services. If John wanted to meet me on a Sunday, we would have to meet on a nearby street. Mama disapproved of his talking to me on Sundays. She was the one spy that I knew for certain was watching John.

Bongoland's Assets

Dar es Salaam did not present an endlessly dangerous and difficult life to the refugees, for they could also rely on a series of assets that the city afforded them. The most important of these was anonymity. In town, the refugee tailors looked like ordinary Tanzanian urban youth. They did not stand out because the city had been overrun with young men who roamed about town with little to do. Newcomers were commonplace. The tailors knew that the multitude of young men had led policemen to largely forego asking strangers in town for identification—a situation quite unlike refugee experiences in other Tanzanian towns.

Dar es Salaam was different in other ways, too. There, it was bad manners for a citizen to inquire about another's name, place of origin or type of employment. Many young men took the further precaution of creating new urban identities for themselves in town, often giving themselves a nickname from American popular culture like Rocky, Rambo, Maiko (for Michael Jackson), or Eddy Muffy (for Eddie Murphy) and proclaiming that they were from the largest town in their home area rather than the village they actually hailed from. They also had to keep up with the rapidly changing urban youth vocabulary to avoid exposure as a *mshamba* in town, which translates as "field man" or "country hick" in English.

Tanzanian rural-urban migrants had to take care not to be identified as *Washamba*, as it might precipitate their exploitation by other urban migrants. This was a strategy the refugee tailors adopted as well. Entering Bongoland as unknowns, Tanzanian migrants and Burundi refugees alike used their anonymity to shield themselves from becoming victims of a swindle. The fact that most young men in Dar es Salaam hid their rural background beneath a created urban facade facilitated the refugees' success in clandestine living.

Concealing the tailors' refugee identities was further helped by the fact that they looked Tanzanian, an asset Somali and some Mozambican refugees in Tanzania lacked.[2] An additional asset the refugees had was their experience in dealing with Tanzanian police.

FIGURE 4.1 Michael Jackson Finals

Prior to Michael Jackson's tumultuous visit to Dar es Salaam in 1992 (when he seemed to be covering his nose while leaving his airplane and then cut his local tour short), the American pop star was extremely popular with Dar es Salaam youth. Efforts to imitate his style of dress and dance were widespread, and dance competitions such as the one advertised here were well attended. Many youth also borrowed Jackson's nickname in Dar es Salaam, *Maiko*, for themselves.

Source: Advertisement from the Empress Cinema, in *Mfanyakazi* [Tanzania] (October 30, 1991: 4).

I heard many stories of policemen stopping refugees in their settlements or en route to Dar es Salaam. If refugees entered a dangerous situation in the capital, every tailor that I met had someone, usually the refugee entrepreneur who served as their patron, to furnish them with emergency assistance. This insurance was considered a necessity for survival in the city.

One Illuminating Incident

The following passage describes what happened during one of my Sunday driving lessons with John. It marked the only time that a third person–Marko–had accompanied us. As it turned out, Marko's presence was an important reason why few driving lessons took place afterwards. The story of the afternoon brought into vivid focus how the refugees' combination of cultural fear and veteran savvy mixed together during a moment of crisis. It demonstrated how, despite their endless descriptions of potential interlopers and secret Tutsi assassins, the refugees' fears circumscribed their lives but did not paralyze them.

John and I had previously arranged our Sunday afternoon appointment to go driving. He had not gone to church that day, and asked me to park my car beyond view of his shop and wait at a store down the street, as Mama would be watching. There I met Marko, who also had not attended church. After I waited for an hour, John softly called to me from fifty feet away. He did not want to come over to me. Asking where the car was parked, I pointed, and he indicated that he'd meet me there.

Sneaking through the back courtyard of the tailoring shop connected to the rival Pentecost church–his presence there representing another act forbidden by the pastor and Mama–John and Marko awaited my arrival by the car. As we quickly drove away, Marko said he wanted to go to the beach, as he had never seen it before and considered it safe to visit as long as he stayed inside my car. But John took charge. He had gone out with me to learn to drive several times already and was anxious to continue.

We drove to a large football field. A path circled the field, and it was often used for student drivers during the searing midday hours before footballers reclaimed the field in the relative cool of the evening. John and Marko pointed out a policeman idly watching in the distance, but John reminded me that he had also been there the last two times we had driven there. Since we had never been bothered before, I stopped the car and let John enter the driver's seat. Marko was astounded by the sight of his friend driving a car.

Gaining confidence, John wanted to talk while driving. We remained aware of the policeman's gaze, realizing that our presence was unusual and probably attracting curiosity—a white man in a shiny new car with a "TX" license plate (signifying that the car was owned by a Tanzanian expatriate) teaching two young Africans to drive. But this was not our first driving lesson together and it still seemed fairly safe.

I asked John what he thought of the policeman's presence. John commented that, unlike in Dar es Salaam, policemen in towns near the settlements usually asked young men to show their identification cards, knowing that they may be one of "the people of '72," a term Burundi refugees used to describe themselves as survivors of the 1972 genocide in Burundi. From the back seat, Marko added that if you lacked identification, as most refugees did, but had money to pay the police, nothing more usually occurred. Left unsaid was their belief that this policeman would not harm us. Similar to John and Marko's perception of safety and danger at the beach, the two believed that my presence would make them immune from trouble on the football field.

After John drove for nearly an hour, Marko insisted on trying to drive. Stopping to switch driving places, I noted the arrival of two more cars with student drivers. Marko's ride was short. He veered the car from one side of the path to the other excitedly before I asked him to brake. While I was becoming nervous about attracting attention, John lowered his guard and laughed loudly—something I had rarely seen any of the tailors ever do. Teasing his friend, he returned to the driver's seat. I told him to drive straight to the road, where I would drive them home.

Marko's very short but wild ride prevented us from noticing the actions of the policeman and his off-duty friend. They had entered one of the other cars on the field and had instructed the student driver to approach our car. Just before passing us, the driver flashed his lights and the two policemen approached on foot. The uniformed policeman casually dangled his machine gun from one hand.

Nothing like this had ever happened to me before. I had consistently taken precautions to minimize my presence and activities with the tailors and maintain their trust in me, always following their instructions. But now two of the refugees, both of whom were usually cautious, had dropped their guard. As usual, I had followed their lead regarding the timing and appropriateness of my actions or conversation. But John and Marko had made a mistake and now it promised to create dire consequences.

The two policemen motioned us to stop our car. What ensued was confused, and created a terror in me that John and Marko would be taken to the police station for questioning. I then saw the red and white sign bearing the letter L in the other car. It signified that the driver had received an official learner's permit to drive, popularly known as a *lena*. We did not have one, as I had thought it better to avoid interactions between John, a refugee living in town illegally, and any government agency.

The policemen began their interrogation by lecturing John and Marko sharply and loudly. They fired most of their questions at John, who had remained in the driver's seat. John's reaction to this verbal assault was instructive. He answered the policemen in a barely audible, respectful voice, claiming he did not know of the need for a *lena*, which the policemen refused to believe (as a white foreigner, the fact that I didn't know about the need for a *lena* was entirely believable). Most of the time, however, he and Marko remained impassive, their faces looking blankly ahead, emotionless. Later they related that this was the behavior refugees had learned to use during interactions with Tanzanian authorities.

The two policemen took turns questioning the two young men. They asked where they were from and whether they were Tanzanian citizens. They demanded to see their identification cards and continued to inquire why they didn't have a *lena*.

Eventually John and Marko answered the policemen's questions in a strange, deadpan way. They were from Kigoma, they said, and had left their ID cards at their father's house in the city. Their father was a pastor, they continued. They didn't know about the need to have a *lena* while learning to drive. This last point the policemen refused to believe, as they pointed to the red "L" sign on the dashboard of the other car.

I tried to calm the policemen, insisting that the problem was my fault alone, since I didn't know about the need for a *lena*. I promised never to teach others to drive without first getting a *lena*. The policemen eventually responded by repeating to all of us "Let's go to the police station" to talk about our violation there.

This scared me. But then John came over to me, asking in a very quiet voice if we could talk in private. We walked behind a tree. I initially thought that he wanted to tell me of his fear of going to the police station. Instead he told me that the policemen simply wanted money to leave us alone. Later, John and Marko told me that one of the policemen had asked them "Why doesn't this *mzungu* [white man] just give us money?" I gave him a one thousand shilling note (equal to about three U.S. dollars). John took the money and gave it to one of the policemen, waving me off so I didn't see the transaction. If I had, John told me later, they would have been embarrassed and might have demanded more money.

Entering the car, I again apologized to the policemen for the mistake. But now all was forgiven. As I started the car, one policeman said in Swahili: "Thank you. Good-bye. Welcome again."

We left.

Victorious, braggadocio mixed with relief out on the road. Wily refugees had outsmarted the Tanzanians again. The incident confirmed John and Marko's view of Tanzanians. "Tanzanians are all like this," John declared. "They are after money, that's all." John also denied he was ever scared, which I privately found hard to believe, and spoke with the confidence of a young man having extensive experience in dealing with authorities. "Tanzanians just want money," he continued, "there's no law [here], nothing." He added that there was nothing to be afraid of in Tanzania if you had money for bribes. (Left unsaid was the fact that my presence appeared to have insured that money, and not questions about their actual identity, would be the focus of discussion with the policemen.) John concluded with a parable he said was commonly recited by refugees: "If you grow a tree in Tanzania, the Tanzanians will try to take it, but if you stand tall next to the tree, they will run away." Tanzanians, the saying implied, are thieving and spineless.

Another issue that arose from the conversation related to their backup defense, which they reserved for dire emergencies. John stated that if the policemen had pressed them, he would have said that Pastor Albert was his father. Marko then explained that they had no other person in town to depend on when "trouble" arose.

Later there was a further indication of their belief in the pastor's ability to protect them. John said he was not worried about getting a *lena* because if officials sought identification he could get a church identification with the pastor's help. John and Marko insisted that any ID card would satisfy a policeman's request, not just government-produced ones.[3] All the pastor said he needed to get a church ID was a passport-sized photo. Soon after their arrival in town they could have gotten a card but had never bothered. They considered the pastor alone as sufficient protection against police harassment.

As we headed home, John summed up his feelings by declaring in a confident, knowing tone: "*Hapa ni pesa tu,*" meaning "Here [in Tanzania] it is just [about] money." In Dar es Salaam, just as in the settlements, he said, breaking the law merely provided an opening for Tanzanian lawmen to make some extra money.

Marko nodded in agreement.

Notes

1. These are ethnic groups in Tanzania. His inclusion of the Chagga (*Wachagga* means "Chagga people" in Swahili) suggested that even ethnic groups from distant regions of Tanzania lived in refugee settlements.
2. Information on other refugee populations in Dar es Salaam can be found in Sommers 1999.
3. In the end, John never bothered to get a church ID because we ventured into town to get him a learner's permit (*lena*) to allow him to drive if accompanied by a licensed driver.

5

Undercover Urbanites

This chapter will describe how young refugee tailors presented, or, as Goffman termed it, "misrepresented" (1959: 58) themselves as Tanzanians. Their strategies are contained in the term *kujificha,* a Swahili verb meaning "to hide oneself," and one that John, William, James, and other young refugees often used to allude to those activities which pertained to hiding.

This chapter describes the public personae of John, William, James, and Luka. James was far more relaxed than the others, since he operated as the only refugee in an otherwise Tanzanian tailoring shop. On the other hand, palpable tension existed in Pastor Albert's shop between John, William, and Luka, caused in part by the conflicting Tanzanian personae each had created. They had all developed a strategy for presenting themselves as Tanzanians in public according to individual perceptions of danger in their immediate surroundings, and these perceptions often clashed.

General Guidelines for Public Action

In spite of the tensions raised by the tailors' clashing personae, all the refugees followed five rules that guided their behavior in the tailoring shops. While working either behind the sewing machine designated for them or standing at the ironing table, the refugee tailors followed the same general rules. In my role as a visiting researcher, I had to obey the code, too.

Never Mention Anything That Refers to Refugees

Refugees should not mention any issues that demonstrate familiarity with refugee camps, refugee issues, or Burundi. Their level of concern about a leak seemed extreme. Only once, for example, did John ever mention the name of his settlement in public, and that came only as a whispered "Katumba" at night while we sat just outside the shop.

Learn the Identities of Regular Visitors

This rule applied to all Tanzanians and those Burundi refugees whom they did not know. A Burundian accent while speaking Swahili could be very distinct and noticeable, Imbo accents in particular. Foreigners could conceivably be spies for the Burundian government, and Tanzanians could secretly be working for either the Burundian or Tanzanian government. When men entered the shop who were suspected spies, the tailors' behavior changed. All conversation stopped. They kept their heads down, worked steadily, and only answered questions the visitors asked. Their answers, however, were always intentionally vague and short, and frequently contained outright lies. Eventually the visitor would leave. Conversation between refugees regarding the visitor's true identity only occurred behind closed doors. In public, silence reigned until long after the visitor had left.

The tailors acted quietly and subserviently with most male customers they did not know. Once, for example, a man with a huge voice entered the pastor's shop. William, whose customary spot was in the back of the shop, motioned for John to serve the customer. John was making a pair of trousers but immediately pushed his work aside and tended to the anxious customer. The man barked, "Stop your work! Measure this!" He pointed to the hem of his pants. John obeyed, and William periodically looked up from his sewing. John worked fast, measuring and noting where the hem should be, and said it would cost him 250 shillings (about one U.S. dollar). The man shoved 220 shillings at John, who did not argue over the difference. As he turned to leave, John looked directly at him for the first time.

John's actions with such a customer were followed by every tailor I observed in similar situations. Such behavior was significant because it was remarkably unlike typical exchanges between Tanzanians. In the presence of adults whom they did not know, the refugees spoke only when spoken to. Their physical movements were quick and economical. They returned greetings curtly. Their manner, in short, separated them from the elongated exchanges that Dar es Salaam residents typically engaged in. Young Tanzanians were expected to say *Shikamoo* to an elder, the appropriate and respectful greeting, which often led to a series of questions and answers between the two, such as "How is work?" (*Habari ya kazi?*), "How did you spend the day?" (*Habari ya Kushinda?*), and so on.

Most refugee tailors would have none of this. They felt compelled to remain reserved and short with people they did not know. Even with people they knew, they were often remote. After visitors received enough short answers to their questions and sat through long silences, they would leave.

Don't Depart from Accepted Conventions

Traditional Tanzanian greetings aside, refugees believed that doing anything unusual in public might attract unwanted attention. This rule aligned with guidelines that most migrant youth followed, as well. Unknowing foreign tourists might accidentally cross this line, and it sometimes led to results that seemed surprising to them but were altogether unsurprising to most Dar es Salaam residents. One tourist related how, while reading a plaque citing the founding of a prominent bridge in Dar es Salaam, he felt the end of a machine gun in his back. The policeman asked him, "What do you think you're doing, reading this?" The foreigner got the point and left.

For the tailors, one of the best ways to blend into the community was to become a *sungusungu*. These government-mandated community night guards required volunteers from every household in the nation to fill its ranks. These volunteers were usually young men, and it was the responsibility of every *Kumikumi* (Ten Cell Leader) to insure that all ten households under his supervision participated. The *sungusungu* patrols were localized guards before Augustine Mrema became the Minister of Home Affairs in 1990. Soon after his appointment, he declared that *sungusungu* participation in its nightly operation would be enforced. Minister Mrema became instantly popular as a protector of Tanzanian homes. For the next three years, his name regularly appeared in newspaper headlines and radio reports.[1]

The *sungusungu* guards were important to Dar es Salaam residents because they could patrol for thieves. What was usually left unsaid was their potential to observe and report on people's movements to their Ten Cell leader. At the very least, the *sungusungu* held the potential of becoming a citizen's arm of the government's system for population control.

John, William, and James all joined the *sungusungu* guard for one night a week. James once bragged that Minister Mrema himself appeared one night on inspection and praised him along with the other night guards in his neighborhood. Still, James played it safe as a *sungusungu*. He said that on his scheduled nights there were so many *sungusungu* patrolling his neighborhood that he didn't have to do much: "I guard our ten houses, sure, but there are others doing it, so mostly I just guard our own house." John described *sungusungu* duty as uneventful and boring, a sequence of circling the ten houses he was assigned to and sitting in front of the shop. William, in contrast, once mentioned that he was a *sungusungu* but refused to comment further.

The refugee tailors' fear of attracting attention crystallized for me during one brief moment with John and William. It had been raining, and the trail of customers had muddied the shop's floor. I grabbed a small broom and started to sweep. John was horrified, declaring that I was a *mzee* (respected man) and had no business sweeping. He was also afraid that the sight of a white man sweeping would draw undesired attention to them. Gently taking the broom from my hand, he ran to the door and anxiously looked out. An empty street. The moment passed.

Lie a Lot

All the refugees lied to keep refugees and Tanzanians at a distance. Often they seemed to be covering over pedestrian, harmless facts, such as whether a person went to a friend's house the night before or saw a certain person in the market or at church. But the refugees retained their caution in such situations by consistently feigning ignorance.

Be Vague

Frequently, the tailors resorted to using intentionally vague words to deflect a visitor's inquiries. One widely used technique in Dar es Salaam was to describe people's actions in the passive verb tense. This device suggested that "things happened" to people ("The car was hit"), instead of people being responsible for actions that took place ("He hit the car"). If someone asked who was responsible for a particular act, the most common response was *sijui* (I don't know). Refugees employed other tools, as well, such as using common references to identify others, such as *rafiki* (friend), *mtu* (person) or *kijana* (young person). Some of the intentionally inexact phrasing had coded meanings. Here are three examples of coded words:

Kwetu Every refugee tailor called themselves an ethnic Ha from Kigoma before strangers. But their refugee colleagues interpreted "Kigoma" or *kwetu* (our family home) as code words for their refugee settlement homes. Between refugees during conversations, "Burundi" also referred to the settlements.

Mjini Whenever the refugees ventured, they would only say they had gone to *mjini* (downtown). But *mjini* could refer either to one of a handful of major marketplaces in town or simply hide the tailor's destination entirely.

Locatives Refugees took advantage of the array of Swahili words that indicate location. These words all translate into English as "there," but they indicate more specific meanings in Swahili. *Hapo*, refers to "there" as a specific place relatively nearby. *Huko* signifies "there" as a general location nearby. *Pale* is used to indicate "there" as a specific location in the distance, while *kule* suggests a generalized distant location.[2] Refugees had taken these Swahili locatives and assigned them specific locations: *huko* for their refugee settlement, *hapo* for their home village within the settlement and *pale* for Burundi. Refugees used these terms even when alone, just in case spies lurked behind a window shutter or doorway.

Restraints on My Behavior

To work with John, William, and James, I had to follow their rules. I could not walk outside with them because their presence in public alongside a white man would attract unwanted attention. I could not visit the refugee tailoring shop across the street from Pastor Albert's shop because it contained refugees whom Albert viewed as untrustworthy ciphers for the breakaway Pentecostal church. I could take notes while sitting in their shops, but only if I wrote quickly and quietly and stopped when visitors or customers entered. I never told John or William when I was going to see James at his tailoring shop, or vice versa, because it seemed to make them uncomfortable. Interviewing John, William, or James in private meant arranging to meet them at a specified point outside of their neighborhood in my car. John and William would agree to these interviews only if I promised not to tell the other one.

Only John explained the reason for this final restriction. He said that the other refugee tailors would suspect him of betraying their shared secrets about their living situation, as well as the history of Burundi and life in the settlements. Other refugees thought that sharing this information with me could only cause them harm. At the same time, most of the refugees I spoke with trusted that I would not betray their secrets to the others (I never did), and seemed to enjoy our private conversations, in part because they were able to visit places in the city they would otherwise never have visited.

Four Public Personae

The five general guidelines for public action merely served to cover evidence of the tailors' refugee identities. Like laws in a courtroom, they were subject to interpretation. But beyond the rules and their various interpretations, a gap remained where a believable public personality needed to take form. To fill these gaps, each refugee tailor developed and presented themselves in public with a viable Tanzanian persona. To do this, they emphasized an aspect of their personality as an instrument for expressing themselves in behavior and language. William became an unusually pious churchgoer and righteous moralist. Luka chose to emphasize his embrace of urban youth culture, which clashed with William's fundamentalist stance. William relied on the persona he assumed upon his entrance into Dar es Salaam: a quiet, subservient, naive apprentice. James, situated in the much more relaxed atmosphere of the Amosi's shop, assumed the persona of a veteran Tanzanian urbanite.

All of these men were far more than the personae they presented in public. William, though a devout Pentecostal, clung to that identification to shield his refugee identity from view. His reliance on a silent, distant manner served to limit the chances that his Imbo dialect might be exposed. John was actually a shrewd analyzer of the social scene and, like Luka, had a strong independent streak which influenced, among other things, his views on politics. James, meanwhile, seemed to feel genuine discomfort in being a refugee. Unlike the others, his Burundi refugee identity seemed more a source of difficulty for him than a source of pride and cultural identification.

Here are descriptions of how each of these tailors presented themselves in public and what aspects of their character they hid from view.

Luka: The Urban Hipster

Luka was bold. He purposely sat at the sewing machine beside the visitors' bench and held court. He engaged nearly everyone in conversation and was an avid follower of neighborhood gossip. Instead of withdrawing into his work whenever a Tanzanian man entered the shop, the stance of safety that most refugee tailors employed, Luka would engage the stranger in idle chatter. He even played football with Tanzanians at the local football field, something no other refugee tailor that I met would even contemplate: such intimacy with Tanzanians whom they did not know directly opposed their strategy of remaining on the edge of Tanzanian society. But Luka was cheerful and cocky and clearly his own man.

While William scared off many strangers with his dark silences and John passively withdrew, Luka engaged. Once, a girl came by and wanted to learn to hem a gown. After John and William silently declined, Luka agreed. He told the girl that it would take one hour to teach her and that he would need to be paid one soda for his services. He also regularly called out to women who passed by. Such behavior may not seem remarkable but it was decidedly unusual for a refugee tailor in Pastor Albert's shop. It drew attention to Luka and seemed to needlessly engage him with strangers. His behavior was singular and it separated him from the John and William, his co-workers.

Luka flaunted his nonconformity. His workmates, especially Yona and William, seemed to hate him. From their perspective, Luka's behavior endangered them all. His daring often confronted the guidelines to which everybody else conformed. Luka, however, considered his actions justified. John had told me of several late night arguments between William and Luka over who should assume charge in the shop when Yona was not there. William won the dispute. Pastor Albert awarded William with the authority to collect and dispense money in the shop following Yona's demise. William had become the head tailor. This state of affairs seemed logical, since Luka could not make suitcoats—a key prerequisite for shop supervisors—while William could. Yet Luka had been in the shop the longest and felt his seniority had been overlooked. His sense of being slighted led to passive aggressive behavior that was intended to threaten William.

As a result, Luka actively assumed the stance of urban hipster in front of Tanzanians, which directly opposed the religious bearing of the tailoring shop generally and its other workers. The shop was, after all, attached to the home of a pastor and supervised by the pastor and assistant pastor. Radio music was forbidden in the shop since disco music invited its listeners to sin. City slang should never cross a tailors' lips. But Luka rebelled against all this. He professed a love for disco and reveled in using youth language words forbidden by Pastor Albert.

Luka's use of *Lugha ya Wahuni* and his constant thumb's up signal broadcast his identification as a veteran urbanite. On several occasions I watched as Luka gabbed with visitors in city slang while William smoldered in silence. When I asked Luka why he used words from the notorious Language of the Ignorant, he proudly responded that he not only had learned the *Lugha* but could speak it expertly. William then added, acidly, that he didn't know the language and didn't like it, which was an understatement.

Yona had once told me that using the city slang was "very bad" because "it identifies you as a *mhuni*." *Mhuni* means "an ignorant person" but could be used to criticize any young man who is unemployed or considered a hoodlum. The pastors and many in the congregation constantly warned that using city slang was a sin: a *mhuni* was by definition a sinner. Luka's use of slang thus seemed to devout Pentecostals like William like an embrace of Satan. And so while William refused to engage anyone in conversation using slang, Luka would initiate it. Worse, he was perceived as recklessly endangering other refugees, particularly when he would suddenly switch from speaking in Swahili to Kirundi. Kirundi was rarely spoken by anyone else in the shop because an ethnic Ha who just happened to pass by might detect it as the language of Burundians. But Luka didn't care. He used Kirundi openly and often with the other tailors, who would always respond to him in Swahili.

Why was Luka so antagonistic to the other refugee tailors he worked with? How was he able to breach the guidelines and still avoid detection as a refugee? More than anyone else, Luka demonstrated the difference between the breadth of the refugees' cultural fear in Dar es Salaam and the actual dangers that lay there. Like John, William, and James, Luka lived in Dar es Salaam illegally, but simply refused to be controlled by his fears. Although he spoke bitterly about the treatment of refugees in the settlements, he had never had similar experiences of mistreatment in the capital. After three extended trips to the capital, Luka was supremely confident of his ability to identify and steer clear of dangerous situations and people. The other tailors, he told me, were much too careful. I had once asked Luka why he talked to me so openly, even mentioning his settlement, Katumba, in the shop. His answer was simple: he spoke to me "because you have no badness. I can tell you. I know it's OK. If I see a Mswahili [Swahili person] coming near I won't tell him. I'll say I'm from Kigoma, a Mha. The [other tailors] are afraid, but you have no badness so I can talk to you." Luka also engaged in casual talk with Tanzanians about everyday topics. When I asked whether any Tanzanians were his friends, he responded forcefully: "No! Three or four, maybe. You can't know who is a [Tanzanian] person to trust. I hide myself. I'm afraid [of them]. Maybe one will bring me trouble.... You can't trust them. You don't know who will hurt you. And so I stay away." Luka, in short, loved wearing his urban hipster identity, but this persona held danger at bay while never, in his view, betraying his refugee identity to any Tanzanian. Luka's persona was public, but his secret remained guarded.

Luka had also managed to safeguard his urban situation in a typically unique fashion. Luka had obtained a church identification card. Although the other refugees in his shop and church congregation could get church identification cards if they pressed Pastor Albert to help them, I met no other tailor who actually owned one. The card was not government issued, for only citizens could obtain those. But many young Tanzanian migrants used similar affiliations to obtain some sort of identification card (*kitambulisho*) in case a policeman asked for one.

Why didn't more refugees get church cards? The process was simple enough: you needed to buy a passport photo, easily obtainable in any town market, and fill out a form. The pastor then got the church to authorize the card with their official stamp. John thought about getting one only after our run-in with the police, but he never did. I can only explain it through the *kujificha* (hiding oneself) ethos that most refugee tailors lived by: stay as quiet and unnoticeable as possible and take every precaution to hide your identity.

Luka's singularity went one step further. He registered and paid his annual development tax in Dar es Salaam, and proudly showed me the receipts. This act secured for himself a heightened degree of personal safety by establishing him as a taxpaying resident of Bongoland. In his own eyes, Luka had outwitted the opposition and increased his degree of security, and had accomplished it all by himself.

William: The Devout Imbo

Luka's strategy and demeanor directly opposed William's. In many ways they were polar opposites. Luka was talkative, he engaged with strangers, and he dared to speak Kirundi in the shop. William sat furthest from the shop doorway in the darkened corner at the back of the shop. In private, William would talk about religious matters, but he rarely spoke in public. Instead, he listened and observed, and seemed to consider Luka's public daring as sins against God and refugees alike.

All of the refugees had imported cultural fear to Dar es Salaam, but William's seemed to have marked him more deeply than the others. In a revealing moment one evening, John and I spoke in hushed voices while William was berated by the assistant pastor in the shop room for failing to complete a large uniform order on time. John then related a rare moment when William had opened up to him. He said that William usually refused to talk about the history of Burundi and the events of 1972 with him. But once, John told me, William crossed his arms over his chest, with his hands resting on his shoulders, and described how the Banyaruguru discriminated against the Imbo in his settlement, Ulyankulu. "He's afraid of us!" John said. "The discrimination [between Banyaruguru and Imbo] has made him afraid to trust us [Banyaruguru]." William believed that the Banyaruguru had frequently deceived him. William was consequently very secretive, John explained, and could be deceptive with Banyaruguru refugees like John.

In response to his sense of isolation from other refugees, William combined three strategies into his tailoring shop routine. He told me that he was a naturally quiet person, and his responses to questions from inquiring visitors or customers were often untrue or exceedingly vague, even about the most casual issues. He also claimed a moral mantle of authority by judging the words and actions of others against the Pentecostal precepts he knew so well. Sin was his favorite conversation topic in the shop. He felt that shop talk, when it was necessary, should deal directly with business or moral issues. Finally, he exacted daily revenge against his Banyaruguru colleagues by insuring that the tailors ate the main Imbo dish—fish—every day. This issue frustrated John, who loved his Banyaruguru food (beans with ugali, or "stiff porridge," made from maize flour), and grew to detest the dried fish meals that William, as the head tailor, was able to mandate. Often William would make lunch and dinner even more miserable for

John by replacing maize ugali with the Imbo favorite–ugali made from cassava.

John's feelings about Imbo food dramatized the tension between Imbo and Banyaruguru refugees. When I ate lunch with John and William, and Luka when he was there, we always ate fish and ugali. Always. Likewise, when John worked at the shop alone, he always prepared beans and ugali. John complained many times about the Imbo meals he had to eat every day. Here he describes his sense of subjugation about this issue:

> He [William] pays for the food, so we only eat the food of the Wanya-mugara ["the people of Mugara," considered the most prominent Imbo town in southern Burundi]. He doesn't like beans, so we never eat them. Only fish and vegetables. Every day, fish! Every day. And Ugali. He doesn't like [maize ugali] much. Their dish is fish with either ordinary cassava ugali and not maize, which we like, or fermented cassava ugali [which they prefer]....
>
> We [Banyaruguru] eat [cassava ugali] too, but not often. And we ferment it for two days. I take it with me on the train, but don't really like it. But it lasts, so we bring it. But it's their food.

Because William was so often silent in public, his control over the tailoring shop was especially noticeable when he wasn't there. In the final months of my fieldwork period William visited his family in Ulyankulu twice. Since Luka had already returned to Katumba, John worked in the shop alone and his behavior changed dramatically with William away. He told me that William made him work and prohibited his attendance in the English classes I held at the pastor's house one night a week. William made John work as much as possible. Diversions of any kind were forbidden. John would refer to refugee issues in coded terms and occasionally even spoke Kirundi while on his own, neither of which William would have allowed. A more dramatic departure, however, was John's sudden friendliness with his neighbors. He took to sitting at the sewing machine next to the front window and calling out to passers-by, especially women. William would have denounced John if he had tried to do this in front of him. For William, as well as Pastor Albert and his wife, this sort of flirting was inappropriate and most probably sinful.

John: The Distant Apprentice

John was seventeen but looked even younger. When spoken to in the shop he raised his eyebrows and looked up alertly from his work

with bright, open eyes. Together with his high forehead and conservative style of dress and haircut, he always appeared impres-
sionable and naive: a schoolboy perhaps. In private John was
perceptive, outspoken and strikingly self-confident, but his public
persona as a shy youth invited his colleagues in the shop, as well as
the pastor and his wife, to endlessly attempt to influence him.

John had arrived in Dar es Salaam shortly before I began visiting Pastor Albert's tailoring shop. Over the next year John became
acclimated to clandestine living and gradually adjusted his persona
into an uneasy balance between those of Luka and William. An
intensely private person, he tried to utilize his aura of young inno-
cence to his advantage by avoiding confrontations and quietly cultivating his popularity. His intentionally youthful demeanor
departed from Luka's sophisticated gregariousness and William's
silent severity. It was an effective act. As time passed he became
friendly with many youths in the neighborhood, gently calling out
to girls he knew and chatting briefly with other young men. Nevertheless, his neighbors rarely entered the shop to socialize even
when William's brooding presence was not there.

John once privately told me that if "I stay quiet in the shop.... I
do nothing wrong, because I don't mention anything about
refugees." While working with Luka, William, or Yona, John almost
always worked silently, talking only when prompted by others. He
kept a piece of chalk at his sewing machine, and several times wrote
messages on the wood for me to read before quickly erasing our
secrets with his hand. A few times he wrote "Imbo" to identify the
visitor as one. Once he related his anticipation of our planned private interview with "we will talk well on Sunday."

By the latter stages of my fieldwork period, John had begun to
see himself as an experienced urbanite. He was proud of his ability
to separate himself from William's gloomy detachment and establish himself as a separate persona before his neighbors. His gradual
popularity marked a change in his view of himself. He bragged that
"Everyone knows me here [in the neighborhood], do you see? I
have so many friends here! Last year I had not gotten accustomed
[to urban life], so I was quiet. I had few friends in those days, but
you see the difference now, don't you?" He had come to be known
simply as *fundi* (craftsman) to his neighbors. John also rarely ventured to church services on Sundays by the end of my fieldwork
period in Dar es Salaam, yet continued to be proud of his popularity with congregation members: "People at church like me a lot. If
I'm not there, they ask: Where is John?"

John had devised a rigid philosophy of a person's character. Every youth entered Dar es Salaam as a *mshamba* (farmer), which he defined as "a person who knows nothing and is amazed by everything." During his first ride in my car he declared himself a *mshamba* for not knowing what a seat belt was, explaining that in the settlements there were almost no cars, only bicycles. Much later, John explained that a *mshamba* was too naive to identify potentially troublesome people. He declared that it was bad to be a *mshamba* since they stuck out in town. They were noticeable and vulnerable. John found the term repugnant, for becoming a city person, a *mtu wa toun,* was very important to him.

According to John, a *mshamba* could veer in one of two directions after migrating to Bongoland—he could become a respectable worker, such as a *fundi,* or become a *mhuni* (ignorant person). Those youths who were *wahuni* or *wasela* (taken from the English word sailor), John and others in his church congregation maintained, were unemployed, drank and smoked, constantly approached women, and seemed able to survive only by robbing others.

Unlike the other tailors in the shop, John was sensitive to being called such names. On one day during his tenure in Dar es Salaam, William, Yona, and Pastor Albert all castigated him for acting too friendly with young women. But privately John disputed their condemnation:

> They call me a *mhuni* [ignorant person] since I talk to girls in the shop, but if I do? So what? I don't care. They're customers! They're also neighbors. And I'm popular here! I know everybody around here. But since they come and visit me and not William—and mama and the Pastor don't want that, they want us to work and keep people out [of the shop]—I can become a *mhuni,* attracted to girls.

Becoming known as a *mhuni* identified someone as a probable criminal, which refugees believed would almost certainly attract government inquisitors. Whereas Luka and James loved to talk about *wahuni,* John shut off even mentioning the terms "because of fear." He was deeply afraid that the mere use of the word in public would attract the worst kind of attention. Unknowingly I once chided him about being a *msela* and provoked the following short dialog:

Me: You're a *msela.*
John: I am not, Bwana! It's impossible.

Me: How can that be so?
John: Fear. I have to stay silent. I can't talk about that here. Mrema is troublesome.
Me: I still say you're a *msela*.
John: No way! I'm not. That's an issue of fear.
Me: Then who are you afraid of ?
John: (Long pause) People.

In this and ensuing private conversations John described his situation as one of being fearful of "people," and described his belief that virtually any Tanzanian could be part of the network of government informants simply identified as "Mrema" here, the name of Tanzania's maverick Minister of Home Affairs at that time.

All of John's public machinations, his innocent demeanor and personal distance from those around him, arose not only from fear of "people" but from his conviction that it was dangerous to trust others. He defined a friend simply as someone whom he could trust. As an apprentice he confided only in Marko, his fellow apprentice, but even that relationship withered over time. By the end of my fieldwork period he seemed to trust no one.[3] He found that people he trusted had later deceived him. In John's view of character, people changed and turned on their friends because their personalities were naturally unstable: "People change fast: one or two beers, just one time, and they change. One or two puffs of a cigarette, or [if they] go with a girl once, they change. Through just one experience like that, [people] can turn on you."

James: The Sophisticated Pentecostal

Although James and John attended primary school together and entered Dar es Salaam at almost the same time, their public personae were entirely different. Where John was private and detached, James was relaxed and warm. Where John deeply distrusted Tanzanians and refugees alike, and eventually came to share no intimate friendships in the capital, James maintained friendships with Tanzanian as well as refugee friends. None of the other refugee tailors that I met, in fact, were as comfortable or relaxed in Dar es Salaam as James. On several occasions he related his plans to me: to first rent his own room near the tailoring shop and save to buy his own sewing machine. Then he would establish his own business in the city. James had no intention of ever leaving Tanzania's capital. Unlike John, William, and Luka, James was there to stay.

Although James and John were the same age, James looked older. Where John embellished his youthful appearance and demeanor to create a safe public persona, James sported a mustache and wore stylish clothing. And while John struggled to shed his image as a *mshamba,* James seemed a natural at urban living. But unlike Luka's jovial embrace of urban life, James was not only an accomplished urbanite—he was urbane, too.

James's parents had lived in a Burundian village near the Tanzanian border before becoming refugees. His aunt had met a Tanzanian trader, an ethnic Ha, on a market day. They later married and settled in Kigoma, Tanzania. One of their children was Amosi, James's cousin and a Tanzanian citizen. Amosi and his brothers all became enterprising businessmen like their father. The family pooled resources so that they both could open and manage tailoring shops. Amosi ventured to Dar es Salaam to establish his, while his brother started one in Kigoma town.

James's father easily arranged for his son to become an apprentice in Amosi's shop. He paid his nephew a fee to teach James tailoring and provide room and board at the back of his tailoring shop. Amosi not only became James's attentive teacher but was a supportive, trusting and reliable friend. Most important, Amosi kept James's refugee identity a secret. The third tailor in the shop was an ethnic Ha named Samuel who was also an apprentice and lived with James in the room behind the shop. James insisted that Samuel never knew he was a refugee. Surrounded by and related to Tanzanian tailors who were ethnic Ha created tremendous security and stability in James's life. His cover as a Tanzanian Ha seemed almost beyond question.

But not quite. James kept to strict precautions in order to keep his refugee identity hidden. Working and living intimately with a Tanzanian meant that James could never reveal any signs of his refugee background. He told me that he had privately taught himself to minimize his *Kirundi* accent while speaking the *Kiha* language. Traces remained, however, so James never initiated conversations in *Kiha* and usually responded to questions asked in *Kiha* by using Swahili.

Although James was the only refugee working solely with Tanzanian nationals, he was still cautious. Unlike John, James rarely used any code words or other means of reference to his refugee identity and settlement home. Such references could only arouse suspicion in Samuel and the Tanzanian neighbors who regularly visited the shop. Even during those rare moments when the two of us were alone in the shop, James forbade discussions on refugee issues. This was a dramatic departure from the other refugee tailoring shops I visited, all of which allowed quiet asides about refugee issues (albeit in coded language) when there seemed to be nobody else around. But James had a secure arrangement and wanted to keep it that way.

Refugees and Tanzanians alike were regulars at Amosi's shop. Most were young men and women from the neighborhood. They entered to use the shop's iron, listen to the radio or just hang out. The shop was a primary site for socializing. This distinction neither displeased nor agitated James. On the contrary, his shop was like many other neighborhood tailoring shops run by Tanzanians, and entirely unlike most shops manned by refugee tailors, which sought to keep the neighborhood at bay.

The young Burundi refugee men and women in James's neighborhood (of which there were many) who took advantage of the shop's social life were all considered Tanzanian Pentecostals. In this context, their identities as refugees were neither mentioned nor questioned. Refugees and Tanzanians alike simply greeted each other as devoted people of Jesus, preferring their Pentecostal salutation *Bwana asifiwe!* (The Lord is praised!) to typical Swahili greetings.

Amosi and James both contributed to the maintenance of their shop as the neighborhood's social center for young Pentecostals. The shop's name announced to all that its workers were Christians. Amosi required Samuel, a Catholic, to attend Pentecostal services in order to work there. And underneath the outward atmosphere of ease in the shop was an adherence to the Pentecostal code of behavior. While city slang was generally forbidden, Amosi played a radio in his shop, although he turned it off when disco music was broadcast.

James once told me that he had to go to church in Katumba or his father would have beat him. When he arrived in Dar es Salaam, he attended church reluctantly and for several Sundays did not go at all. Later he joined the church choir, and now kept the songbook near his sewing machine, so that other choir members could access it easily. This choir book contained dozens of songs written by choir members or copied from cassette tapes or other choirs. James himself had composed several of them.

Perched at the sewing machine at the center of the shop, James kept working while participating in discussions. He was almost always relaxed and at ease, entering conversations about religion or neighborhood gossip. He silently listened to potentially dangerous topics, such as Tanzanian politics, since a person's opinions could eventually reach the ears of the Ten Cell Leader and cultivate suspicions about them. As long as he avoided conversations on politics or refugee life, James felt safe his cousin's tailoring shop.

James consistently invited me to his shop, something he did either after church services or while we both were visiting Albert's shop. He also enjoyed an easy relationship with his boss. In contrast, John, William, and Luka were all under pressure to produce. They were keenly aware that they could be replaced by other refugee tailors if they failed to work hard enough.

James lacked the characteristic distrust and consequent distance that pervaded most of my relationships with refugee tailors. He succeeded in large part by relating to refugees and Tanzanians as fellow Pentecostals. This strategy effectively skimmed over potential trouble spots that social relationships presented for William, a fellow choir member in their congregation. William did not use his association with other Pentecostals to insure socially unthreatening situations. His approach toward his religion was resolute and private, and seemed to afford him little solace when dealing with other Pentecostals. At choir practices, William was all business, while James participated both socially and musically. William never seemed able to shed his deep suspicions about Banyaruguru refugees and all Tanzanians, while James was entirely comfortable acting Tanzanian.

Notes

1. No television existed in Tanzania during my stay there (1990–92).
2. These precise definitions are taken from Hinnebusch and Mirza 1979.
3. Except, apparently, me: I had become his confidant, for I had proved I could keep secrets. He enjoyed teaching me about hidden realities underneath those I observed. He also found explaining situations to me an acceptable exchange for learning to drive my car.

6

Satan's City

Perhaps no aspect of African refugee society and culture is as over-looked by researchers and most humanitarian relief agencies as the refugees' religious lives. This may also apply to religious studies: Pirouet, for example, observed that she was "not aware that theol-ogy [had] ever addressed itself to [the refugee] phenomenon" (1996: 82). For young Burundi refugees searching for opportunities outside the isolated settlements they grew up in, their Pentecostal faith, and the networks that emerged from Pentecostal congregations, played a critical role in facilitating their escape to Dar es Salaam.

The rise of Pentecostalism among Burundi refugees is actually part of a much larger demographic phenomenon: the expansion of Pentecostalism across Africa. "In Africa," Harvey Cox observed, "Pentecostal congregations … are quickly becoming the main expression of Christianity" (1995: 15). But its arrival as "the salient sector of African Christianity today" (Gifford 1998: 33) is due in large part because Pentecostals have targeted and accommodated youth needs. One can immediately see the appeal for urban migrant and refugee youth, because Pentecostal churches, as Cox has noted, "give people a sense of dignity, a place in a community of friends which often stands as a surrogate for an extended family fractured by mobility and change" (1995: 259). Gifford, moreover, has found that the churches "re-order society for the benefit of youth," creating a bond with "many who previously would have been regarded as different" (1998: 347).

This chapter will attempt to account for the remarkably strong presence of Pentecostalism in Burundi refugee society existing both in the settlements in Tanzania and in Dar es Salaam. It will consider the impact of Pentecostal teachings on the refugees' *kujificha* coping strategies, with particular attention paid to Pentecostalism's appeal and utility for young refugees. The chapter will also examine why the Imbo-Banyaruguru rivalry became part of a contentious division between two competing Pentecostal churches.

Tracing Religion in Burundi Refugee Lives

Despite numerous studies on various aspects of Burundi refugee life in settlements, there is little information on the role religion has played in refugee lives. Christensen, for example, simply described "Sundays and holidays" in Ulyankulu settlement, when "the rhythm differs":

> During church hours the compounds are deserted. In the morning almost all the refugees attend the services, which are characterized by an exuberant "togetherness" as churches resound with familiar hymns. Afterwards there is a gathering to greet relatives and friends from other parts of the settlement. (1985: 98)

Ogbru's survey (1983) found that Burundi refugees were overwhelmingly Christian but did not examine the variety of churches they belonged to. He did, however, find that refugees from Kenya, South Africa and Uganda, many of whom resided in Dar es Salaam, "tended to record higher percentages of free thinkers or atheists than other larger groups of refugees" (1983: 33). This finding, Ogbru contended, "may be explained by possible urban life influences" (ibid.). The implication that urban life may corrode religious faith is supported by the perspectives of urban sin expressed by Pentecostal church leaders in this chapter. Most of the refugees in this study, however, were found to have remained devout Pentecostals despite their urban residence. As will be described, Pentecostalism was an essential tool for navigating the stresses and dangers of urban life.

Pentecostalism's appeal appears to have been at the forefront of a significant religious transformation in Burundi refugee society. Although Burundi's population remains predominantly Catholic, Ayok and Mbago's survey of Katumba and Ulyankulu found that nearly 68 percent of the respondents were Protestant, most of them Pentecostal, while Catholics comprised only 25.8 percent of the surveyed population (Ayok and Mbago 1987: 31). Pentecostal missionaries reported a lower figure for the population of "true" refugee followers of their faith, but their numbers did not include those on the periphery of their movement and members of related churches. Regardless of the disparity in the two sets of numbers, missionaries proudly cited the remarkable growth of refugee converts to Pentecostalism since the creation of Katumba and Ulyankulu settlements almost thirty years ago.

The Pentecostal Expansion

Why have so many Burundians converted to Pentecostalism as refugees? The seeds of the answer appear to emanate from southern Burundi, where most of the refugees from the 1972 genocide came from. Donald Hohensee, a missionary for the World Gospel Church in Burundi, conducted a survey in 1977 of Burundi's major churches' activities and their effectiveness at gaining converts. He initiated the study because his church had been largely ineffective in expanding its membership since 1960, and its members seemed resigned to accepting their fate. By citing passages in the scriptures, however, he challenged this view and set out to discover why missionaries for other churches had been more effective in gaining converts.

Of particular interest to him was the dramatic upsurge that Pentecostal churches had achieved, their membership expanding at a rate far higher than any other church in Burundi. Since 1960, Pentecostal conversions far outdistanced all other Protestant churches.[1] His comparative survey begins and ends with the following problem:

> I couldn't explain our [World Gospel Church] smallness purely on doctrinal grounds for the Free Methodists and the Pentecostals were similar to our own. Nor could the Pentecostals have all that advantage just because they spoke in tongues. I was forced to the conclusion that growth must have more to do with method than with doctrinal beliefs and practices. (Hohensee 1977: 2)

Later in the book Hohensee expresses his quandary more succinctly: "The question that is crying out for an answer is why did the Pentecostals come out of the harvest field with nearly 50,000 communicants [members] when others came out with only 1000 to 5000 communicants" (Hohensee 1977: 99).

Hohensee's cites the Pentecostals' "people movement" method of evangelism as the central reason for their success. This method jointly attracts a "tribe, a caste, or any homogenous unit where marriage and intimate life take place" (McGavran 1970: 29). Members of communities become Christian converts without experiencing social dislocation. The new religion fits into the existing lifestyles by seeking group conversions. Christians had successfully used this method, Hohensee states, to evangelize Asia Minor and Europe, but its influence had waned. In Burundi, most Protestant churches attempted to attract individuals to Christianity one at a time, often by luring them with offers of education or medicine. These types of converts frequently became distanced from their family and community members. In a people movement, this failing isn't possible, because "the people have not needed the works by the Mission to help keep them true. There is the social support which they receive because they made the decision together.... Reversion [to their original beliefs] becomes harder because now it means breaking the unity of having decided for Christ as a unit" (Hohensee 1977: 101).

Hohensee's work suggests that Burundi's Pentecostals employed methods which enabled them to establish themselves quickly in Tanzanian refugee settlements. The Pentecostal church had other advantages, too. Swedish Pentecostal missionaries arrived in Burundi in 1935, settling in the southern province of Bururi. The epicenter of the 1972 unrest occurred in the Pentecostal stronghold, and the towns of Mugara and Bururi figure prominently in descriptions of the conflict. Burundi's Pentecostal mission was comparatively decentralized, leaving pastors in each district to assume the administrative and legal duties on behalf of their church. The pastors were also very well paid, because Pentecostals emphasized financial self-reliance. Finally, the pastors' Bible school in Burundi used Swahili as the language of instruction, something Hohensee considered a "weakness" in Burundi but was an obvious strength for pastors who fled to Tanzania in 1972, since Swahili was a national language there.

Thus, in applying Hohensee's observations in Burundi to the flight of refugees into Tanzania, several comparative advantages seem to have positioned the Pentecostals to assume a position of strength against other churches in Burundi's refugee communities. Their pastors were accustomed to assuming additional duties of legal representative and administrator. They were used to leading highly organized, self-sufficient congregations. And they spoke Swahili well, having learned it at their Bible schools.

Burundian Pentecostal pastors also benefited from the presence of Swedish Pentecostal missionary organizations on each side of the Tanzania-Burundi border. According to a senior Swedish missionary in Tanzania, the Pentecostals in Burundi contacted their associates in Tanzania by radio at the outset of trouble in 1972. When Burundi refugees entered Tanzania, the Pentecostals had the first organized support program at the border to provide new refugees with food, shelter and medicine. This must have left them in great standing with non-Pentecostal Burundi refugees and helped them gain converts. The Pentecostal refugees also benefited by having the Pentecostal Church's Tanzanian headquarters in Tabora, which is situated close to both Ulyankulu and Katumba settlements.

Although research in Dar es Salaam two decades after the refugees' original flight made it difficult to get a complete story of the rise of Pentecostalism among Burundi refugees, it appears that Pentecostalist missionary doctrine and strategies fashioned in Burundi were especially portable and transferable to Tanzanian soil. The people movement approach, which targeted communities rather than individuals, seems to have easily aligned the group experience of Burundians becoming refugees together. The refugees were likely drawn to Pentecostalism because it offered solace from the past and empowerment for the future through a spiritual rebirth:

> When a Pentecostal speaks of life as delivered once again by a second birth in experiences of light and wind and fire, he or she dramatically symbolizes dissolutions of the past in catalytic and cataclysmic recoveries of wholeness. In Pentecostal language, that is an achievement of holiness. Such recoveries spread like forest fires along linked chains of kin and neighbours, re-forming families or creating communities which are themselves extended families-in-God. The importance of these networks for facilitating conversion can hardly be exaggerated. (Martin 1990: 203)

The philosophy and process of this conversion to Pentecostalism (and "rebirth" in Tanzania for those already Pentecostal) may also explain the evidence of their strength in numbers and degree of devotion within the Burundi refugee population. This would advance the likelihood that Malkki's descriptions of a Burundian Hutu mythico-history and shared consciousness arising in the refugee settlements may have been significantly, perhaps even profoundly, influenced by Pentecostalist interpretations of the ethnic genocide and the meaning of refugee existence. As Martin concluded, "Pentecostalism, after all, is about spiritual power and empowerment" (ibid.: 204). These themes, taken together with

Pentecostalism's explanatory powers, reveal how the religion could have influenced the ideas and activities of a large, and still growing, proportion of the Burundi refugee population.[2] Indeed, Martin argued that in Latin America Pentecostalism was "truly indigenous" and "was also more truly embedded in the local cultures and reflected them even as it altered them" (1990: 231). If this can be said for Burundi refugees, then Burundi refugee ideas of history, ethnicity and nationalism may have also contained a stronger, more sculpting religious influence than has been previously suggested.

Pentecostal Refugee Dynamics

Pentecostal conversions notwithstanding, the Burundi refugee settlements contained a solid contingent of Catholics in their population. Given the rich Catholic heritage in Burundian colonial and postcolonial history, this might be expected. Yet Catholic refugees from the settlements were scarcely present in Dar es Salaam at all. This finding was surprising, and led to a careful re-assessment of my sampling techniques to determine whether they were leading me to overemphasize the influence of Pentecostalism among urban refugees. As part of this re-assessment, I held interviews with the handful of Catholic refugees in town, and Catholic Church officials, on this issue. These efforts turned up no evidence whatsoever of a larger Burundian Catholic refugee population in Dar es Salaam, and led me to estimate that at least 90 percent of the Burundi refugee population in the capital were either Pentecostal or members of a closely related faith.[3] Prevented from examining this problem inside the refugee settlements themselves, the reasons for this seemed fairly mysterious. Most Pentecostal and Catholic refugees professed not to understand why more Catholics had not migrated from the settlements to the capital. A few cited one possible reason: that "the Catholics don't help each other" like Pentecostals do. Their settlement-city networks, in other words, appeared to be weak.

The same could not be said for Pentecostal refugees. They lived in many areas of the city, they actively participated in "Hutu Network" activities, they maintained reliable economic networks for themselves, and many were heavily involved in church activities and rivalries. To gather an understanding of the religious environment from which most Pentecostal refugees in town had come from, and lacking direct access to the Burundi refugee settlements, I interviewed, in addition to Burundi refugees in town, members of the central Pentecostal mission, the Pentecostal Church Association in Tanzania (PCAT). These missionaries helped provide an overview of Pentecostalism in the settlements. They estimated that about one fifth of the two hundred thousand Burundi refugees were full members of Pentecostal churches, with twenty-six thousand in Katumba and six thousand each in Ulyankulu and Mishamo (these figures do not include the numbers of refugees either loosely associated with the PCAT–those that may periodically attend PCAT churches–or other churches related to the PCAT, such as the Assemblies of God churches). In the mid-1970s, there were only nine thousand full-member Pentecostals in Katumba–their numbers have nearly tripled since then.

The churches in Katumba were highly organized. Most of the settlement's twenty-nine villages had churches. Some of these were called division churches, and on the first Sunday of each month up to five thousand members attended services there. As in Burundi, the members' contributions provided considerable sums for church activities and personnel.

The Pentecostal missionaries also described a curious paradox. They stated that many Burundi refugee *wasomi* (intellectuals) were Pentecostals, including exiled elites in Europe. This implied that a disproportionate number of leaders of exiled political groups were Pentecostals. At the same time, however, they refused to admit that Pentecostal refugees were divided as Imbo and Banyaruguru, and one missionary even stated that "The Pentecostals don't get into politics." Pentecostals in the settlements all get along, they contended.

Evidence of religious strife among Dar es Salaam's Pentecostal refugees challenged this position. In fact, the PCAT missionaries had their hands full with a divisive feud involving a breakaway Pentecostal church within their ranks. One foreign Pentecostal missionary spoke of the difference between Kenya and Tanzania regarding the registration of churches. While Kenyan policy allowed individual churches to register separately with the government (an Anglican missionary once told me that Kenya was "the missionary capital of the world"), the Tanzanian government allowed only one registered church per religion. This had forced Pentecostal missionaries from a variety of countries to work within a single administrative structure. The administration itself arose from the Swedish Free Mission, which had established the first Pentecostal church in colonial Tanganyika in 1932 and was later managed by Tanzanian nationals and called the PCAT.

The Pentecostals' problem arose in 1964, when the PCAT originally registered with the government. In an oversight, they forgot to assign a registration number to one Dar es Salaam church. That church felt slighted, and used this lapse to assert itself as the primary Pentecostal church in the land. Interviews with church leaders indicated that the chance to resolve the dispute and unite as one church had already passed. PCAT leaders continued to fight with the breakaway church leaders over the ownership and leadership of various Pentecostal churches.[4]

The PCAT administration is located in Tabora, close to Ulyankulu and Katumba settlements. The Pentecostal refugees have imported their tradition of strong support for the central church administration from Burundi. As one missionary commented: "The refugee churches are the ones who are supporting PCAT the most. They are the most loyal to the original organization. They give more *pesa* [money] than the Tanzanian churches [give to PCAT]. So if [the refugees] go home to Burundi, PCAT is in trouble, their financial base endangered." Refugee pastors and elders attend the yearly meetings in Tabora, representing an unusually well-organized block of Pentecostals in Tanzania.

In Dar es Salaam, the dispute between the PCAT and the breakaway church split the refugees into opposing sides. During one interview, one foreign missionary surmised that education had divided them: in his view, the breakaway church had leaders with a higher level of formal education than the PCAT pastors in Dar es Salaam. This difference, he believed, had attracted educated Tanzanians and refugees to the breakaway church, for their presence in PCAT churches seemed to automatically challenge the pastors' authority:

> Educated people don't feel accepted [in PCAT churches] anymore. Only at [the breakaway church] are they attracted and feel comfortable. If an educated man speaks at a [PCAT] congregation, nobody dares to contradict him—even pastors feel that they are lower than the educated people, so there's tension—pastors feel that they're stupid in front of the educated people.

The missionary concluded that PCAT pastors needed to receive more education. At the time of our interview, he said, many PCAT pastors could not read. The literacy requirement used for the Burundi Pentecostal system, as well as the Catholics and Lutherans in Tanzania, should be applied to PCAT to reduce the risk of alienating educated followers.

Visits to the breakaway church and interviews with refugee members indicated that the church had attracted well-educated as well as less-educated refugees.[5] More significantly, all of the refugees who told me that they attended the breakaway church were Imbo.[6] Many Imbo denied that this was true. The Imbo-Banyaruguru dispute could not possibly involve their religious devotion—they went to church, they insisted, simply to praise Jesus. Yet many reserved harsh language for Banyaruguru refugees who had risen to positions of authority in PCAT churches.

Analyzing the Imbo refugees' apparent attraction to the breakaway church revealed several probable motivations. Numerically smaller than the Banyaruguru refugee population, both in Dar es Salaam and in the settlements, Imbo refugees appeared to have severed themselves from the PCAT only after entering the capital. This break constituted a means both for maintaining their Imbo identity and separating themselves, symbolically and socially, from the Banyaruguru. Joining the breakaway Pentecostal church also seemed to have enabled the Imbo to congregate together without attracting undue attention. It also set them into the familiar position of opposing Banyaruguru refugees and allowing them to claim the mantle of being the educated refugee group, as even the uneducated Imbo attending the breakaway church considered its membership to be educated.

The Pentecostal Congregation

I regularly attended church services at the tailors' Pentecostal church. Pastor Albert conducted services there infrequently, as he often preached at other churches, but his assistant pastor attended every Sunday, and all of the refugee tailors in this study were congregation members. I often attended choir practices too, as James and William were devoted members and occasionally went to church-related activities that the tailors infrequently attended, such as the "Young People's Organization" and the occasional afternoon *Semina* (Seminar) designed to teach young people how to avoid sin and follow Jesus. I also went to several evening crusades, one of which was sponsored by the tailors' church.

The crusades were intended to attract new followers and "crusade" against the sinful attractions that Pentecostals considered so prevalent in Dar es Salaam. They took place in open spaces near churches, equipped with microphones and screeching amplifiers, and a long extension cord winding behind a makeshift podium toward someone's back door. The crusades, which normally extended from a Thursday through the weekend, began with choir music comprised of electric and bass guitars, and perhaps a Casio electric organ, together with young men and women from the sponsoring congregation. The music always attracted a crowd, followed by speakers with announcements and mini-sermons. The microphone then entered the hands of the guest pastor, usually an experienced evangelist who worked the crowd into a fervor just as the tropical sunset, immersed in the glow of city dust, entered full bloom.

Just under three-quarters of the entire population of Tanzania's capital is comprised of men and women under the age of thirty (1988 Census Regional Profile: Dar es Salaam). In Pastor Albert's church, at least 90 percent of every Sunday service were young adults and children. Total attendance varied between forty-five and sixty, with slightly more than half of the church comprised of young men. Some of the young women had children in tow.

When I asked the Assistant Pastor of the church to explain why practically the entire congregation was comprised of young people, his response underscored the image of his church as one in service to rural-urban migrants:

> Originally, [Dar es Salaam] was *Wazaramu*.[7] Most were Muslim. Those who came from Mbeya, Kigoma, Burundi, Morogoro, and all over Tanzania, came to Dar es Salaam for work. Young men and women came here [and their parents and elders] remained in the villages.... The *Wazee* [parents and elders] here in the city are mostly Muslim, and they are not interested in changing their religion.

The African religion scholar, Ogbu Kalu, added an additional reason for the youthful accent of Pentecostal congregations: "Pentecostals provide a community which helps the urban dweller build a survival network."[8] Surrounded by sin and danger, the young refugees' Pentecostal faith not only mapped out how to avoid trouble but identified where refugees could relax, if only a little—in what Kalu considers "the youthful atmosphere of Pentecostal groups."

Fear among the Faithful

The Assistant Pastor of Pastor Albert's church was a Tanzanian national who was very aware of the presence of Burundi refugees in his congregation. John, William, and James all singled him out as wily and untrustworthy. They seemed forever afraid that he would report them to the Tanzanian authorities. Indeed, he often appeared curious about refugee issues, intentionally raising them with me in the presence of the tailors. In turn, the refugees seemed to feel that he was toying with them.

The tailors reserved even more suspicion and dislike for another Tanzanian in the congregation. Kathbert was a church officer who frequented the tailoring shops on weekdays. John and William consciously ignored him whenever he entered, and their dislike for him was palpable. Kathbert also made James nervous. None of the tailors ever explained why they held Kathbert in such contempt, but John and James did admit their conviction that he was most definitely a spy, and dangerous. If anyone was going to root them out of the neighborhood, they believed it very well could be him.

The Tanzanian Assistant Pastor's knowledge of refugees in his congregation could hardly have been avoided, since Pastor Albert himself was of Burundian extraction. The more difficult question lay in discovering just how many refugees were actually in the congregation. Even Pastor Albert was unsure of the precise number. This was intentional. He told me that he only tended to refugee concerns when people privately approached him and identified themselves as refugees. He was always open to private consultation with them.

Pastor Albert's congregation crystallized Burundi refugee life in town better than any other venue I visited. The church was the only site where Burundi refugees in the neighborhood gathered together, yet because they kept to themselves, refugees could be sure of the identities of few people in their congregation. The refugees had all arrived by themselves in Dar es Salaam, having come from huge rural settlements. They worked in different places, entered church on Sundays to worship, and then returned to their city homes. I always found it interesting to watch the congregation's young men and women exit the church doorway and shake everyone's hand just outside, as they formed a large circle of singing believers. For as they smiled, sang, and clapped together, in what looked like a warm, intimate community, John, William, James, and others kept their blinders on. They did not want to know who among them were fellow refugees.

For William and James, ignorance supported their desire for self-protection. William, who already felt isolated as an Imbo refugee among Banyaruguru, and James, who maintained a satisfactory urban situation by promoting his Pentecostal identity above all others, clearly followed this course. John, on the other hand, considered himself an expert at silently identifying who were actually refugees. Yet he used this information to protect himself, not to reach out to others. Revealing one's refugee identity there was thought especially perilous because Tanzanians were mixed in with the group, some of whom may have been government spies. Within the intimate confines of the small Pentecostal church, retaining a Tanzanian shield over one's refugee identity was considered the only viable strategy.

The most remarkable public incident relating to this issue occurred during my first visit to church. At one point in the service all of the *wageni* (strangers, or guests) were asked to introduce themselves to the congregation. A young woman stood and said with great passion that she was a Burundian from Ulyankulu settlement. "We are also in Katumba and Mishamo," she declared, mentioning the other two Burundi refugee settlements. "We come here [to Dar es Salaam] illegally," she said, and cursed the *wapelelezi,* an astonishingly direct reference to spies and informers. The life is hard in all three refugee camps, she added, and ended with "We are all *wasafiri* (travelers, visitors) when we come here [to Dar es Salaam]." She then translated for her mother, who was visiting Dar es Salaam with her and spoke only Kirundi, the language of Burundi.

Following the young woman's startling speech, the Assistant Pastor gently said that "you don't have to mention your tribe here [in church]." Afterwards, the refugees dismissed her, saying that she was nuts. The Assistant Pastor later told me with a laugh that "this woman was not all right."

But it was clear that the young woman's outburst had touched a nerve. Mentioning one's ethnicity as a Tanzanian in such a context is unusual enough. Government policy had de-emphasized ethnicity publicly, although there were standard ways of expressing it in code. When a person said that they were from the town of Moshi, the home area of the ethnic Chagga, it inferred that they were Chagga; if they were from Tabora, it inferred Nyamwezi ethnicity; from Kigoma, Ha; from Bukoba, Haya, and so on. But for a Burundi refugee to openly state their identity and condemn the spies that pursued them was more than unusual. Her behavior must have strengthened all of the refugees' individual resolve to cloak their own identity and maintain a Tanzanian identity in church. This woman not only seemed mad, she was dangerous.

In private individual discussions, I asked John, William, and James how many refugees were in their church congregation. Their responses were characteristic of their personalities, revealing how their shared cultural fear could be expressed in different ways. William did not answer my question, responding with "I don't know."

James was contradictory, a sign of his general tendency to shy away from sensitive issues. He once told me that most of those in the congregation were ethnic Ha from western Tanzania: "I figure most are Ha there, but I really don't know [if they are Burundi refugees or not]. We [refugees] can all imitate *Kiha*, since it's not a big difference [from *Kirundi*]." James later contradicted himself by commenting that those Ha in church might actually be refugees who are skilled in speaking *Kiha* just like an ethnic Ha: "Many who say they are Waha are really refugees living in Kigoma. They were there, maybe [for] two years, and in that time learned to speak Kiha [without being detected as a refugee]—then they came here to Dar es Salaam." James's commentary indicated that people who have lived in proximity to ethnic Ha would have learned to speak *Kiha* well. This would also include Katumba and Mishamo settlements, which are also situated in areas where ethnic Ha live. He also confessed his inability to be sure just who is a refugee and who is a Tanzanian Ha:

> "I can't ask another if they're refugees because I can't tell if they are Ha or Hutu.… If they [the Tanzanians] find out I'm not a Ha, he'll tell another, and it will spread, until a *mkubwa* [big man] finds out … then he'll say "Let's go look for him!" We'll [the refugees] be chased [from Dar es Salaam]!"

James professed knowing for sure of only four other refugees in Dar es Salaam: John, William, and two others living in other parts of town. In fact, James shunned learning about the presence of other refugees nearby—by pretending that everyone around him was a Tanzanian. For James, practiced ignorance was the safest strategy for coping in the capital, and most especially within the intimate setting of the church, where Tanzanian Ha sit and pray and sing alongside Burundi refugees. Surrounded by Tanzanians and unsure of who among them were actually refugees, he considered it a particularly dangerous setting for identifying refugees. As James related with fervor: "In church, we never say to another that we're refugees—never!"

John, on the other hand, issued his view of the facts in blunt terms: "Most of the people in the church are refugees! Most! All are afraid to say [or admit this fact]. I know the truth by the way the speak Swahili, that's how I know. They are refugees. I can make it out from their accent, the way they speak [Swahili].… Nearly all … are from there [refugee settlements] … the accent is there. I can tell." John then proceeded to name nearly every person I knew in the congregation and identify them as refugees. He insisted that detecting refugees in church was easy for all Burundi refugees to do.

The difference in accent was too obvious. We all know who the others are, John explained, but we all stay silent about the truth. Then he described the nature of the refugees' interactions as fellow church congregation members: "We never say it [that we are refugees] to each other, though. Never! [There is] nothing to talk about, anyway. But I know that most are [refugees]." After stating that he is still a member of the church no matter how infrequently he attends, John cut our talk short.

Since I knew that other refugees in the congregation were actively hiding their identity just as John, William, and James were, it was hard to decipher who was a Tanzanian national and who was Burundi refugee. Over time, however, some signs were revealed to me. After several of the Sunday church services, while I was preparing to leave, different congregation members indicated, while we stood apart from the rest, that they were refugees. Two others asked to speak to me about refugee issues by discreetly passing me notes on small pieces of paper during church services.

I also had come to consider John's statements as closer to the truth than those of either William or James. William was suspicious of most people, and his tendency to answer questions with brief replies frequently applied to our discussions as well. He may have been lying by professing not to know who was a refugee in his church. However, it was also perfectly conceivable to interpret his response to my inquiry as an indication that he did not want to know. His secretive and socially withdrawn behavior in the tailoring shop was the same during choir practices and Sunday services. Although he was the co-leader of the choir and an accomplished guitarist, he rarely sang, and when he did speak to others in the choir, it was usually to critique their performance in some way. The other choir leader, in contrast, communicated his displeasure to the singers by encouraging them to improve. During services William was a rapt listener who prayed with great fervor. But socially he remained detached, a respected but distant figure.

James's behavior in church and in the choir (he was one of the lead singers) was unlike William's. James enjoyed himself, and his relaxed, cheerful demeanor made him popular and always approachable. Other choir members would pass by his shop to accompany him to church, while William arrived alone and never passed by James's workplace, even though it was on his way. During choir practice James remained sociable, and after church services he remained outside with friends. Church and choir were safe extensions of his workplace, and he enjoyed them.

By 1992, after months of getting to know each other during conversations in Pastor Albert's tailoring shop or in conversations during and after our driving lessons, John had assumed the role of teacher in our private talks, informing me of hidden refugee realities with an authoritative manner. In truth, much of what he related was corroborated when I checked it against the views of other refugees. He had proven himself as an unusually reliable source. John had no interest in joining the choir, and only once, to my knowledge, went to a church crusade. The services appeared to bore him. His periodic attendance seemed an attempt to deflect suspicions among the church membership about whether he was still a devout, "saved" Christian who had not embraced sinful ways. Church attendance preserved his position with Pastor Albert, who otherwise might have replaced him with a more devout refugee churchgoer from the settlements.

Neither John, William, nor James used the church as a network. In a strange way, refugees attended church together, and probably outnumbered the Tanzanian membership, but did not use this social setting to share information or provide mutual support regarding the problems of hiding in Dar es Salaam. The presence of Tanzanians, in this case, seemed to make their participation in church services and activities relatively safe. In that environment, they were Pentecostals, fellow followers of Jesus, joined together because all of them had been "saved." The setting provided a temporary outlet from the stress and worry of hiding and the strain of working under demanding circumstances.

Refugees joined with Tanzanians to worship at Pastor Albert's church, not to expand their connections with other refugees. As John stated, there was "nothing to talk about" with other refugees in any case. This comment was indicative of how the refugees coped in Tanzania's capital. Large support networks in the city were not only unnecessary—they were considered potentially disastrous. Your parents or friends arranged a position for you, and you worked long hours and rarely ventured from the haven of the workplace. If you had a person to rely on in case of trouble—Pastor Albert served this purpose for John and William, and Amosi matched this role for James—then it was better to have very few friends. In John's words, "Too many friends could only bring trouble." Intimacy with refugees you did not know served no useful purpose.

Such a perspective may have applied to William and other Imbo refugees in the congregation even more, as they appeared to be vastly outnumbered by Banyaruguru refugees. An Imbo dialect is usually so distinct that even I could detect it, and I heard it used by very few congregation members. In addition, the Pastor was a Banyaruguru, and it struck me as unlikely that his congregation would attract many Imbo in the first place, especially since so many Imbo attended the breakaway Pentecostal church instead. I would also check my suspicions of Imbo or Banyaruguru refugees in the congregation with John, the self-described language expert. William's awareness that he was part of the minority refugee group was probably behind his unending distance from others in church.

Satan in Bongoland

> *Ni wewe tu, Yesu, ni wewe tu.*
> [It's only you, Jesus, it's only you.]
>
> *Shetani! Rudi nyuma, naenda na Yesu.*
> [Satan! Return behind me, I go with Jesus.]
>
> —Two common hymns at Pentecostal services

Even though refugees did not attend church together to expand their social networks, their church did serve other very useful purposes. Most members of the congregation seemed to be exceedingly devout followers of church doctrine, and their faith in God was strong. Every Sunday, the services were sites of extraordinarily energetic worship.

The Pentecostals of Dar es Salaam, like other Pentecostals, based their devotion on a literal interpretation of the Bible and by becoming infused with the Holy Spirit. A Swedish Pentecostal missionary in Dar es Salaam put it this way: "The only difference [from other fundamentalist churches] is in [our] feeling the power of the relationship with the Holy Spirit; we are known for speaking in tongues, we Pentecostals are, and it's true. We believe the Book is only it; that it unites us—only [that]." He went on to say that what Jesus taught in the New Testament "is the center of all."

The practice of Pentecostalism in Dar es Salaam differed somewhat from this institutional emphasis on the New Testament. As the Swedish missionary explained, "We say: the Bible has two sharp edges: the Old and the New Testament, though the basic word is Jesus, of course. He [Jesus] says He's fulfilling the Old Testament." But he added that the Pentecostal pastors in Dar es Salaam and other parts of Tanzania tended to focus on the Old Testament, particularly the Ten Commandments, instead of the New Testament. Local pastors, he said, don't look at "Jesus fulfilling their lives but more on the Ten Commandments; [preaching] to do this, don't do that ... and so on. That's their focus! And it's too bad." He suspected the reason for this had to do with the pastors' lack of education and understanding. Yet the emphasis on the laws of God presented the pastors with an especially effective way of instructing their followers about how to avoid sin.

Life in Dar es Salaam seemed to highlight the need for this sort of instruction. Most congregation members were migrant youth who lived in the city without guidance from their parents or the community structures that existed in the settlements. Potential avenues that led toward sinning also abounded in the capital city: the pastors were forever warning against the dangerous presence of Satan lurking in Dar es Salaam. Unless young people steeled themselves to oppose urban sin, they warned, youths were vulnerable to Satan's influence. According to Pentecostal pastors and many of their followers, Satanic temptations saturated Bongoland.

The Pentecostal pastors considered young men especially vulnerable to vices such as drinking, smoking tobacco or marijuana, and attending discos. The worst example of young urban sinners were the *machekibob*; unemployed young men who seemed to advertise their departure from acceptable urban lifestyles. These *machekibob* were everywhere, too, huddled in groups at street corners or school playgrounds in every neighborhood. To the pastors, the lurking *machekibob* suggested a seductive option to an upright life. The Ten Commandments helped the pastors address what they considered their greatest challenge: making sure their congregation's young men did not become *machekibob*.

Models of Urban Sin

The word *chekibob* (the plural is *machekibob*) was apparently lifted from an English language action film. Young men watched such films either at the outdoor drive-in or in one of the dilapidated downtown cinemas.[9] In one scene, Tanzanian and refugee youth explained to me, some "fashion design" men went to "check" on "Bob." Some disagreement existed over whether Bob was a person or a group called the "BoB," or "Boys of Britain," but regardless of its origin, its meaning was the same: people going to "check Bob" were those who identified with Western models of screen outlaws.

The *machekibob* fascinated John, William, and James, and were a frequent conversation topic in the tailoring shops. When young men that they considered a *chekibob* passed by, it usually spurred animated conversations. In the process, the tailors taught me the other words in the *Lugha ya Vijana*. A *chekibob* was a *mhuni* (ignorant person), a *msela* (sailor), a *junki* (junkie), a *shua boy* (show boy). He was a young man who drew on his pants and wore his hair *punki* (punk), meaning that his hair was cut very short along the sides and high on top. He enjoyed all kinds of *dawa ya kulevya* (medicine for getting drunk), which included marijuana, alcohol, and drugs. He also stole for a living. And of course, his language was full of the most current city slang.

The *machekibob* were significant to the refugee tailors because they identified and delineated the opposing side of urban life. The *machekibob* were unemployed hoodlums while the refugees were hardworking and upright young men. In their view, a young man in Dar es Salaam became one or the other. There could be no in-between, a depiction reinforced by Sunday sermons–young men either avoided sin or quickly became *machekibob*. The *machekibob* helped keep the threat of failure close by.

The City as Satan's Lair

> ... to say "I forgot," well, you really remember, so to say "I forgot" is a lie. If you use it, Satan enters.
>
> –Assistant Pastor, speaking to the church's
> Young People's Organization

> Satan is in you, he talks to you and invites you to continue to sin. And it leads you to do worse and worse things.
>
> –Pastor Albert

In the view of Pentecostal pastors, Satan was everywhere. Dar es Salaam abounded with bars. There were several downtown movie theaters, as well as the notorious drive-in, which young people flocked to each night. They sat on the hill behind the drive-in's walls and watched the movies for free. Every night people went there to socialize and buy snacks under the stars, and gaze up at Indian or Western films on the huge, distant screen, the movie's soundtrack faintly wafting from the car speakers inside the drive-in's walls.

Listening to Pentecostal pastors warn about urban sin in conversations and sermons identified a handful of guiding principles. One was that young people needed to be kept busy with religious activities. As Albert noted: "[Y]ou have to keep people out of trouble. This is why we try to have many activities for the young ... to keep them from the attractions of Satan. *Shetani!* So, we have a choir, bible study, and a *vijana* [young people's] group. They keep [Satan's] temptations away." Pastors regularly criticized those youths in their congregations who didn't attend the daily activities planned for them at church. The tailors in Pastor Albert's shop felt defensive about this issue. Even though there was something for them to do every day, few participated regularly. They could, Albert insisted, go to crusades and attend Bible study classes. But the tailors usually refused.

Pastor Albert explained that the purpose of daily activities was to help young people remember the sermon's message between Sundays. He made a distinction between how all information is received and how religious information should be processed. In young people, the message of a Sunday sermon

> rests in the head, and there it gets mixed with all the other ideas of the week; troubles of money, what their friends say, thinking of hunger, and so on.... They do not lower the ideas [of the sermon] into the heart.... It is hard to get it into their hearts. That is the difficulty. So, they remember for a few days, but it does not stand out for very long. Whatever the sermon says on Sunday, it is mostly forgotten by the next Sunday.

Religious instruction needed to descend into the heart to avoid being forgotten and make a lasting difference in a person's life, for Satan thrived in the mind. As Albert explained on another occasion, sinful ideas and experiences that entered the head were hard to remove. They poisoned a young person's thoughts. The magazines with naked or scantily clad women,[10] Albert noted, encourage young men "to do bad things. So we don't want our young people to see them. Because [the pictures] stay inside your head. And this is Satan." Implicit in this conception is the belief that young people had a hard time avoiding Satan since experiencing or seeing something sinful drew them toward the Devil.

The pastors also considered sin addictive. As one explained:

> If you drink one glass of alcohol, already you are sinning. [And] tomorrow you will drink two, then a bottle, and then soon you will remain in the bar for twenty-four hours, drinking.
>
> If you steal one shilling or one thousand, it is the same. Tomorrow [it will be] five shillings ... and then it continues from there. Thus, all drinking, all stealing, is equal, is the same.... By sinning, by stealing even a shilling, you are inviting in Satan.

Once the sinning began, the pastors believed that young people could not control themselves and their sinning would only increase. One lie led directly to a bigger lie; petty theft to grand larceny. And unless the sinners repented they would surely burn in Hell.

To explore this philosophy, here are descriptions of what Pentecostal pastors viewed as the three prime activities that led to extravagant sinning: visiting bars, watching movies and using the *Lugha ya Wahuni* (Language of the Ignorant).

Bars and Catholics

> If you go to the bar, your good ideas migrate.
>
> –A devout young Pentecostal

Pentecostal refugees refrained from offering specific views on Catholic refugees. They could not supply exact information on why Catholic refugees had failed to migrate to Dar es Salaam. Whether in the settlements or the city, they simply preferred to stay away from Catholics, citing the same reason that Tanzanian Pentecostals invariably supplied: Catholics were sinners.

The Pentecostal leaders I interviewed all believed that God told Moses not to drink alcohol, and that Jesus never drank wine containing alcohol.[11] They told me that this was a major difference between Pentecostals and Catholics. The Assistant Pastor characterized it this way: "We follow the Bible as it's written, but Catholics follow only a part of it. They drink alcohol a little, although the Bible says not to take any." The Pastor's outrage against Catholics was strong. "You can drink as a Catholic," another pastor told me, "even with the priest!" One young woman in the Pentecostal congregation told me, in a voice laden with disgust, "*Waroma* (Roman Catholics) allow the drinking, dancing, disco, everything!" Taking one sip of alcohol was sinful without a doubt, Pentecostals explained to me. That Catholics allowed moderate drinking raised questions about their credibility as Christian leaders, because moderation in activities considered sinful was unacceptable: one cannot partake in a little sin and be saved. Sin is addictive. As one pastor told me: "People get drunk and then go to Catholic and other churches and pray, sing to God. They're hypocrites!"

Pentecostals considered bars as Dar es Salaam's primary venues for sin. In Pastor Albert's view, they harbored the two worst sins of all: drinking alcohol and fornication. The music one heard in bars, the alcoholic beverages sold there, and the dancing and sexual activity they could inspire, all represented sinful temptations on their own. But to Pentecostals, their combined availability in bars seemed to represent venues where people totally embraced Satan's ways. A person thus must avoid even listening to music normally heard in bars, as it would inevitably lead a person to celebrate the sin-laden values expressed in the music and toward the bars where the music was regularly played. As Pastor Albert's eldest son explained: "If you hear something [sinful like disco music], it will challenge your faith, so that it's better not to hear it. When you hear something is when you can start to believe in it." According to this approach, it was sinful to listen to any music except Christian choir music. Dancing outside the church's confines, Albert declared, would lead you to dance in a bar, since drunks would want to dance with you. And once inside a bar, dancing would inspire you to drink and "get caught up with prostitutes [if you are a man] and drunks [if you are a woman].... Dancing is the Devil, because just look [what goes on] in a bar!" Sinful dancing included both disco and traditional dancing, Albert sermonized one Sunday, because they both invited "Satan into your mind and [would] lead you to bars, to dance disco, a bad music that teaches you to sin. Just listening to the music, just dancing, leads to the sinful life."

Movies The notion that single sins led directly to extravagant sinning implied that young people could not control themselves. This was a central tenet of the Pentecostal preachers' teaching to youths in Dar es Salaam. Young men were especially vulnerable to Satan's temptations, which is why pastors warned against even glancing at a movie at the outdoor drive-in. Pastors urged young men in their congregations to avoid the drive-in at all costs—it was a central social spot for the *machekibob*, and if you went there you became one. The movies had the power to transform youths because they contained images of sex and nudity that were difficult to erase from memory. These images, Pastor Albert sermonized, "affect you. They are of Satan, and He will remain in you, too, and the ideas will lock in your head and influence you. Those beautiful girls, they are prostitutes.... The pictures of women influence you to do bad things, so we don't want our young men to see them."

Language Given the pastors' contention that the *Lugha ya Wahuni* was sinful, using even the mildest words became a way that youths walked the dangerous edge between sinner and saved. Throughout the city, people used mild slang words like *safi*, which literally meant "clean" but was widely used to mean "Okay," was so common that it did not seem to youths especially sinful. Even Albert admitted that *safi* was probably more disrespectful than emphatically sinful. On the other hand, he considered much of the *Lugha*'s vocabulary utterly damning. Speaking, or even hearing, phrases like *Sista Du* (short for Sista Dunia, or Worldly Sister), which young men conferred upon highly attractive or sexually available women, was a sin. Worse, it indicated that you were becoming a *chekibob*.

The Gray Area: Bribery for Survival

With few exceptions, the Pentecostals' perspective of the urban environment was black and white: either you followed Satan or you were saved. This philosophy allowed Burundian Pentecostal refugees to consider themselves superior to Tanzanians by highlighting a flaw in Tanzania's political and economic system: the inability to live on a normal Tanzanian salary. To Pentecostal refugees, this made sinning a necessity for Tanzanians and enabled refugees to retain a sense of superiority over them.

Pastor Albert spoke openly and expansively about Tanzania's problems. He reminded me several times that the Tanzanian government was corrupt. Its primary role was to collect money from its citizens: "Nobody knows where the money goes. They [Tanzanian government officials] steal it. That's all. We all know the money comes in, but it goes into pockets in the government. That's how it works! What can we do? Tanzania is just like that." His expression of powerlessness was echoed in another conversation, when Albert told me that Tanzanian government officials "take the money, and there's nothing to do [about it]."

Many Tanzanian citizens would have agreed with Albert's description. Corruption was frequently discussed in the local media. But Pastor Albert stated Tanzanian corruption as a fact and then detached himself from it, a position taken by many Burundi refugees. The system was wrong, even sinful, but as they were outsiders, there was nothing they could do to reform it.

I heard many Pentecostal leaders condemn the acceptance of bribes, yet the Assistant Pastor, a Tanzanian, confessed that pastors must ultimately make an exception for corruption. "People must take bribes here, since the salaries are too low to live on," he explained to me. "People take bribes because of low salaries, so in no sense is it bad." In moral terms, taking bribes in the cause of survival was not a sin. God would understand.

But many refugees said that they were victims of such corruption. At the same time, I knew that some of the tailors failed to report all of the money they took in from customers. But clearly this sort of thing was, in their eyes, simply in the cause of survival and so not morally wrong. Yet such actions were private and secret and thus beyond the realm of the corruption of the Tanzanian state. The refugees generally considered themselves detached from and opposed to the Tanzanian system, and considered Tanzanians their moral inferiors.

Pentecostalism for Coping

For Burundi refugees, the cultural fear they imported from their settlement homes led to frequent expressions of powerlessness. Their remarkable success at establishing a fugitive presence in Dar es Salaam failed to extinguish their abiding sense of vulnerability. Pentecostalism, too, spoke of powerlessness, but it also provided a possible way out by concretizing fears and offering spiritual support. The religion encouraged its adherents to develop intimate relationships with Jesus Christ through prayer. Although cultivating this spiritual relationship may have been more important to William than John or Luka, all of the Pentecostal refugees were capable of deep religious fervor while praying at church services. Their faith was a buoy amidst the sea of inner fears that each refugee navigated.

While Pentecostalism could not erase the refugees' near-constant fear of a shadowy Tutsi presence in their lives, Pentecostal pastors could tell them where another danger, Satan, reigned (in bars and movie houses) and how he operated (by getting you to sin). Pentecostalism thus supplied refugees with a coping strategy that worked: avoid sin, and you avoid trouble. Stay on the straight and narrow path by reading the Bible, attending church activities, and working hard in tailoring shops—that Pentecostal regimen would also help you avoid notice as an illegal urban resident or become a potential Tutsi victim.

The economic dimension of Pentecostalism provided refugees with the opportunity to infuse their productivity with religious virtue. John, William, and James all worked extremely hard, and many of their conversations while working centered on Pentecostalist themes. Weber's general commentary provides a useful frame for viewing their lives:

> the religious valuation of restless, continuous, systematic work in a worldly calling, as the highest means to asceticism, and at the same time

the surest and most evident proof of rebirth and genuine faith, must have been the most powerful conceivable lever for the expansion of that attitude toward life which we have here called the spirit of capitalism. (Weber 1958: 172)

The refugee tailors of Dar es Salaam demonstrated capitalistic behavior, although Martin refined this contention to apply more specifically to Pentecostal followers: "the people who become Pentecostals are small people and their 'capitalism' is … mostly 'penny capitalism'" (Martin 1990: 206). But above and beyond this, Pentecostalism also supported the refugees' clandestine style of urban living. The refugee tailors' efforts to learn a trade and send money to their families in the settlements rewarded them with empowerment instead of powerlessness, and recognition in the settlements while maintaining public invisibility in the city. Their motivation to accumulate wealth in town was seen as virtuous, in a way similar to Marshall's description of Pentecostal behavior in Nigeria: "In the 'Pentecostal' churches … material success is not shunned, but seen as a mark of God's favour." (1991: 27).

Tensions within Burundi refugee society complicated the influence that Pentecostalism could have in their lives. Pentecostalism provided connections between Pentecostal believers in the settlements and Dar es Salaam, which directly facilitated opportunities for young refugees to become clients to Pentecostal refugee patrons in the capital. These connections, however, were vertical; from a young refugee in town to his patron and his family in the settlement. The refugees' connections rarely moved horizontally to strengthen social cohesion among young refugees in town. The breakaway Pentecostal church had certainly created a place where Imbo refugees could congregate, while also institutionalizing the urban rivalry between Imbo and Banyaruguru refugees. Yet even at the breakaway church, Imbo refugees worshipped alongside Tanzanian Pentecostals. Imbo refugees might occasionally congregate together outside church, but such meetings appeared to be rare, and large gatherings of refugees were generally avoided.

Social interactions between refugees in Pastor Albert's church resembled chess games. Refugees eyed each other but followed their own game plans, worshipping together without connecting. At church, everyone was a Pentecostal, refugee and Tanzanian alike. Everyone interacted as fellow "saved" Pentecostals; never as refugees. So while Pentecostalism provided the Burundian urban refugees with an avenue for getting to Dar es Salaam, a code of behavior for succeeding in the city after reaching there, and a source of spiritual uplift and empowerment, for most refugees it did not dramatically expand or improve relations between refugees. The church also did not necessarily protect refugees from the potential invasions of the Tutsi or their various possible accomplices. It could even enhance suspicion, because it brought one together with refugees and Tanzanians who might be spies, such as Kathbert, whom John, William, and James had all identified as dangerous.

John, William, and Jesus

John's endeavor to secure and live by his own moral code was regularly confronted by William's lectures on immorality. One evening, while dining with William and John, William began to castigate John for not going to church. William proclaimed that since it is written in the Bible that you must go to church, you cannot get into Heaven if you don't attend. John silently listened to William's vigorous pronouncements, and then stated that he led a moral life. He didn't steal, have girlfriends, or lie, so not going to church every Sunday was acceptable. "Isn't that enough?" he asked William. "Isn't that what Jesus demands?"

The argument was longstanding, and each man stood his ground. It illuminated how John had developed his own way of leading a life without, in his view, sinning, while enduring the condemnation that accompanied his Sunday absences from church services. Even before the church, its rules and its conditions for a righteous life, John had somehow sculpted a small space to call his own.

Notes

1. Perhaps fearing a negative Burundian government reaction, Hohensee makes little of the tumultuous effects of the genocide and refugee exodus in 1972. He merely notes that the number of Pentecostals declined dramatically during the "political unrest" (Hohensee 1977: 99) of that year. Not mentioned is the larger fact that the combination of death in and flight from Burundi caused the nation's population to drop by nearly 10 percent in 1972.
2. Examples of Rwandan refugee religious group responses to genocide are described in Sommers 1998c.
3. Leaders of the Pentecostal churches, the Assembly of God, and independent evangelical churches all told me that the differences of philosophy and approach between them were not particularly significant. The churches often coordinated activities together.
4. One of the disputes has resulted in an unusual settlement. One Dar es Salaam church allowed the PCAT pastor and his following to use the church for half of the day while the pastor from the breakaway group led his followers during the other half.
5. I did not interview those at the refugee tailoring shop opposite Pastor Albert's, which was run by a breakaway church leader, as he had warned me against it. Since I did not wish to endanger my access to Pastor Albert's shop, I followed his rule.
6. This is not to say that there are more highly educated Imbo than Banyaruguru refugees.
7. The *Wazaramu*, or "Zaramu people," are the indigenous ethnic group of the area that became Dar es Salaam.
8. Private interview.
9. The indoor movie theaters were often filled with mosquitoes. Some joked that if a person had malaria, it proved that they had been to the movies.
10. For some reason, women's clothing catalogs from the West, which included women modeling underwear, were commonplace in Dar es Salaam. I entered many young men's rooms who had papered their walls with pictures of white women posing in varieties of underwear.
11. None of the Biblical citations they mentioned to support this claim directly prohibited alcohol entirely, but one can see how the spirit of abstinence (as well as moderation) could be construed from scripture. In Leviticus 10:8–11, God commands Aaron that drinking when entering the tabernacle is a sin punishable by death. In John 14:12–15, Jesus asks his followers to "keep the commandments which I give you" (although it must be noted that Jesus never commanded others to abstain from alcohol). And in Ephesians 5:18, Paul commands "Do not besot yourselves with wine; that leads to ruin."

7

Conclusion

A Second Refugee Generation

Three weeks before completing my field research in Dar es Salaam in 1992, I hired John and James to each make me a pair of pants. I could not ask William because he was visiting his family in Ulyankulu settlement, and would not return until just before I left town. John and James helped me choose the material, but I asked that they design the sort of trousers that they preferred to wear.

John selected a sedate, blue-gray polyester material. The trousers had neither pleats nor cuffs, and seemed emblematic of his public persona in Dar es Salaam: practical, conservative, and intended to blend in with respectable Dar es Salaam residents. James designed a very different pair of pants. His were made of lightweight, blue-purple plaid polyester, and were both pleated and cuffed. They were also roomier than John's pair–far from the baggy style favored by the many of the *machekibob* in the neighborhood, but certainly lean-ing, if only a little, in that direction. The stylishness of the trousers that James made was signaled by the *lebo* he sewed into seams along one front pocket (which said "Mr. Dor") and above the back pocket (which read "Non-Iron Van Brook 65% Teturon"). It was the sort of trousers James would wear: understated but contemporary.

John and James were justly proud of the trousers they had made, and delighted by how well they fit me. Both also smirked a little when I wore trousers made by one of them into the shop of the other. John shook his head when I showed him the *lebo* James had incorporated into his design. Not his style by any means, but very much what his cousin preferred. James carefully examined the craftsmanship of the trousers John had made for me, breaking into a knowing grin while pointing out the narrow leg and lack of cuffs, pleats and *lebo*. John's seriousness and competence were very evident in the product I was wearing.

The trousers that James and John had made for me (James's cost slightly more, due to the two *lebo* he had added) symbolized the different ways that each kept to the goal shared by all refugee tailors in town: to hide their refugee identities by being seen as model Tanzanian citizens. This goal stood at the core of their strategy for coping in the capital, and it was made fairly clear by members of the Tanzanian government's Ministry of Home Affairs that it helped preserve their urban situation. Very few of the thousands of Burundi refugees in Dar es Salaam were troublemakers, and the Tanzanian government did not bother with them. Their ability to blend into Dar es Salaam's teeming migrant society only strengthened their position.

This aspect of urban refugee life was illuminated early in 1992. Joseph Karumba, the outspoken leader of the mainly Imbo refugee political party, Ubumwe, aroused the consternation of Tanzania's Minister for Home Affairs, Augustine Mrema, after one very public outburst in Katumba settlement. When Mrema responded by seeking his arrest, Karumba went into hiding. Given the vastness of Tanzania's thinly populated rural areas, the diversity of hiding places that Karumba could have chosen seemed broad. Strangers in rural Tanzanian communities tend to stick out, however, and Karumba undoubtedly knew, if he even had such an option, that the likelihood of Ten Cell Leaders locating a stranger in a small village or town was high. Instead, Karumba chose the one place in the country where anonymity was readily available: Dar es Salaam. Karumba may have spent his months in hiding no more than a mile or two from Mrema's downtown office.

Cultural Fear

Considerable attention has been paid to refugee fears in this book, as they constituted the dominant emotional characteristic of Burundi refugee life in Dar es Salaam. Fear sculpted the clandestine niche that young Burundi refugee men, who so dominated Burundi refugee society in the capital, created for themselves there. But describing fearful refugees is, in and of itself, hardly exceptional. On the contrary: more than anything else, fear defines people who are categorized as refugees. Referring to the 1951 United Nations Convention relating to the Status of Refugees (UNHCR 1995), the authors of a UNHCR document entitled "Handbook on Procedures and Criteria for Determining Refugee Status" asserted that "The phrase "well-founded fear of being persecuted" is the key phrase in the [refugee] definition. It reflects the views of its authors as to the main elements of refugee character" (UNHCR 1992: 11). Fear may also constitute the primary factor separating refugees living inside organized camps, settlements, or "schemes" from those living outside them (often called self-settled or spontaneously settled refugees). Hansen's research with Angolan refugees in Zambia found that "scheme-settled refugees were more dependent and self-settled refugees were more fearful" (1990: 32). The self-settled refugees, Hansen added, were especially "fearful of exposing their identity as refugees" (ibid.).

Just as the United Nations definition and Hansen's finding collectively suggest, John, William, James, and all the other refugees interviewed for this book, shared a fear of persecution, and those Burundi refugees residing illegally in Dar es Salaam—the overwhelming majority of the Burundi refugee population there—were afraid of being exposed as refugees. The experience of surviving genocide transformed these inherent fears into feelings of profound terror. Burundi refugees were raised to believe that the Tutsi, or their accomplices, could be anywhere at any time, planning to eliminate Hutu people. Such fears aligned with time-worn ethnic stereotypes suggesting Tutsi superiority and Hutu inferiority: should the two ever meet, most refugees believed that the Tutsi's innate cleverness would undermine Hutu defenses against them. The problem was, it may not ever be clear just who a Tutsi was, due to the fundamental ambiguity inherent in Central Africa's ethnic identities. While the Twa might be seen as a more or less distinct ethnic category (short and Pygmy-like), the colonial codification of Hutu and Tutsi was far more conclusive than the reality. Belgian overlords, Des Forges observed, "believed Tutsi, Hutu and Twa were three distinct, long-existent and internally coherent blocks of people, the local representatives of three major population groups, the Ethiopid, Bantu and Pygmoid" (1999: 36). But grounds for the ethnic—or, indeed, racial—differences the Belgians and other Europeans claimed to exist in Rwanda and Burundi were, over time, reduced to simple belief. The colonial rulers could only assert that the evolutionary scale they had designed was valid. "Unclear whether [the Tutsi, Hutu and Twa] were races, tribes, or language groups," Des Forges commented, "the Europeans were nonetheless certain that the Tutsi were superior to the Hutu and the Hutu superior to the Twa—just as they knew themselves to be superior to all three" (ibid.).

Alongside the myth of Tutsi (and European) superiority was the myth of Hutu inferiority. If this belief in the Hutu's own inherent inferiority has led many Hutu themselves towards self-hatred, it may have been supported by, and announced within, Burundian culture. A pamphlet published by the Centro Studi Michel Kayoya in the aftermath of the 1972 genocide in Burundi reflects on a finding uncovered by Father Rodegem, the Catholic Priest, scholar and author of a number of books on Burundi. Rodegem, the pamphlet states, "has been able to [establish] that a notable percentage of the names collected in Burundi express hate, rivalry, enmity" (Centro Studi Michel Kayoya 1975: 9). It then proceeds to list five examples of Burundian surnames that support the claim—Nzikobanyanka (I know I am hated), Barampama (I am persecuted), Bandyambona (I am eaten alive), Barampema (I am laughed at), and Ndimurwanko (I live in enmity)—and contends that these sorts of names, still very much in use in Burundi, "reveal internal tensions and rivalries that rage within a group; the permanent enmities, endogenous source of conflicts; the violent or obsessive antagonism which go as far as the creation of such names for the babies born to them" (ibid.).

While the issue of Hutu self-hatred extends beyond the bounds of the research undertaken, and will only be suggested here, the subject of collective victimization does not. As Uvin has described, Hutu and Tutsi in Rwanda and Burundi feel victimized by their ethnic adversaries. "The Tutsi," he noted, "increasingly define themselves as a small minority faced by a genocidal majority, while the Hutu image of itself as a socially marginalized, forever misunderstood and exploited majority has become greatly strengthened" (1999: 267–68). For the case of John, William, James, and virtually every Burundi refugee interviewed in Dar es Salaam, the sense that the Tutsi and their spies lurked in the shadows of their urban lives was ever-present. They often felt trapped by unseen Tutsi hands, whose innate superiority made a Hutu victory over them seem virtually impossible, particularly when the Burundi refugee community was divided upon itself and the rival refugee group (Imbo or Banyaruguru) was thought to be aligned with their hidden Tutsi enemies.

This state of affairs had an array of consequences for Burundi refugees in town, the most pervasive of which was fear. This fear was experienced at a personal level which mirrored that on a larger scale. While it has been argued here that the succession of inter-locking violent events in Rwanda and Burundi made fear a critical element in the region's collective psychology and culture, Uvin has contended that, of the two, fear has played an even larger role in Burundi, where "the most prevalent motive for violence is fear" (ibid.: 263). The events of the 1972 genocide still "constitute the defining moments in independent Burundi's history," Uvin argues, having "crystallized Hutu and Tutsi identities and created a climate of permanent mutual fear" (Uvin 1999: 258).

The extent and power of this high level of collective fear is dram-atized by the cultural fear felt by John, William, James, and their second generation Burundi refugee colleagues in Dar es Salaam. Cultural fear was the product of fear and trauma that the older refugee generation had transferred, through stories of Tutsi domi-nation and surviving genocide, to a younger generation that had not experienced genocidal killing first-hand but acted as if it had. The traumatizing experience of surviving the genocide that took place either before they were born or when they were very young children dominated their emotional lives in the Tanzanian capital.

Douglas and Wildavsky have observed how, for all of us, "Stand-ing inside our own culture, we can only look at our predicament through our culturally fabricated lens." In the case of young Burundi refugees, cultural fear was the lens through which they per-ceived reality. This explains why urban life for John, William, and James seemed far more threatening and dangerous to them than it would appear to an outside observer. The tensions, illegalities, and surveillance existing in everyday Dar es Salaam life exacerbated the refugees' tendency to feel terrorized when others, faced with similar circumstances, merely felt anxious.

If one applies Douglas and Wildavsky's concept of culture to Burundi refugee culture or, indeed, the cultures of Burundi or Rwanda, the idea of Central African cultures as traumatized comes into focus. According to Farrell's definition, Burundian and Rwan-dan cultures have been traumatized for many years, given that trau-matic injuries to individuals injure their cultures in the process: "In trauma, terror overwhelms not just the self, but the ground of the self, which is to say our trust in the world. In this way trauma is an injury not just to the central nervous system but also to the culture which sustains the body and soul" (1998: xii). Having experienced a succession of violent episodes—genocide among them—together with decades of political repression, it appears safe to assume that many, if not most, Burundian and Rwandan citizens have become traumatized, and perceive reality through cultural lenses that contain a degree of trauma, as well.

The definition of trauma in the Comprehensive Textbook on Psychiatry (1985) as a feeling of "intense fear, helplessness, loss of control, and threat of annihilation" (Andreasen, in Herman 1997: 33) links to Uvin's argument that Burundians are ruled by fear. It also supports the perception of Burundi as having a traumatized culture. Such a conception should undoubtedly apply to post-genocide Rwanda as well. Herman's own definition of trauma connects feelings of victimization more directly to the experience of trauma itself: "Psychological trauma is an affliction of the powerless. At the moment of trauma, the victim is rendered helpless by overwhelming force.… Traumatic events overwhelm the ordinary systems of care that give people a sense of control, connection, and meaning" (1997: 33). Both of these definitions describe the terrors, real and imagined, that continue to overwhelm Burundians and Rwandans. It may be that the creation of a national cosmology in Burundi refugee camps, which Malkki has described, will help Burundi, as a traumatized nation, address its "need to remember, grieve, and atone for their wrongs in order to avoid reliving them" (Herman 1997: 242). But there are signs that such a conclusion is premature. A Physicians for Human Rights (PHR) report, for example, has labeled Burundi "a profoundly sick society" in which Burundians still experience "physical violence, displacement from their homes, and an almost continuous state of terror" (PHR: 1994). Moreover, the national cosmology that Malkki described points to an imagined, Burundian Hutu entity existing separately from the Burundian Tutsi perpetrators of the genocide and their trauma. Two worlds, of enmity and hatred, still remain. Burundi seems a very long way from recovering from its violent and traumatic past and present.

The Pentecostal Present

Pentecostalism, with the ability, as Martin has described it, to "console and buttress those who lose from social change" (1990: 231), might seem a logical a kind of emotional bulwark against the tide of ethnic terror that Burundi refugees have faced. But the influence of Pentecostalism on refugee lives was actually more complicated than this. On the one hand, Pentecostalism could help route a refugee's life towards moral and economic success. The "high ethical demand" on African Pentecostals, which Kalu has described (1997: 15), served as a road map away from sinful temptations and towards quiet success for urban refugees seeking to succeed in Dar es Salaam. Pentecostal services also provided a safe place where Burundi refugee youth could play a community role while hiding in the city. During church services, they could sing in a choir, perhaps occasionally as a featured soloist, lead the congregation in prayers, or read scripture. There was also the opportunity to receive spiritual support, consolation and, to some extent at least, power through prayer, a critical component of every Pentecostal church service and a mainstay in the lives of most Pentecostal refugees.

On the other hand, the refugees did not feel that their Pentecostal faith provided them with impermeable protection against perceived evils, despite Kalu's claims that it lent believers "power over evil powers" (ibid.). Faith may help keep one away from Satanic temptations in bars or at the cinema, but being a Pentecostal did not seem able to protect anyone against Tutsi evil. William, one of the most fervent Pentecostal believers among the refugee tailors, was also one of the most fearful of invasions by Tutsi, or Tutsi accomplices. That Pastor Albert urged eventual reconciliation with Tutsi adversaries, whom the tailors believed were much more powerful than they were, was undoubtedly unnerving to them. The problem, as Pastor Albert viewed it, lay in "the [ethnic] discrimination. It's still inside all of the Burundian churches and everywhere else." Peace and protection, Albert continued, would only come through "peaceful resolution." However, Hutu political leaders "want confrontation [with the Tutsi] and that will never solve the problem. There is no answer in their methods. They want the impossible from the [Tutsi] government. In reality, they want to replace the government, and the government knows this, so the deadlock is always there." The specter of ethnic stalemate and vengeful violence between Burundians kept the refugee's future in limbo. It also coated their present with an uncertainty that kept imaginings of Tutsi invaders alive and limited the Pentecostal church's ability to provide, in Cox's words, a "powerful cosmic ally" against "sinister powers" (1995: 259).

Africa's Urban Refugee Phenomenon

As migrant refugees, the youthful, mostly male, Pentecostal-dominated Burundi refugee population in Dar es Salaam represent both the emergence of a new kind of African refugee and an example of the continent's surge toward cities and Pentecostalist faiths.

That urban refugee populations in Africa have been growing has already been demonstrated. To begin with, a growing body of research has posited that "most refugees in Africa are spontaneously settled" and not residing in refugee camps or settlements (Kuhlman 1994: 124). Local governments and the United Nations High Commissioner for Refugees (UNHCR) are aware of this: by 1989, Cuenod was able to estimate that three quarters of all African refugees were living outside planned settlements (Cuenod 1989: 8, cited in Kuhlman 1994). As a result, refugees may only be accepting the combined local government and international community's offer of assistance and protection in camps if they are unable to leave them. If refugees, and refugee men in particular, can leave the settlements, no regulation seems able to stop them. Because most refugees live outside camps illegally, however, they are difficult to track.

In response, UNHCR, whose mandate is to protect and assist all refugees but whose funding constraints are considerable, tends to focus their attention on camp refugees. This presents refugees with a clear choice: either welcome the protections and provisions that camps promise to provide and UNHCR is mandated to assure, or accept considerable risks for the chance to pursue a life outside the camps. Many if not most refugees, given the chance, appear to be willingly assuming the risk of living outside the camps illegally. The result of this split in refugee demographics is that refugee camps may actually be the primary home only for those who reject the risks of spontaneous settlement. Refugees with the capital, savvy, or networks to survive outside camps do so. Indeed, as Kuhlman has observed, the decision to accept or reject settlement life "may be part of some refugees' survival strategy to let relatives who are less capable of fending for themselves live in a settlement where they can depend on aid" (1994: 130).

It thus should not be so surprising that women and children dominate settlement demographics. Indeed, the gender dimension of refugee sociocultural dynamics remains largely undescribed. If refugee camps contain mostly women and children, where have the refugee men gone? The gender imbalance in and of itself can be remarkable—in 1997, Koloumba, the largest of Guinea's camps for Sierra Leonean refugees, was 75 percent female, and "the number of young men in the camps continues to decrease" (Sommers 1997c: 18). This is indicative of a larger refugee phenomenon in which "those who are able to fend for themselves gradually drift out of the camps, while those who are not remain behind" (Kuhlman 1994: 130). Most of those refugees able to fend for themselves, it appears, are men.

As increasing numbers of these refugee men have set their sights on cities, they join the migrants in a movement from countryside to city that is transforming the continent. The refugees in urban Tanzania constitute a particularly useful case for examining this phenomenon. Dar es Salaam is, after all, the site of urbanization of the highest order, and Burundi refugees have lived within its borders for an uncommonly long period of time. Dar es Salaam, too, has a specific relationship to rural Tanzania, located as it is "in a multiethnic political economy, dependent on a poor and drought-susceptible agricultural hinterland" (Guyer 1987:7). Young Tanzanians have also been motivated to migrate to town as a means of escaping the boredom of and government restrictions on rural life. Omari's description of rural Tanzania underscores the impact of youth migration on local societies: "Many rural areas nowadays are left with old people. Go to the villages, and you will observe this phenomenon instantly as you set your foot there. Such a situation very much affects the development of the rural areas" (1981: 2).

Upon reaching the cities, the issue of gender for young urban refugee men again surfaces. Refugee youth in cities can be difficult to identify not only because they are actively hiding their identities but because they are part of a much larger phenomenon: the fact that young adult men tend to dominate urban migrant populations in Africa. In Dar es Salaam, the urban youth culture that emerged celebrated the youth's separation from the rest of society. Many believed that these young men were probably engaged in illegal economic activities and outright crime. It was also commonly believed that such youngsters were not merely acting "cheeky" when they used their *Lugha ya Wahuni* vocabulary–they were signifying their presence beyond the bounds of acceptable urban society. Living in a city dominated by young men, and influenced by their urban youth culture, made it much easier for the young male-dominated Burundi refugee contingent in Dar es Salaam to hide.

The fact that most of these young, urban refugee men were also Pentecostals is part of a much larger phenomenon. In Dar es Salaam, the Pentecostal refugees' ability to dominate urban migration from the settlements was no doubt supported by what Martin called the Pentecostals' "protective network" (1990: 231). His description of such networks in Guatemala, for example, were echoed by Pentecostal missionary descriptions of Burundi refugees in Tanzania, which explained how the Pentecostal refugees sacrificed to help each other in Burundi refugee settlements. The expansion of this communal assistance between Pentecostal refugees to incorporate rural-urban networks seems to have only been a matter of time. It may well be that the pronounced linkage between successful urban migrant youth and Pentecostalism in Burundi refugee society is part of an emerging trend in African migration.

Finally, and particularly important in cases as seemingly intractable and harrowing as Burundi's, as surely as a first generation of refugees yields to a second, the second will yield to a third. Will a third refugee generation eschew its connections to its homeland and more directly identify with the host nation? Should they still be considered refugees in legal terms? Where, and by what means, will these refugees choose to live? Moreover, if refugee networks to cities continue to expand and stimulate a surge of urban migration, how will this affect their host nation's political and social environment? All of these questions have serious implications for the growth and stability of the great African cities of the twenty-first century.

Facing a Crisis

Kuogopa and *kujificha*; fear and hiding oneself. Near the end of the fieldwork period, it was possible to view a significant twist in the relationship between the two concepts that played such dominant roles in the lives of the refugee tailors.

A crisis in the lives of all Burundi refugees in Tanzania arrived early in 1992. It arose from plans to return Burundi refugees to their original homes in Burundi. A series of meetings in Tanzania, Burundi, and Switzerland between the UNHCR and Tanzanian and Burundian government officials produced a repatriation blueprint for Burundi refugees in Tanzania by late 1991. In it, there would be three options Burundi refugees could choose from: either voluntarily return to Burundi, elect Tanzanian citizenship, or maintain their refugee status in Tanzanian settlements.

In the ensuing months, Tanzanian and Burundian government officials visited the settlements in an effort to assure refugees that conditions in Burundi were stable and peaceful. UNHCR also dispatched delegates of refugees from all three Burundi refugee settlements to inspect conditions in Burundi and then report back to their settlement colleagues. Burundi officials warmly urged their return.

Some refugees immediately began repatriating: unofficial estimates reported that as many as twenty thousand refugees secretly returned to Burundi without any outside recognition or support. Their desire for secrecy was no doubt critical to their decision, because leaders from the two major refugee political parties (Palipehutu and Ubumwe) were reportedly pressuring refugees in the settlements to boycott the initiative until after their parties had assumed power in Burundi.

In Dar es Salaam, there were a series of meetings on the three future options. These meetings were attended by the elite refugee contingent in town. Non-elite refugees, nearly all of whom were in town illegally, stayed away. They disagreed with the condition of having free and fair elections before repatriating, which most elite refugees were insisting on. Many of the elites were representing themselves as spokesmen of the larger, Burundi refugee majority— *Watu wa Juu* (the High People) representing *Watu wa Chinichini* (the Very Low People). But many among the younger, non-elite male refugee majority set a different condition. All of those I interviewed on this issue maintained that their return to Burundi would only take place once the army was no longer dominated by Tutsi soldiers but became a joint, integrated Hutu and Tutsi institution. Luka was fond of repeating the non-elite refugee refrain on this: "The army is the government." Many also repeated what would happen to Hutu civilians if a Hutu were to be elected as President of Burundi: they would start warring with the Tutsi, and the conflict would force the refugee returnees to flee to Tanzania a second time.

In the second half of 1992, after I had left Tanzania, refugees were allowed to select their preferred option. A reliable source (who did not wish to be identified) reported that the overwhelming majority opted to retain refugee status. Others were preparing to return in 1993 after Melchior Ndadaye became Burundi's first Hutu President. President Ndadaye's subsequent assassination on October 21, 1993, and the ensuing conflict and outpouring of new refugees into Zaire, Tanzania, and Rwanda, halted the repatriation effort in its tracks.

Before these catastrophic events occurred, however, in late March 1992, something took place that illuminated the difference between refugee perceptions of danger and their consequent actions. Refugee apprehensions greatly increased when Minister Mrema, speaking to refugees at Mpanda settlement, announced that refugees had three months to decide whether to repatriate or become Tanzanian citizens, adding that "Tanzania did not want to entertain the idea of Burundi refugees becoming freedom fighters, especially when the situation in their country of origin that made them run away had changed in their favour" (Daily News 1992a: 1). Two days later, Mrema explained that "we are encouraging [the refugees] to go back to avoid forming another Burundi in Tanzania" (Kitururu 1992: 1). Commenting on Africa Refugee Day to the media in June 1992, Minister Mrema addressed the claims by "the emerging [refugee] political groups" of a conspiracy: that the Tanzanian and Burundian governments sought to lead refugees to their death in Burundi. In response, the Minister asked "What is so special about [the refugees] that the [Burundi] government would carry out a vendetta against Hutus who left the country 20 years ago?" He added that "We certainly cannot continue harbouring refugees indefinitely as this would create a political problem for us" (Daily News 1992b: 8).

Minister Mrema's dramatic March ultimatum, proclaimed in newspaper headlines and in Voice of Tanzania radio news broadcasts, was never upheld, but it effectively forced refugees to realistically reconsider their aspirations.[1] The fact that Mrema did not immediately mention the third option in the UNHCR-sponsored plan—retaining refugee status—agitated the entire refugee community. Everyone had to start considering what they would do, given the options. Some began to panic. Minister Mrema soon allowed that refugees could retain their refugee status, but since it was mentioned in the Daily News, an English language newspaper that few refugees could read, word of the third option spread slowly.

Augustine Mrema's zenith-like rise to the heights of popularity in Tanzania appears to have had no precedent in modern Tanzanian history. After assuming the post of Minister of Home Affairs in November 1990, he quickly became Tanzania's predominant populist figure. For a time, his flamboyant and highly public presence attracted almost daily attention, making him a common topic of conversation across Tanzania. Stories casting Mrema as a reformer, advocate for victims of injustice or leader against urban crime and filth made the newspapers on a regular basis. Mrema became a folk hero to many Tanzanians either because he made things happen or, at least, projected the appearance of constant reforming activity.

Many Burundi refugees seemed to believe that Minister Mrema had used his ultimatum to personalize his relationship with them. The refugees considered Mrema's statements not as part of a Tanzanian government initiative but a direct challenge from Mrema himself. This seemed to make every Burundi refugee I spoke with unusually uneasy. Some clearly felt terrified and helpless. Discussions about their future usually included direct references to the Minister.

The following descriptions compare stated concerns to eventual actions by John, William, and James. I could not record Luka's reactions, since he returned to Katumba just before Mrema issued his ultimatum. Luka stayed in Katumba for the remainder of my time in Tanzania.

John's Fear

John insisted that I have dinner with William and himself the night after Minister Mrema's announcement came across the local media. Before sitting down to an Imbo dinner of dried fish and *ugali*, which William had insisted upon, John and I spoke privately.

He was scared, to a degree that I had never seen before. "How can we decide in three months?" he asked. Then he turned to me: "Why did he [Mrema] do it?" Yet John's method for making this critical decision was characteristic of his personality. He insisted that "I can't talk to others! Not even to James! We must all decide for ourselves. I don't know what [others will] do. It's a private matter…. I can't have another's help. I must decide alone." John thus decided not to consult with anyone in town. His essential distrust and desire to maintain distance from other refugees meant he would have to solve this quandary by himself. The two options— to repatriate to Burundi or become a Tanzanian citizen–both filled him with considerable apprehension. "To be a refugee is anxiety" or "To be a refugee is fear" became his evening refrains. Returning to Burundi was impossible, he said, because he was convinced that "the Tutsi people will kill us, they will fight us." This thought awakened stories that family members had related about their flight from Burundi: ten relatives approaching starvation while sheltering under a tree because the Tutsi wanted to kill them all. These kinds of stories of hardship and terror–always caused by the same unquenchable Tutsi evil–made John's cultural fear particularly palpable during these uneasy days. In his view, repatriating to Burundi meant a certain, horrible death at the hands of Tutsi. The Tutsi, John explained, were unusually clever, untrustworthy and unspeakably vicious. You could not reason with them. He recalled when Pastor Albert mentioned to us that even when a Tutsi acts friendly toward a Hutu, in the back of his mind he wants to kill him.

Yet John also believed that he would be immersed in a sort of living purgatory if he became a Tanzanian citizen. Refugees used the verb *kukata* (to cut) to refer to accepting Tanzanian citizenship, for the act itself symbolized cutting oneself away from one's own Burundian identity forever. This option was considered drastic by most refugees that I interviewed, John among them: "If I get the Tanzanian [citizenship] paper, I'll only be apart from my family.... Our culture will be in Burundi, but I must stay [in Tanzania]." John assumed that his parents and younger siblings would all repatriate, but that he would not. Why? "Because I'm already accustomed to Tanzania," he said. In the view of John's family, living and working in Dar es Salaam brought him closer to Tanzanians and enlarged the realm of personal opportunity. Unlike the rest of his family, John was no longer sequestered in Katumba. After much thought following dinner, and with great reluctance, John decided that he would become a Tanzanian citizen. Given the two options, it seemed he had no other choice.

Faced with the same two options, John later said he expected older refugees to repatriate because refugee life, for them, was so unbearable that "it was better [for them] to die in Burundi" than remain refugees in Tanzania. Returning to *kwetu* (our homeland) would be worth the risk. But it wasn't for John and for more than half of the refugee men that I interviewed during this period. One refugee youth explained their situation in the following way: "When [our families] go [to Burundi], we are lost. Our family traditions, our culture will be there ... with our families; [young refugee men] will be stranded in Tanzania, without family or our cultural traditions." This comment exemplifies how many young refugees felt somewhat distanced from Burundian culture. It did not seem theirs to own or inhabit–younger generation refugees accessed it through their elders. The traditions, the mythico-history and the fears that connected them to Burundian identification had be received from the generation of refugees who had fled Burundi in 1972.

Gender played a role, too, for while most unmarried young women lived with their parents and seemed destined to follow their parents' movements, many young men in town believed that they had to act independently, even if this meant being stuck in Tanzania. Even if they became Tanzanian citizens, they explained that, in their hearts, they would never actually become Tanzanian. If abandoned in the alien country of Tanzania, they would simply exist as exiles from Burundian culture.

William's Silence

William had little to say about Mrema's ultimatum. His infrequent comments consistently expressed his "grief" at the situation and his contention that "Yesu" (Jesus) would guide him. This perspective was characteristic of the views of a segment of young refugees in town, and it exasperated educated refugees who analyzed the situation in political terms. A number of refugee devotees to Pentecostal, Assemblies of God, or evangelical churches seemed passive in their reliance on Jesus for guidance, and it nourished a certain fatalism about possible Tutsi violence against them. William, for example, once said that he was prepared to go to heaven. Stating that he would only return to Burundi when God showed refugees the way, William also expected to die in Tanzania. For him, only divine intervention could resolve the Burundian situation satisfactorily enough to allow him to return "home." William also had no intention of accepting Tanzanian citizenship. Like a number of other devout Pentecostal refugees, William had decided to do nothing, put his trust in Jesus, and take his chances.

James's Calm

James once told me that he did not know what village he came from in Burundi. All he knew was that it was somewhere near the Tanzania border. His father, he explained, never told him and he never bothered to ask for details. They weren't necessary. Reflecting on the future, James related how his father's interpretation of the Pentecostal creed had led him to urge his children not to anticipate return to Burundi but accept their present situation in Tanzania instead:

> My father didn't want to explain [about Burundi]. He doesn't want us to hate others. He says we're all humans, so I never heard about differences between different kinds of people out there ... about the Tutsi there.... I've never been [to Burundi], so I don't know [the Tutsi's] character. I can live with all people, though. We're religious people [who] don't care about differences among people.

The fact that James had Tanzanian relatives separated him from virtually every young Burundi refugee I interviewed in Dar es Salaam. He implied that his family's border heritage erased inner quandaries over national identification because it had enabled his

Burundian family to settle in Tanzania: "I only know Tanzania, and [I will] get my citizenship. My father is from the border, but he'll never return [to Burundi]. He has a farm here now, and he gets a profit selling his surplus. He'll never return. [And] return to what? We don't know. My father has a life here." Refugees from the border area, James's statement implied, were sufficiently familiar with both countries before they became refugees that accepting host nation citizenship was a reasonable alternative. James was also the only refugee to use the verb *kupata* (to receive) with reference to obtaining Tanzanian citizenship (most refugees had used *kukata*, meaning "to cut"). While his peers felt that being forced to choose between repatriation and Tanzanian citizenship would mean permanent exile in Tanzania, the fact that James's family had come from a part of Burundi that bordered Tanzania lessened the significance of national affiliation for him. It made James an exception.

After the Burundi refugee community in Dar es Salaam initially responded to Minister Mrema's ultimatum with expressions of fear and agitation, few refugees ever acted on their concerns. Eventually anxieties over having to choose between returning to Burundi and accepting Tanzanian citizenship receded. Most Burundi refugees in Dar es Salaam simply continued everyday life, and returned their focus to their familiar set of anxieties, fears, and suspicions.

The refugees' inaction suggested an allegiance to refugee identification that stood above all others. Retaining refugee status meant retaining their clandestine situation in Dar es Salaam, which made their perception of Dar es Salaam as dangerous seem somewhat self-fulfilling. Vague talk about waiting for a safe time to return to Burundi surfaced in private conversations from time to time, yet the perception of the Tutsi as their evil oppressors kept that option remote. Refugee historians promoted the idea that the Tutsi would eventually slaughter them if they returned. At the same time, becoming a Tanzanian citizen was generally regarded as an unsavory option. The application process was expensive, Tanzanian authorities might either trick them and send them back to Burundi or ask for bribes, and besides, Tanzanians would treat them as undesirable refugees whether they became citizens or not. It did not seem worth the bother. Mrema's ultimatum had not, in the end, transformed the lives of the young Burundi refugees in town at all. Excepting James, it merely strengthened their identification as refugees.

Turning Outward

By the end of the fieldwork period, in mid-1992, the refugee tailors that had become my informants had all decided to engage in one new leisure activity. This enlarged the boundaries of their urban lives, and signaled an enhanced degree of comfort in town.

This process began even before Mrema's ultimatum. Luka, who left Dar es Salaam as repatriation plans were still being developed, was, as always, a dramatic case in point. One steamy afternoon, while sitting in Pastor Albert's tailoring shop, Luka suddenly asked me a question about his favorite pastime: the cinema. How many people are watching, he inquired, when a woman takes her shirt off in front of a movie camera? I guessed about thirty people, which yielded a huge grin from Luka together with his trademark thumb's up sign. It also produced an embarrassed smile from John and a dark scowl from William. To Luka, movies revealed fascinating avenues into life in the West, while demonstrating Western decadence and immorality, and Luka's evident fascination with sin, to William.

This brief exchange in the tailoring shop illuminated the different directions that the refugee tailors had chosen as they settled into urban life. While retaining the necessary precautions for continuing a clandestine existence, they had selected something new to do outside of the church and their shop. For Luka, it was irregular but obviously memorable visits to Dar es Salaam's only drive-in theater. There he joined Tanzanians in buying spiced cassava or soda from vendors and sitting in the field beyond the drive-in walls, gazing up at the huge movie screen in the distance. For William, the activity of choice was venturing to Pentecostal crusades in different parts of town. On such occasions, William left the shop before it closed at dusk and returned to eat a late dinner, saying little about his evening adventures.

For James, it was a walk at dusk. He referred to his evening strolls with the slang phrase *kunyoshanyosha miguu* (to make shoes straight), which meant walking slowly without any definite destination. He loved to walk casually around his immediate neighborhood and chat with people he knew. Though James never ventured far from his tailoring shop, an apparent precaution against dangerous encounters, he was at ease in the familiar setting that his neighborhood offered.

John kept the details of his new activity almost as concealed as William did. He loved to voyage either alone or with Marko to

Bongoland's central market at daybreak on Sundays, when shops were closed and streets were virtually empty. It was the only time that venturing there felt safe. Leaving at that time also meant that John wasn't around to be scolded by William, Pastor Albert, and Mama for not going to church. And so every Sunday morning John exited into his own ritual, a quiet walk into the city he had come to love.

Note

1. This incident was also examined in Sommers 1993.

Epilogue

The Forgotten People

The years since the end of the fieldwork period for this book (mid-1992) have been unusually tumultuous and unforgiving for Burundians. Yet the immediate signs for the future in 1992 were almost entirely positive. The government-endorsed constitution in March of 1992, which had set the stage for attempts to persuade Burundi refugees to repatriate (described in the previous chapter), were followed by the rise to prominence of an opposition party called Frodebu (Front pour la démocratie au Burundi). Formed by a cadre of Hutu intellectuals who had been refugees following the 1972 genocide, and "against all odds" (Lemarchand 1996b: 178), Frodebu swept into power following the general election of June 1993. Stunningly, after three decades of Tutsi hegemony, the last two of which were marked by severe state repression against Hutu civilians, Burundi had held a multiparty election that was widely thought to be free and fair. The election had produced Burundi's first Hutu President, an engineer-turned-politician named Melchior Ndadaye.

The democratic miracle proved a mirage. Soon after the election, on July 2, 1993, forty Tutsi soldiers attempted to overthrow Ndadaye even before he had officially assumed power. They failed, and Ndadaye charged ahead with a distinctly multi-ethnic government and plans for expanding democratic reforms. Tragically, former President Pierre Buyoya's four and a half years of preparations for a multiparty democracy in Burundi had failed to adequately heed the non-elite Burundi refugee refrain that "the army is the government." In this particular refugee view, democracy in Burundi is considered dangerous if dramatic national army reforms do not take place first. The non-elite refugees maintained that only a truly multi-ethnic army could pave the way for lasting peace and democracy in Burundi. They were right. On October 20, 1993, members of the armed forces again staged a coup, and this time they succeeded.

News of Ndadaye's assassination further demonstrated the power, pervasiveness, and lasting influence of the 1972 genocide over Burundians. Memories of those terrible times inspired pre-emptive strikes by Hutu civilians against Tutsi neighbors and authority figures across the country, something that also took place on a smaller scale in northern Burundi in 1988, when, as one Hutu survivor noted, "Everyone was saying '1972! 1972!'" when army soldiers advanced (Watson 1989: 53). Lemarchand characterized the 1988 violence as marked by, for Hutu civilians at least, "a sudden outburst of rage, followed by intense fears of an impending reenactment of the 1972 carnage" (Lemarchand 1996b: 128). Five years later, in the wake of Ndadaye's fall, Lemarchand similarly described the immediate and violent reactions of Hutu civilians against their Tutsi compatriots: as a "spontaneous outburst of rage fueled by memories of 1972" (Lemarchand 1996a: 8).

There was one very significant difference, however, between the violence that exploded in Burundi in 1988 and 1993. In 1988, massacres carried out by Hutu civilians were followed by swift and extensive reprisals against them by the armed forces, leaving the estimated death toll at several thousand Tutsi and twenty thousand Hutu (Human Rights Watch 1998: 13). But within a few weeks the violence essentially ended. The violence starting late in 1993, on the other hand, has yet to end. It started with a similar spasm of Hutu massacres and Tutsi reprisals, though the violence stretched across a much larger geographic area of Burundi and left larger numbers of Burundians dead. One source estimated there were up to fifty thousand deaths, the casualties appearing to be equally divided between the two ethnic groups (ibid.: 15), while a second source thought the final figure was double that amount (Economist Intelligence Unit 1999: 46). Yet unlike the 1988 violence, the 1993 events have been followed by a spiral of destruction that has enveloped the entire Burundian population in a combination of despair, terror, and violence whose end, as of this writing, still seems distant.

This post-democracy period has witnessed a dramatic expansion of ethnically based parties and militias in Burundi. The Hutu side has been especially active in this regard. Though coalitions continue to form, ebb, and flow, their general disunity recalls the dismay

Burundi refugee elite men in Dar es Salaam regularly expressed to me about the inability of Hutu refugees to unite against their Tutsi enemies. Among those parties still involved is Palipehutu, though it has lost its standing as the dominant Burundi refugee party to the Conseil National pour la Défense del la Démocratie (CNDD). Still around, too, is Joseph Karumba, now based in southern Burundi and head of Frolina (Front de Libération National) (Africa Confidential 1999b: 2). Whether the current Frolina has fully absorbed the membership from Karumba's earlier, Imbo refugee-based party, which was mainly known as Ubumwe, is uncertain.

Locating, identifying, and assisting forcibly displaced Burundians has become a constant challenge for humanitarian and human rights groups. Since armed groups rarely battle each other directly, Hutu attacks on Tutsi civilians are inevitably followed by Tutsi attacks on Hutu civilians, and vice versa. This has caused massive displacements, internal and external, of Burundians over different periods of the conflict. The U.S. Committee for Refugees estimates that more than 500,000 Burundians (more than 8 percent of the total population) are internally displaced. Since the outbreak of violence in October 1993, a number of sources have approximated that two hundred thousand Burundians have been killed.

The chaotic instability emanating from Burundi's ongoing civil war make all figures necessarily unreliable. Statistics alone also cannot reflect the breadth of Burundi's forced displacement because tens, if not hundreds, of thousands of civilians have returned to their homes only to be displaced from them again. On the Hutu side, insurgent groups, Palipehutu and Frolina among them, are thought to have killed or displaced relatively few Tutsi, due to a number of factors, among them the fact that they are generally poorly equipped and have comparatively few targets—Tutsi civilians—to attack, since the Tutsi comprise a fairly small part of the Burundian population. Most Tutsi now live in areas well defended by the national army (Human Rights Watch 1998: 2).

Burundi's armed forces, on the other hand, have been employing a series of tactics to variously control, terrorize, and kill members of the Hutu majority. Perhaps their most notorious tactic was the creation of "regroupment" camps, wherein as many as seven hundred thousand Hutu civilians (out of a total population of approximately six million Burundians) were removed from their homes and ordered into specific locales under army control (Economist Intelligence Unit 1999). Among the Hutu civilians that the army has targeted for violence includes the chronically malnourished. The

Burundian army reportedly believes that "malnutrition is evidence of having lived in rebel-controlled areas where food is scarce" (Human Rights Watch 1998: 1–2). Together with the government, the army has been able largely to control the access of international humanitarian organizations to internally displaced Burundians. As a result, many members of the humanitarian community have accepted government and army restrictions while tens, and perhaps even hundreds, of thousands of displaced civilians remain unable to access their services.

As in 1972, the lion's share of the recent Burundi refugee population resides in Tanzania. Current population estimates hover around 300,000, nearly all of whom are in camps in Western Tanzania, though lately new influxes have steadily enlarged that figure. Significantly, current refugee statistics count only those Burundians who have become refugees since Ndadaye's assassination in 1993. Refugees from the 1972 genocide are not included. This is a new development, and it deserves some consideration. "Some 100,000 Burundians who settled in Tanzania in the 1960s, 1970s and 1980s," the U.S. Committee for Refugees (USCR) states, "are not included in [USCR's] refugee total" for Tanzania (USCR 1997: 63). These Burundians, a mixture of immigrants and refugees that included "the people of '72" among them, "appear to be socially and economically integrated into Tanzania and are largely self-sufficient. Although they are no longer considered to be refugees in need of protection or assistance, they live a 'refugee-like' existence" (ibid.). A UNHCR sub-office head interviewed in 1998 in western Tanzania further refined USCR's definition. The official explained that UNHCR now considered all Burundi refugees who had arrived in Tanzania before 1995 as "old caseload" refugees who "have not legalized their status and can look after themselves." Accordingly, UNHCR would "only look after the newcomers," providing "protection and support to them based on our mandate."

To be sure, the circumstances of the Burundi refugees who arrived in Tanzania following the 1972 genocide had not changed since the end of my fieldwork period in mid-1992. Most of them still lived in Katumba, Mishamo, and Ulyankulu settlements, while others resided in Dar es Salaam and a few other towns. Still others continued to live in Kigoma and in Tanzanian villages near the Burundian border. But the civil war in Burundi had dramatically altered how these refugees were perceived. The huge new influx of Burundi refugees had relegated "the people of '72" to the background. Their relative success at economic self-sufficiency, and their lengthy stay in Tanzania, had reduced their standing, in the eyes of international observers, as refugees. This had occurred even as the "old caseload" refugees' "fear of being persecuted" for returning to Burundi appeared to have become more "well-founded" after Ndadaye's death in 1993 than at any time since their original flight in 1972. The 1972 refugees have become a truly forgotten people.

The lack of adequate provisions for protecting these "old caseload" Burundi refugees in Tanzania was exposed in 1997–98 when the Tanzanian government embarked on a "round-up" of all Burundian nationals living in western Tanzania (Burundi refugees and migrants in other areas of Tanzania were not targeted). Despite its prior determination, following the outbreak of war in Burundi late in 1993, that all Burundian nationals in Tanzania "qualified for prima facie refugee status" (Human Rights Watch 1999: 9), the Tanzanian government nonetheless forcibly deposited nearly 100,000 Burundians into Burundian refugee camps near the Burundi border (Sommers 1998a).

Late in 1996, just before this round-up in western Tanzania began, I was able to briefly visit Dar es Salaam. In many ways, not much seemed to have changed. Broken streetlights still kept city streets almost completely dark at night. Augustine Mrema was still dominating the newspaper headlines, only this time as an opposition party leader. Tanzania's founding President, Julius Nyerere, had figured heavily in Mrema's break with the ruling CCM party by "following him around the country and making better speeches to the *wananchi*" (citizens) (Africa Confidential 1999a: 1) during the campaign for the CCM presidential nomination in 1995 (Nyerere's chosen candidate, Benjamin Mkapa won that nomination and was then elected to succeed another of Nyerere's chosen candidates, Ali Hassan Mwinyi, as Tanzania's President).

Though there were a number of signs of improvement in Dar es Salaam, such as repaired roads, an improved telephone network and the introduction of both email and television broadcasting (Tanzania was the last country in Africa to make this last move), the press of urban growth was more noticeable than ever. More cars and more kiosks brought increased traffic problems. Urban and peri-urban neighborhoods around the city's edges had continued to expand.

Dar es Salaam's garbage removal had also remained as an issue of national debate. In 1996, I arrived in Dar es Salaam during "Dar es Salaam City Cleanliness Week," a campaign announced by Prime Minister Frederick Sumaye to inspire city residents "to participate in city development programmes morally and materially instead of relying on donor assistance" (Mbiro 1996: 1). In a front page editorial supporting Sumaye's initiative (entitled "Yes, let us always keep Dar clean") the *Daily News* reflected on how "Dar es Salaam has over time been sinking deeper and deeper into an abyss of garbage" (1996: 1). In an almost comic twist, the development potential of garbage had also made the front page of the *Daily News* the month before. Pantaleon Chuwa, a microbiologist at the University of Dar es Salaam, presented a paper estimating that ten to 13 percent of the two thousand tons of solid waste daily produced by Dar es Salaam residents consisted of organic waste arising from marketplaces which "can be used to grow [edible] mushrooms" (Mgusi 1996: 1). Tanzania's Minister for Science, Technology and Higher Education immediately responded by declaring that "the government will put the knowledge into practical application as a tool of economic and social development" (ibid.).

During my visit, I was delighted to find that no amount of garbage on the street—or in stories in the press—could suppress the vibrancy of the urban youth's *Lugha ya Wahuni*. There had continued to be an outpouring of new words and phrases. Kids had concocted one set for use during their attempts to find employment. Before venturing forth, a youth might tell his friend "*Nakwenda juu*" (I'm going up). If his attempt to secure employment had failed, the youth would explain that "*Nimeteremka chini*" (I've come back down). My giving a tie to Marko as a gift revealed another new phrase. Holding the gift in his hands, he thanked me for the *Clinton tie*. A *Clinton tie*, Marko explained, was a wide tie, the same as those worn by U.S. President Bill Clinton. Several youths hawking ties downtown later confirmed that *Clinton ties* had become high fashion in Dar es Salaam.

In my visit to the neighborhood where John, William, James, and Pastor Albert had all lived and worked during my fieldwork period, I saw a number of changes in their lives, some upbeat, others truly tragic. James had previously written to tell me that he had married Pastor Albert's eldest daughter, but there was more news after arriving at his house. The newlyweds had just had a child and lived together in a rented room across the street from his former tailoring shop. The room was thickly furnished, with a double bed, a full sofa set and a bureau containing dishes and clothes. Sitting there in his room, next to his wife and young daughter, James looked more content and calm than I had ever seen.

James was obviously doing well in Bongoland. He explained that he had finally left Amosi's shop across the street a year ago and carried out the plan he had described to me many years before. He had bought two sewing machines, rented a small storefront in another part of the city, hired another tailor, and started his own tailoring business. He still did not know how to make a suitcoat, but explained that another refugee tailor in town was teaching him how to do it.

James had hired a Tanzanian, not a Burundi refugee, to work as his assistant in his tailoring shop, and it proved only one of many signs of his growing separation from many of the other refugees in town. For the first time, James talked with me about refugee politics. "I don't like segregation, so I stay away from politics," he explained. James explained that he felt John and William both hated him because they believed he was untrustworthy, and blamed both of them—John the Banyaruguru and William the Imbo—for being involved in the "*ubaguzi*" (segregation), which he clearly despised. He seemed especially bitter about John, his cousin, who "didn't share his ideas and always stayed separate" from him.

Even so, James wanted to talk about the "segregation" in Imbo and Banyaruguru politics. "Ubumwe is for the Imbo only," James explained, but since there were only a small number of party members, their leader, Joseph Karumba, "is not powerful." James also condemned Palipehutu, the leading Banyaruguru party, because "they just want violence." His preferred politician was Leonard Nyangoma, the CNDD leader, whom he lauded for allowing "all Burundians in: Imbo, Banyaruguru, even Tutsi."

James also mentioned that his parents had returned to Burundi following Ndadaye's election as President. He said "they were not worried about war because they live near the border." When civil war eventually reached their home area in Burundi, James's parents simply returned to Tanzania. James explained that his parents then sent two of his siblings, a younger brother aged twenty-two and a sister aged twenty, to Dar es Salaam. He did not elaborate on where they lived or what they were doing in town.

I asked James for news about other refugees that I had known. John, he said, had shifted to another refugee tailoring shop in Dar es Salaam and married a woman in Katumba settlement. His wife remained in Katumba raising their two children. William had left Dar es Salaam for good in 1993, traveling to Arusha for a job in a refugee tailoring shop that, in the end, did not materialize. James said he'd heard that William was back home in Ulyankulu settlement. James also mentioned Marko, but only said "he's different." James's wife, Pastor Albert's daughter, explained that they were not sure why Marko was so troubled, though she said her father knew why. Albert had once told her that "it was important to know about Marko's past," but then refused to elaborate.

While John, William, and Marko had retained their refugee identities, James had made another change in his life. Together with five other Burundi refugees in his Pentecostal church congregation, James was applying for Tanzanian citizenship. The example of tens of thousands of "old caseload" Rwandan refugees, who had returned to Rwanda following the 1994 genocide after entering Tanzania beginning in 1959, had made a strong impression on James. Julius Nyerere had awarded these "old caseload" Rwandan refugees Tanzanian citizenship (even if they were not seeking it), yet the refugees returned to Rwanda thirty-five years later, and did so peacefully. This proved to James that he could cross between Tanzania and Burundi as easily as the Rwandans had repatriated to Rwanda or, indeed, as his parents commuted across the Burundi-Tanzania border.

I did not find John in town when I visited his new tailoring shop. Marko was there, however, if only as a visitor, together with one of John's new tailoring colleagues. He seemed to have aged considerably since I last saw him. He remained hesitant and soft-spoken, with a look of worry deeply etched across his face. Marko said he now worked for a small tailoring shop located just near the ocean. But he had not returned to the ocean shore since he accompanied John and myself there years before.

Marko had much to say about John, with whom he seemed to have patched up his relationship. John now regularly went to church, he said. He said neither he nor John had yet learned to make a suitcoat, but Marko was aware that James was now learning that skill; recognition of James's relative success compared to John and himself. Marko also said that John would not be returning to Dar es Salaam for another six weeks. This was due to the fact, he explained, that "there are so many people coming to Dar es Salaam these days, including from the refugee camps, that all the trains are booked." After Marko introduced us, the sole tailor working in the shop whispered that he was from Katumba.

Just before leaving Bongoland, I finally met with Pastor Albert. I had visited his home twice previously, but each time was told that he was working. On the first visit I also entered the same tailoring shop adjoining his house that I had regularly frequented when John, William and Luka worked there. There were four new young men working there (Albert later confirmed that they were all refugees from the settlements), and the shop's atmosphere seemed as tense as ever. No radio played, the men worked in silence, and they responded to my greetings and questions as John and William used to respond to strangers: by being brief, sullen, and evasive. "Where is Pastor Albert?" I asked. "Out," came the reply. "Where did he go?" I inquired. "He's working." "When might he come back?" I asked again. "I don't know," one of the tailors answered.

I was shocked by Pastor Albert's appearance when I finally met him one evening at his house. He had aged considerably. He looked tired and haggard, his memorable smile replaced with an expression of deep sadness. He was in mourning: Mama had died a few months earlier. She had been standing in line at a petrol station, waiting to fill a container with kerosene. Somehow the kerosene had caught fire. An explosion followed, and Mama was among those who had burned to death. After he told me this, I suddenly realized that I was sitting on the left-hand side of the sofa and beneath a framed photo of Albert and Mama (with Albert grinning and Mama looking, as always, serious), the place in the living room where she had always sat. The room fell into an uncomfortable silence, after which I expressed my shock and condolence.

I was grateful when Pastor Albert changed the subject to mention his delight at having recently become a grandfather. He then shifted our discussion to politics. "Most refugees want their rights as refugees respected while in Tanzania," he said, "but keep their Burundian citizenship, too." He was convinced that, left on their own, Burundian Hutu and Tutsi could not settle the war peacefully. He suggested employing a multinational African military force "to force peace" in Burundi. If this happened, Pastor Albert explained, "then the Hutu and the Tutsi could learn to love each other and live together." Albert concluded his plan for lasting peace for his country of origin, but one he no longer was a citizen of, with a changed, brightened expression. Cultivating love and togetherness between ethnic enemies would require guidance from above. "Only God," he said, gently but confidently, "can heal the Hutu and the Tutsi."

Bibliography

Abrahams, R.G. 1987. Sungusungu: Village Vigilante Groups in Tanzania. *African Affairs* 86: 179–196.

Andreasen, N. C. 1985. Posttraumatic Stress Disorder. In *Comprehensive Textbook of Psychiatry, 4th ed.*, H. I. Kaplan and B. J. Sadock, eds. 918–24. Baltimore: Williams and Wilkins.

Africa Confidential. 1999a. After Mwalimu. *Africa Confidential* 40(21) (October 22): 1.

———. 1999b. Losing a peacemaker. *Africa Confidential* 40(21) (October 22): 2.

African Rights. 1995. *Rwanda: Death, Despair and Defiance*. London: African Rights (Revised Edition).

Albert, Ethel M. 1963. Women of Burundi: A Study of Social Values. In *Women of Tropical Africa*, Denise Paulme, ed. 179–215. Berkeley and Los Angeles: University of California Press.

Anduru, Agoro. 1982. *This is Living and Other Stories*. Dar es Salaam: Press and Publicity Centre.

Ankerl, Guy. 1986. *Urbanization Overspeed in Tropical Africa, 1970–2000: Facts, Social Problems, and Policy*. Geneva: INU Societal Research Series, Dirk Pereboom, ed. INU Press, Interuniversity Institute.

Armstrong, Allen M. 1988. Aspects of Refugee Wellbeing in Settlement Schemes: An Examination of the Tanzanian Case. *Journal of Refugee Studies* 1(1): 57–73.

———. 1987a. *Urban Control Campaigns in the Third World: The Case of Tanzania*. Occasional Paper Series, No. 19. Glasgow: Department of Geography, University of Glasgow.

———. 1987b. *Evolving Approaches to Planning and Management of Refugee Settlements: The Tanzanian Experience*. Dar es Salaam: Tanganyika Christian Refugee Service, Special Report No. 3.

———. 1986. *Motivating Tanzania's Refugee Communities*. Dar es Salaam: Tanganyika Christian Refugee Service, Feature Report, October.

Armstrong, Allen M., and M.L. Garry. 1988. *Development Status Report on Mpanda District, Rukwa*. Dar es Salaam: Tanganyika Christian Refugee Service, October.

Aronson, Dan R. 1980. *The City is our Farm: Seven Migrant Ijebu Yoruba Families*. Cambridge: Schenkman Books (Second Edition).

Ayok, A.C., and M. Mbago. 1987. *Problems and Prospects for Integration of Burundi Refugees in Tanzania: A Case Study of Katumba and Ulyankulu Settlements*. Refugee Management Series, No. 2.

Baker, Jonathan, and Tade Akin Aina. 1995. *The Migration Experience in Africa.* Uppsala: Nordsika Afrikainstitutet.

Balfour, Patrick. 1939. *Lords of the Equator: An African Journey.* London: Hutchinson and Co.

Barke, Michael and Clive Sowden. 1992. Population change in Tanzania 1978–88: a preliminary analysis. *Scottish Geographical Magazine* 108(1): 9–16.

Bascom, Johnathan. 1995. The New Nomads: An Overview of Involuntary Migration in Africa. In *The Migration Experience in Africa,* Jonathan Baker and Tade Akin Aina, eds. 197–219. Sweden: Nordiska Africainstitutet.

Belgian Congo and Ruanda-Urundi Information and Public Relations Office. 1960. *Ruanda-Urundi: Geography and History.* Translated from French by Goldie Blankoff-Scarr. Brussels: Belgian Congo and Ruanda-Urundi Information and Public Relations Office.

Bernhard, H. Russell. 1988. *Research Methods in Cultural Anthropology.* Newbury Park, London, New Delhi: Sage Publications.

Bohannan, Paul. 1960. Conscience Collective and Culture. In *Essays on Sociology and Philosophy, Emile Durkheim et* al. Kurt H. Wolff, ed. 77–96. New York: Harper and Row.

Briggs, John. 1993. Population change in Tanzania: a cautionary note for the city of Dar es Salaam (Comment). *Scottish Geographical Magazine* 109(2): 117–118.

———. 1991. The peri-urban zone of Dar es Salaam, Tanzania: recent trends and changes in agricultural land use. *Transactions of the Institute of British Geographers (New Series)* 16(3): 319–331.

Centro Studi Michel Kayoya. 1975. *Burundi: An atrocious tragedy which leaves the world unconcerned.* Brescia (Italy): Centro Studi Michel Kayoya.

Chant, Sylvia and Sarah A. Radcliffe. 1992. Migration and development: the importance of gender. In *Gender and Migration in Developing Countries,* Sylvia Chant, ed. 1–29. London and New York: Belhaven Press.

Che-Mponda, Chemi. 1993. Be wary of trouble makers Mrema. *Daily News* (Tanzania) May 7: 3.

Chrétien, Jean-Pierre. 1985. Hutu et Tutsi au Rwanda et au Burundi. In *Au Cœur de l'Ethnie: Ethnies, Tribalisme et État en Afrique,* Jean-Loup Amselle and Elikia M'Bokolo, eds. 129–165. Paris: Éditions la Découverte.

Christensen, Hanne. 1985. *Refugees and Pioneers.* Geneva: UN Research Institute for Social Development.

Clark, Lance. 1987. *Country Reports on Five Key Asylum countries in Eastern and Southern Africa.* Washington, D.C.: Refugee Policy Group (April).

Colson, Elizabeth. 1971. *The Social Consequences of Resettlement: The Impact of the Kariba Resettlement upon the Gwembe Tonga.* Manchester: Manchester University Press. Published on behalf of The Institute for African Studies, University of Zambia.

Cox, Harvey. 1995. *Fire from Heaven: The Rise of Pentecostal Spirituality and the Reshaping of Religion in the Twenty-first Century.* Reading, MA, Menlo Park, CA, New York, et.al.: Addison-Wesley.

Cuenod, J. 1989. EC Assistance to Regions with Large Numbers of Refugees. Paper presented at the International Conference on Refugees in the World: The European Community's Response, held at The Hague, Netherlands, December 7–8.

Daily News (Tanzania). 1996. Yes, let us always keep Dar clean (Comment). *Daily News* October 8: 1.

——. 1993a. Mwinyi cites youth help priority area. *Daily News* June 15: 1.

——. 1993b. Mrema calls for *sungusungu* revival. *Daily News* September 2: 5.

——. 1993c. Hawkers go on rampage: shops looted, several hurt. *Daily News* September 4: 1.

——. 1992a. Mrema gives option to Burundi refugees. *Daily News* March 27: 1.

——. 1992b. Tanzania: Home of the persecuted. *Daily News* June 20: 8.

Daley, Patricia. 1991a. Gender, Displacement and Social Reproduction: Settling Burundi Refugees in Western Tanzania. *Journal of Refugee Studies* 4(3): 248–266.

——. 1991b. The Politics of the Refugee Crisis in Tanzania. In *The IMF and Tanzania*, Horace Campbell and Howard Stein, eds. 175–199. Harare: Southern Africa Political Economy Series (SAPES) Trust.

Des Forges, Alison. 1999. *"Leave None to Tell the Story": Genocide in Rwanda.* Based on research by Alison Des Forges, Timothy Longman, Michele Wagner, Kirsti Lattu, Eric Gillet, Catherine Choquet, Trish Huddleston, and Jemera Rone. New York, Washington, London, Brussels: Human Rights Watch.

Douglas, Mary and Aaron Wildavsky. 1982. *Risk and Culture: An Essay on the Selection of Technical and Environmental Dangers.* Berkeley, Los Angeles, London: University of California Press.

Economist Intelligence Unit. 1999. *Rwanda Burundi: Country Profile 1999–2000.* London: Economist Intelligence Unit.

Farrell, Kirby. 1998. *Post-traumatic Culture: Injury and Interpretation in the Nineties.* Baltimore and London: Johns Hopkins University Press.

Finnegan, R. 1989. *The Hidden Musicians: Music-Making in an English Town.* Cambridge: Cambridge University Press.

Frederick, Adolphus, Duke of Mecklenburg. 1910. *In the Heart of Africa.* Translated by G.E. Maberly-Oppler. London, New York, Toronto and Melbourne: Cassell and Co.

Gasarasi, Charles P. 1987. The tripartite approach to the resettlement and integration of rural refugees in Tanzania. In *Refugees: A Third World Dilemma*, John R. Rogge, ed. 99–114. Totowa, NJ: Rowman and Littlefield.

Gifford, Paul. 1998. *African Christianity: Its Public Role.* Bloomington and Indianapolis: Indiana University Press.

Goffman, Erving. 1959. *The Presentation of Self in Everyday Life.* Garden City, New York: Doubleday Anchor Books.

Gourevitch, Philip. 1996. The Poisoned Country. *New York Review of Books*, June 6: 58–64.

Greenland, Jeremy. 1980. *Western Education in Burundi 1916–1973: The Consequences of Instrumentalism.* Brussels: Les Cahiers du CEDAF 2–3.

——. 1976. Ethnic Discrimination in Rwanda and Burundi. In *Case Studies on Human Rights and Fundamental Freedoms: A World Survey, Vol. IV*, Willem A. Veenhoven, ed.-in-chief. 97–133. The Hague: Martinus Nijhoff. Published for the Foundation for the Study of Plural Societies.

——. 1973. Black Racism in Burundi. *New Blackfriars* 54(640): 443–451.

Grohs, Gerhard. 1972. Slum Clearance in Dar es Salaam. In *Urban Challenge in East Africa*, John Hutton, ed. 157–176. Nairobi: East African Publishing House.

Guyer, Jane I. 1987. Introduction. In *Feeding African Cities: Studies in Regional Social History*, Jane I. Guyer, ed. 1–54. Bloomington and Indianapolis: Indiana University Press.

Hannerz, Ulf. 1992. *Cultural Complexity: Studies in the Social Organization of Meaning.* New York: Columbia University Press.

———. 1980. *Exploring the City: Inquiries Toward an Urban Anthropology.* New York: Columbia University Press.

Hansen, Art. 1990. *Refugee Self-Settlement Versus Settlement on Government Schemes: The Long-Term Consequences for Security, Integration and Economic Development of Angolan Refugees (1966–1989) in Zambia.* Geneva: United Nations Research Institute for Social Development (November).

Harris, Nigel. 1992. Introduction. In *Cities in the 1990s: The challenge for developing countries,* Nigel Harris, ed. ix-xxiii. New York: St. Martin's Press.

———. 1990. Urbanization, economic development and policy in developing countries. *Habitat International* 14(4):3–42.

Herman, Judith Lewis. 1997. *Trauma and Recovery.* Second edition. New York: Basic Books.

Hinnebusch, Thomas J. and Sarah M. Mirza. 1979. *Kiswahili: msingi wa kusema, kusoma na kuandika, Swahili: a foundation for speaking, reading and writing.* Lanham, MD, London, New York: University Press of America.

Hohensee, Donald. 1977. *Church Growth in Burundi.* South Pasadena, CA: William Carey Library.

Hope, Kempe Ronald, Sr. 1998. Urbanization and Urban Growth in Africa. *Journal of Asian and African Studies* 33(3): 345–358.

Horner, Rosalind. 1967. *The Nature of Political Conflict in Burundi.* Manchester, England: University of Manchester. Unpublished Masters Thesis.

Human Rights Watch. 1999. *In the Name of Security: Forced Round-Ups of Refugees in Tanzania.* New York: Human Rights Watch Report, Vol. 11 (4a) (July).

———. 1998. *Proxy Targets: Civilians in the War in Burundi.* New York, Washington, London, Brussels: Human Rights Watch.

Hyden, Goran. 1980. *Beyond Ujamaa in Tanzania: Underdevelopment and an Uncaptured Peasantry.* Berkeley and Los Angeles: University of California Press.

Iliffe, John. 1979. *A Modern History of Tanganyika.* Cambridge: Cambridge University Press.

Ishumi, Abel G.M. 1984. *The Urban Jobless in Eastern Africa: A Study of the Unemployed Population in the Growing Urban Centres, with Special Reference to Tanzania.* Uppsala: Scandinavian Institute of African Studies.

Kalabamu, Faustin T. 1992. Tanzania: Developing Urban Residential Land. *Journal of Urban Affairs* 14(1): 61–78.

Kalu, Ogbu U. 1997. The Third Response: Pentecostalism and the Reconstruction of Christian Experience in Africa, 1970–1995. Paper presented at the Yale-Edinburgh Seminar, Yale Divinity School, New Haven (June).

Kaluba, Saitiel. 1989. Local Government and the Management of Urban Services in Tanzania. In *African Cities in Crisis: Managing Rapid Urban Growth,* Richard E. Stren, and Rodney R. White, eds. 203–246. Boulder: Westview Press.

Karadawi, Ahmed. 1987. The Problem of Urban Refugees in Sudan. In *Refugees: A Third World Dilemma,* John R. Rogge, ed. 115–129. Totowa, NJ: Rowman and Littlefield.

Kerner, Donna O. 1988a. *The Social Uses of Knowledge in Contemporary Tanzania.* New York: City University of New York. Unpublished Dissertation.

———. 1988b. "Hard Work" and Informal Sector Trade in Tanzania. In *Traders Versus the State: Anthropological Approaches to Unofficial Economies,* Gracia Clark, ed. 41–56. Boulder and London: Westview Press.

Kesby, John D. 1977. *The Cultural Regions of East Africa.* London, New York, and San Francisco: Academic Press.

Kimenyi, Alexandre. 1989. *Kinyarwanda and Kirundi Names: A Semiolinguistic Analysis of Bantu Omomastics.* Lewiston, Queenston, and Lampeter: The Edward Mellen Press.

Kitururu, Moses. 1992. Burundi refugees plan return after assessing situation at home. *Sunday News* (Tanzania), March 29: 1.

Kopytoff, Igor. 1987. The Internal African Frontier: The Making of African Political Culture. In *The African Frontier: The Reproduction of Traditional African Societies,* Igor Kopytoff, ed. 3–84. Bloomington and Indianapolis: Indiana University Press.

Kuhlman, Tom. 1994. Organized Versus Spontaneous Settlement of Refugees in Africa. In *African Refugees: Development Aid and Repatriation,* Howard Adelman and John Sorensen, eds. 117–142. Boulder, San Francisco, Oxford: Westview Press; North York: York Lanes Press.

Lamb, David. 1982. *The Africans.* New York: Random House.

Last, Murray. 1991. Adolescents in a Muslim City: The Cultural Context of Danger and Risk. In *Kano Studies 1991: A Special Issue by the Youth Health group,* BUK, H.I. Said mni and Murray Last, guest editors. 1–21. Kano, Nigeria: Bayero University.

Lemarchand, René. 1996a. *Burundi: Genocide Forgotton, Invented and Anticipated.* Copenhagen: Centre of African Studies, University of Copenhagen. Occasional Paper.

——. 1996b. *Burundi: Ethnic Conflict and Genocide.* Cambridge and Melbourne: Woodrow Wilson Center Press and Cambridge University Press.

——. 1970. *Rwanda and Burundi.* New York, Washington, London: Praeger Publishers.

Lemarchand, René and David Martin. 1974. *Selective Genocide in Burundi* (Report No. 20). London: The Minority Rights Group.

Linden, Eugene. 1993. Megacities: Our Urban Future. *Time Magazine* 141(2): 28–38 (January 11).

Livre blanc sur les événements survenus aux mois d'avril et mai 1972. 1972. *Livre blanc sur les événements survenus aux mois d'avril et mai 1972.* Bujumbura: Ministère de l'Information.

Lugalla, Joe. 1995. *Crisis, Urbanization, and Urban Poverty in Tanzania.* Lanham, New York, London: University Press of America.

Lugusha, E. 1981. *Socio-Economic Survey of Burundi Refugees in Kigoma Region.* Dar es Salaam: Economic Research Bureau, University of Dar es Salaam.

Malkki, Liisa. 1996. The Poisoned Country (Letter to the Editor). *New York Review of Books,* September 19: 79.

——. 1995. *Purity and Exile: Violence, Memory, and National Cosmology among Hutu Refugees in Tanzania.* Chicago and London: University of Chicago Press.

——. 1990. Context and Consciousness: Local Conditions for the Production of Historical and National Thought among Hutu Refugees in Tanzania. In *Nationalist Ideologies and the Production of National Cultures,* Richard G. Fox, ed. 32–62. Washington, D.C.: American Anthropological Association. American Ethnological Society Monograph Series, No. 2.

——. 1989. Purity and Exile: Transformations in Historical-National Consciousness Among Hutu Refugees in Tanzania. Cambridge, MA: Unpublished Dissertation, Harvard University.

Makinson, Carolyn. 1993. Estimates of Adult Mortality in Burundi. *Journal of Biosocial Science* 25: 169–186.

Marshall, Ruth. 1991. Power in the Name of Jesus. *Review of African Political Economy* 52: 21–37.

Martin, David. 1990. *Tongues of Fire: The Explosion of Protestantism in Latin America.* Oxford, U.K., and Cambridge, MA: Blackwell Publishers.

Masamba, Nyambona. 1993. Dar es Salaam: City of kiosks. *Daily News* (Tanzania), June 6: 5.

Masendo, Zaphania. 1993a. NEMC criticizes valley invasion. *Daily News* (Tanzania), September 3: 1.

———. 1993b. Kariakoo Riots: Vendors blame the government. *Sunday News* (Tanzania), September 5: 1.

Maunya, Morice. 1993. Army of jobless haunts Nation. *Daily News* (Tanzania), August 3: 1.

Mayer, Philip, with contributions by Iona Mayer. 1971. *Townsmen or Tribesmen: Conservatism and the Process of Urbanization in a South African City.* Cape Town: Oxford University Press (Second Edition).

Mbiro, Michael. 1996. Dar residents told to keep city clean. *Daily News,* October 8: 1.

McGavran, Donald A. 1970. *Understanding Church Growth.* Grand Rapids: Eerdmans.

Mgusi, Constantine. 1996. Wastes may produce mushrooms–Don. *Daily News,* September 16: 1.

Mitchell, J. Clyde. 1969. The Concept and Use of Social Networks. In *Social Networks in Urban Situations: Analyses of Personal Relationships in Central African Towns,* J. Clyde Mitchell, ed. 1–50. Manchester: Manchester University Press. Published for the Institute for African Studies, University of Zambia.

Mwampembwa, G. 1991. ... East ... West Dar is Worst! *Daily News* (Tanzania), October 8: 3.

Nelson, Nici. 1992. The women who have left and those who have stayed behind: Rural-urban Migration in Central and Western Kenya. In *Gender and Migration in Developing Countries,* Sylvia Chant, ed. 109–137. London and New York: Belhaven Press.

Newbury, David S. 1980. The Clans of Rwanda: An Historical Hypothesis. *Africa* 50(4): 389–403.

Nyerere, Julius K. 1968. *Freedom and Socialism: A Selection from Writings and Speeches, 1965–67.* Dar es Salaam: Oxford University Press.

———. 1966. *Freedom and Unity: A Selection from Writings and Speeches, 1952–65.* Dar es Salaam: Oxford University Press.

Oberai, A.S. 1992. Population growth, employment and poverty in Third World mega-cities. *Courier* 131: 64–66.

Ogbru, Benjamin A. 1983. *Tanzania Refugee Caseload Survey.* Dar es Salaam: UNHCR, August.

Ogbu, Osita and Gerrishon Ikiara. 1995. The crisis of urbanization in sub-Saharan Africa. *Courier* 149 (Jan.-Feb.): 52–59.

Omari, C.K. 1981. *Youth and Development: Proceedings of the Workshop held at YMCA Moshi, Tanzania, September 20th-27th, 1980.* Dar es Salaam: National Council of Social Welfare and Services.

Physicians for Human Rights (PHR). 1994. Rwanda and its Aftermath: The Looming Crisis in Burundi. Adapted from a PHR delegation report by Benoit Nemery, Rosa Njee Befidi-Mengue, Anna Cirera Viladot, and Susan B. Walker. *Medicine & Global Survival* 1(3) (September): 125–127.

Pirouet, M. Louise. 1996. The Churches and Refugees in Africa. In *Christianity in Africa in the 1990s.* Christopher Fyfe and Andrew Walls, eds. 82–91. Edinburgh: Centre of African Studies, University of Edinburgh.

Prunier, Gérard. 1995. *The Rwanda Crisis: History of a Genocide.* New York: Columbia University Press.

Rakodi, Carole. 1997. Introduction. In *The Urban Challenge in Africa; Growth and Management of its Large Cities*, Carole Rakodi, ed. 1–13. Tokyo, New York and Paris: United Nations University Press.

Rechenbach, Charles W. 1967. *Swahili-English Dictionary.* Catholic University of America Press.

Reyntjens, Filip. 1995. *Burundi: Breaking the Cycle of Violence.* London: Minority Rights Group International.

Rogge, John R. 1986. Urban Refugees in Africa: Some Changing Dimensions to Africa's Refugee Problem, with Special Reference to Sudan. *Migration World* (Staten Island, NY) 14(4): 7–13.

———. 1985. *Too Many, Too Long: Sudan's Twenty Year Refugee Dilemma.* Totowa, NJ: Rowman and Allanhead Publishers.

Rutake, Pascal and Joseph Gahama. 1998. Ethnic Conflict in Burundi. In *Ethnic Conflicts in Africa*, Okwudiba Nnoli, ed. 79–103. Dakar: CODESRIA.

Sanjek, Roger. 1990. Urban Anthropology in the 1980s: A World View. *Annual Review of Anthropology* 19: 151–186.

Sawers, Larry. 1989. Urban Primacy in Tanzania. *Economic Development and Cultural Change* 37(4): 841–859.

Scott, James C. 1986. Everyday Forms of Peasant Resistance. *Journal of Peasant Studies* 13(2): 4–35.

———. 1985. *Weapons of the Weak: Everyday forms of Peasant Resistance.* New Haven: Yale University Press.

Scudder, Thayer and Elizabeth Colson. 1982. From Welfare to Development: A Conceptual Framework for the Analysis of Dislocated People. In *Involuntary Migration and Resettlement: The Problems and Responses of Dislocated People*, Art Hansen and Anthony Oliver-Smith, eds. Boulder: Westview Press.

Segamba, Léonce, and Vincent Ndikumasabo, Carolyn Makinson, and Mohamed Ayad. 1988. *Republique du Burundi: Enquête Démographique et de Santé au Burundi 1987.* Gitega, Burundi: Ministère de l'Intérieur, Départment de la Population, and Colombia, MD: Institute for Resource Development/Westinghouse.

Sommers, Marc. 1999. Urbanisation and its Discontents: Urban Refugees in Tanzania. *Forced Migration Review* 4(April): 22–24.

———. 1998a. *A Child's Nightmare: Burundian Children at Risk.* New York: Women's Commission for Refugee Women and Children.

———. 1998b. Power and the Powerless. *New Routes: A Journal of Peace Research and Action* 2(4): 11–12.

———. 1998c. *Reconciliation and Religion: Refugee churches in the Rwandan camps.* Uppsala: Life and Peace Institute. Occasional Paper.

———. 1997a. Book Review of Purity and Exile: Violence, Memory, and National Cosmology among Hutu Refugees in Tanzania, Liisa H. Malkki. *American Anthropologist* 99 (1): 38.

———. 1997b. Book Review of The Migration Experience in Africa, Baker, Jonathan and Tade Akin Aina, eds. *International Journal of African Historical Studies* 30(3): 636–638.

———. 1997c. *The Children's War: Towards Peace in Sierra Leone.* New York: Women's Commission for Refugee Women and Children.

———. 1995. Representing Refugees: The Role of Elites in Burundi Refugee Society. *Disasters* 19(1): 19–25.

———. 1994. Hiding in Bongoland: Identity Formulations and the Clandestine Life for Burundi Refugees in Urban Tanzania. Boston: Unpublished Dissertation, Boston University.

———. 1993. Confronting the Future: The Effects of the Repatriation Program on a New Generation of Burundi Refugees. *Refuge: Canada's Periodical on Refugees* 12(8): 27–29.

Speke, John Hanning. 1922. *Journal of the Discovery of the Source of the Nile.* London and Toronto: J.M. Dent and Sons; New York: E.P. Dutton and Co., Fourth Reprinting of first 1906 edition (Originally published in 1864, in New York: Harper).

Stren, Richard E., and Rodney R. White. 1989. *African Cities in Crisis: Managing Rapid Urban Growth.* Boulder, San Francisco and London: Westview Press.

Taylor, Christopher C. 1997. Sons of Kigwa, Sons of Kanyarwanda? The Hamitic Hypothesis in Rwanda and Burundi. Paper presented at the American Anthropological Society's Annual Meeting, Washington, DC, November 5 (unpublished).

Torrey, Barbara Boyle. 1998. We Need More Research on the Impact of Rapid Urban Growth. B6. *Chronicle of Higher Education,* October 23.

Tripp, Aili Mari. 1997. *Changing the Rules: The Politics of Liberalization and the Urban Informal Economy in Tanzania.* Berkeley, Los Angeles & London: University of California Press.

———. 1989a. *Defending the Right to Subsist: The State vs. the Urban Informal Economy in Tanzania.* Wider Working Paper No. 59, World Institute for Development Economics Research of the United Nations University. Helsinki: Wider Publications.

———. 1989b. Women and the Changing Urban Household Economy in Tanzania. *Journal of Modern African Studies* 27(4): 601–623

Tueros, Mario and Nichoderms B. Mwaduma. 1993. Policy Options and Insitutional Framework for the Promotion of the Informal Sector. Paper presented at the National Workshop on Informal Sector Policy in Tanzania, Dec. 1–3, in Morogoro, Tanzania.

Turner, Simon. 1998. Representing the Past in Exile: The Politics of National History among Burundian Refugees. *Refuge: Canada's Periodical on Refugees* 17(6): 22–29.

United Nations Department of Economic and Social Information and Policy Analysis. 1993. *World Urbanization Prospects: the 1992 Revision.* New York: United Nations.

United Nations Development Programme (UNDP). 1998. *Human Development Report 1998.* New York, Oxford: Oxford University Press.

United Nations High Commissioner for Refugees (UNHCR). 1998. *Refugees and Others of Concern to UNHCR: 1997 Statistical Overview.* Geneva: Statistical Unit, UNHCR.

———. 1995. *Collection of International Instruments and Other Legal Texts Concerning Refugees and Displaced Persons, Volume I: Universal Instruments.* Jean-Pierre Colombey, ed. Geneva: Division of International Protection of the Office of the United Nations High Commissioner for Refugees.

———. 1992. *Handbook on Procedures and Criteria for Determining Refugee Status: under the 1951 Convention and the 1967 Protocol relating to the Status of Refugees.* Geneva: UNHCR (reedited), (January).

U.S. Committee for Refugees (USCR). 1997. *World Refugee Survey 1997.* Washington, DC: Immigration and Refugee Services of America.

Uvin, Peter. 1999. Ethnicity and Power in Burundi and Rwanda: Different Paths to Mass Violence. *Comparative Politics* 31(3) (April): 253–271.

——. 1998. *Aiding Violence: The Development Enterprise in Rwanda.* West Hartford, CT: Kumarian Press.

Waller, David. 1996. *Rwanda: Which Way Now?* Oxford, UK: Oxfam (UK and Ireland).

Washokera, Ibra (Radi). 1992. *Wo Wo Wo: Scud La Vitabu.* Dar es Salaam: Jacaranda Publications, no. 2.

Watson, Catherine. 1993. *Transition in Burundi: The Context for a Homecoming.* Issue Paper, September. Washington, D.C.: U.S. Committee for Refugees.

——. 1989. After the Massacre. *Africa Report* 34(1) (January-February): 51–55.

Watts, Kenneth. 1992. Urban policies: some conclusions. *Courier* 131 (January-February): 62–63.

Weber, Max. 1958 [1904–1905]. *The Protestant Ethic and the Spirit of Capitalism.* Translated by Talcott Parsons. New York: Charles Scribner's Sons.

Weinstein, Warren. 1976. *Historical Dictionary of Burundi* (African Historical Dictionaries, No. 8). Metuchen, NJ: Scarecrow Press.

——. 1972. Tensions in Burundi. *Issue: A Quarterly Journal of Africanist Opinion* 2(4): 27–29.

Weinstein, Warren, with Robert Schrire. 1976. *Political Conflict and Ethnic Strategies: A Case Study of Burundi.* Syracuse, NY: Syracuse University, Maxwell School of Citizenship and Public Affairs, Foreign and Comparative Studies/Eastern Africa XXIII.

World Resources Institute and International Institute for Environment and Development. 1988. *World Resources 1988–89.* New York: Basic Books.

Index

Studies in Forced Migration

General Editors: **Dawn Chatty** and **Chaloka Beyani**

Volume 7

PSYCHOSOCIAL WELLNESS OF REFUGEES

Issues in Qualitative and Quantitative Research

Edited by **Frederick L. Ahearn, Jr.,** School of Social Service
at the Catholic University of America

In recent years, scholars in the fields of refugee studies and forced migration have extended their areas of interest and research into the phenomenon of displacement, human response to it, and ways to intervene to assist those affected, increasingly focusing on the emotional and social impact of displacement on refugees and their adjustment to the traumatic experiences. In the process, the positive concept of "psychosocial wellness" was developed as discussed in this volume. In it, noted scholars address the strengths and limitations of their investigations, citing examples from their work with refugees from Afghanistan, Cambodia, Vietnam, Palestine, Cuba, Nicaragua, Haiti, Eastern Europe, Bosnia, and Chile.

The authors discuss how they define "psychosocial wellness," as well as the issues of sample selection, measurement, reliability and validity, refugee narratives and "voices," and the ability to generalize findings and apply these to other populations. The key question that has guided many of these investigations and underlies the premise of this book is "what happens to an ordinary person who has experienced an extraordinary event?" This volume also highlights the fact that those involved in such research must also deal with their own emotional responses as they hear victims tell of killings, torture, humiliation, and dispossession.

2000, 272 pages, bibliog., index
ISBN 1-57181-204-0 hardback **$69.95/£47.00**
ISBN 1-57181-205-9 paperback **$19.95/£14.00**

www.berghahnbooks.com

Studies in Forced Migration

General Editors: **Dawn Chatty** and **Chaloka Beyani**

Volume 9

WHATEVER HAPPENED TO ASYLUM IN BRITAIN?

A Tale of Two Walls

Louise Pirouet

Refugees and asylum-seekers are high up on many people's political agenda. Even so, there is a remarkable lack of information. Who are these asylum-seekers? Aren't they almost all "bogus"? How do Western immigration authorities decide whether or not they are genuine? Is the UN convention on Refugees out of date and in need of renegotiation?

This book brings insider knowledge to the study of asylum in Britain today. It is based on visits to places where asylum-seekers are detained, on working with lawyers representing asylum-seekers, and on a close knowledge of many of the refugee organizations. It argues passionately that Britain shall not throw away, through ignorance and misunderstanding, a reputation for providing a place of safety for the persecuted, and the chance of welcoming people who have much to contribute to national life and culture.

Louis Pirouet has been involved with refugee concerns for many years both in Africa and Britain. She is a trustee of Asylum Aid, helps to run a group in Cambridge that works for safeguards for asylum-seekers held at a detention center near Cambridge, and assists Kenyans and Ugandans appealing against refusal of asylum.

Spring 2001, ca. 208 pages, bibliog., index
ISBN 1-57181-991-6 hardback ca. **$59.95/£40.00**
ISBN 1-57181-468-X paperback ca. **$19.95/£13.50**

www.berghahnbooks.com

Studies in Forced Migration

General Editors: **Dawn Chatty** and **Chaloka Beyani**

Volume 10

DISPLACEMENT, FORCED SETTLEMENT, AND CONSERVATION

Edited by **Dawn Chatty** and **Marcus Colchester**

Wildlife conservation and other environmental protection projects can have tremendous impact on the lives and livelihoods of the often mobile, difficult-to-reach, and marginal peoples who inhabit the same territory. The contributors to this collection of case studies—social scientists as well as natural scientists—are concerned with this human element in biodiversity. They examine the interface between conservation and indigenous communities forced to move or to settle elsewhere in order to accommodate environmental policies and biodiversity concerns.

The case studies investigate successful and not so successful community-managed, as well as local participatory, conservation projects in Africa, the Middle East, South and Southeast Asia, Australia, and Latin America. There are lessons to be learned from recent efforts in community-managed conservation, and this volume significantly contributes to that discussion.

Dawn Chatty is General Editor of Studies in Forced Migration and teaches at the Center for Refugee Studies of the University of Oxford. **Marcus Colchester** works for the Forest Peoples Programme.

Winter 2001/02, ca. 304 pages, bibliog., index
ISBN 1-57181-841-3 hardback ca. **$69.96/47.00**
ISBN 1-57181-842-1 paperback ca. **$25.00/£17.00**

www.berghahnbooks.com